HIMALAYAS

Photographs and Text by **YOSHIKAZU SHIRAKAWA**

HIMAL

Testimonial by

MAHENDRA BIR BIKRAM SHAH DEVA,

KING OF NEPAL

Preface by

ARNOLD TOYNBEE

Introduction by

SIR EDMUND HILLARY

Essay, ''The Great Himalayas,'' by

KYUYA FUKADA

ABRADALE PRESS / HARRY N. ABRAMS, INC., PUBLISHERS, NEW YORK

Library of Congress Cataloging-in-Publication Data
Shirakawa, Yoshikazu, 1935–
    Himalayas.
    Translation of: Himaraya.
    1. Himalaya Mountains—Description and travel.
I. Title.
DS485.H6S42713 1986   954   86–3495
ISBN 0-8109-8065-7

Original Japanese edition published by
Shogakukan Inc., Tokyo

Times Mirror Books

Printed and bound in Japan

CONTENTS

श्री ५ महाराजाधिराजबाट श्री शिराकावाद्वारा
रचना गरिएको 'हिमालय' नामक पुस्तकको निमित्त
बक्सेको प्रस्तावना

पन्ध्र सय माइल लामो भूभागमा फैलिएको हिमालय पर्वतमालाको अद्वितीय
सौन्दर्यको केहि मात्रामा यो चित्रमय पुस्तकद्वारा सकेसम्म धेरै मानिसमा बोध गराउने
रचनाकार श्री शिराकावाको प्रयासको सराहना गर्दछु ।

धेरै ढुराले हिमालय पर्वत श्रृंखला महत्त्वपूर्ण छ । सर्वोच्च पर्वत चुद्रामा चढ्ने
आकांक्षा राख्नेहरूको निमित्त यो प्राकृतिक आकर्षण केन्द्र छ । वन्य जन्तु र पर्वत
शिखरमा पाइने जडिबुटीको पनि यो स्रोत ठूलो भण्डार मानिएको आएको देखिन्छ ।
स्कान्तमा रमाउने विचारवान् पण्डितहरूको निमित्त हिमालय मन्दा दोश्रो उपयुक्त
स्थान कमै पाइएला । अर्को दृष्टिले हिमालय पर्वतमालाको टाकुराहरू पृथ्वीको
श्रृष्टिकर्ता भगवान प्रतिको पुकार र पूजाको रूपमा उठेका हुन् कि भनी कल्पना गर्न
सकिन्छ, वा समस्त पृथ्वीका श्रृष्टिप्रति यो धरती मन्दा माथि उठ्न पर्दछ भन्ने
निरन्तरको संकेत मान्न सकिन्छ । यिनै पर्वतमालाहरूबाट बगेका जलश्रोतहरूबाट यो
सम्पूर्ण प्रदेशको उद्धार भएको छ । वास्तवमा हिमालयको महत्त्व यसको छायांमा रहने
प्राणीहरूको लागि अवर्णनीय महत्त्व राख्दछ । हिमालयको आश्रयमा रही यसै भूभाग
बाट गौतम बुद्धले ज्ञानको आलोक संसार भरी फिंजाएका हुन् । यस उच्च पर्वतको
व्याख्याले परिपूर्ण वेद, पुराण, उपनिषद् तथा महाभारत लगायत प्रशस्त प्रमाण छन् ।

यो पुस्तक तस्वीरहरूले भरिएको छ, भाषा, चालचलन, रीति रिवाज र
जातपातको कारणवाट हुने भेदभाव र कठिनाई पन्छाई तस्वीरको माध्यमवाट
हिमालयको भव्यता र महानता स्वं यस इलाकामा रहने मानिसहरूको दृष्टिकोणलाई
अधिकांश जनतामा फैलाउन यो पुस्तकले मदत गर्ला भन्ने मलाई लागेको छ र लेखकको
प्रयासको हार्दिक प्रशंसा गर्दछु ।

२०२७ श्रावण १२गते सोमवार ।   --------

Principal Private Secretary,
Royal Palace,
Nepal.

PREFACE BY HIS MAJESTY THE KING TO
THE BOOK "HIMALAYA" BY MR. SHIRAKAWA

The attempt made by the author Mr. Shirakawa to acquaint
the people at large with the unique beauty of the Himalayan
mountain-ranges spreading over 1500 miles, is commendable.

The Himalayan mountain-range is of much significance from
various view-points. It is a natural centre of attraction to
explorers wishing to climb the highest peak on the earth. This
region has been regarded as the great store-house of alpine fauna
and flora. For the great saints and learned people who like and
seek solitude there is hardly a place more suitable than the
Himalayas. From another view-point, it can be fancied that the lofty
peaks of Himalayan mountain-range stand as a symbol of prayer and
worship to the Creator Lord of the earth or it can be regarded as an
everlasting emblem indicating that created beings should rise
higher than the terrestrial consciousness. The water resources
flowing out of these mountain-ranges have sanctified this entire
region. Truly speaking, the Himalayas occupy an ineffable position
for all living-beings dwelling on its shade. Gautam Buddha
contributed to the world the light of Knowledge from his sheltering
place under the domain of the great Himalayas. The Vedas, Puranas
and Upanashids including the Mahabharata — all these sacred books
speak very highly of the Himalayas and are full of descreptive
proof regarding the significance of the mountain-ranges.

This book is full of photographs. I believe, overcoming
the difficulties born of differences in language, customs and
manners, and anthropology with photographs as its media, the book
will help a lot in enlightening the people at large on the grandeur
and greatness of the Himalayas and the out-look of the people
dwelling in its region. I heartily appreciate the author's efforts.

July 27, 1970   ————

Arnold Toynbee

I have gazed, with awe, at some of the high peaks of the Himalayas on a journey by air from Rawal Pindi to Gilgit. From an aeroplane the traveller's glimpses of the World are brief. Sometimes, indeed, he sees nothing, from taking-off to landing, except the upper surface of a continuous blanket of cloud. On this journey I was fortunate. I did see the mighty mountains, and my vision of them has made an ineffaceable impression on my mind. I was overwhelmed by their beauty, and their majesty, and at the same time I realised that here Nature was revealing to me something that is beyond herself. The splendour that shines through Nature is imparted to her from a source which is beyond Nature and which is the ultimate reality. If there were not this invisible spiritual presence in and beyond the visible universe, there would be no Himalayas and no mankind either; for mankind is part of Nature, and, like non-human Nature, we owe our existence to the reality that is the mysterious common source of non-human Nature and ourselves.

As I flew over the Himalayas, I felt the cold rise from the peaks far down below me and shoot up through the floor of the plane to chill my feet and legs. For a moment, Nature seemed more powerful than even modern Man. Surely the Himalayas are inviolable. Yet this man-made man-piloted plane was soaring over them, and one peak after another had already been scaled to the summit.   So are the Himalayas really secure against Man's assaults, now that Man is armed with a scientific technology?   May it not now be within Man's power to desecrate the Himalayas if he finds this economically profitable and militarily advantageous?

We have not yet succeeded in defiling and defacing the Himalayas.   For the time being, they remain inviolate.   But we have already polluted and marred the more easily accessible parts of the land and water surface of our planet.   One of the most beautiful countries on Earth is Japan.   Yet the Japanese people themselves have been spoiling their homeland.   They have been obliterating the plains under a hideous man-made crust of streets and apartment-houses and factories.   They have been gashing the shapely mountains to cut speedways through them.   They have been poisoning their air with fumes and their waters with refuse.   And, over plain and mountain alike, they have been spreading a pall of smog which veils the country and starves it of sunlight.

This brutal treatment of non-human Nature has now been carried to extreme lengths in Japan, but it was started at the opposite end of the Old World, in Britain. This was the birthplace of the Industrial Revolution that has spread all round the globe within the last two hundred years.   Within these two centuries, Man has enormously increased his power by harnessing the inanimate forces of Nature on an unprecedented scale.   He has only just begun to realise that, in enslaving Nature, he is threatening to liquidate himself.   Man is a part of Nature, and he will not be able to survive if he destroys the natural environment in which his pre-human ancestors became human in the act of awaking to consciousness.

From the beginning of this human chapter of his history, Man has been bent on mastering Nature, and he has now succeeded in mastering the whole of terrestrial Nature except himself.   This is an ironical achievement and an ironical failure.   Self-mastery is, for Man, the key to happiness, to welfare, and to survival.   Yet human nature is still recalcitrant to Man's command, and this unregenerate human nature is a threat to Man's existence, now that Man has armed himself with inanimate Nature's titanic forces.

Man has now fallen into conflict with human and non-human Nature alike.   This is why, today, his enhanced power and wealth are causing him increasing anxiety and unhappiness.   But this present-day disharmony dates only from the invention of mechanised industry.   Pre-industrial Man, the hunter and the cultivator, managed to make Nature minister to his needs without going to War with her.   Upper Palaeolithic Man's cave-paintings show that he was fascinated by the beauty and prowess of the animals on whom he preyed.   Neolithic Man made the face of the Earth more beautiful by transmuting the wilderness into rice-paddies and corn-fields.   Till the Industrial Revolution in England, only two hundred years ago, Man still lived at peace with Nature.

He still felt the awe of Nature that he had inherited from ancestors who had been at Nature's mercy. Cannot we regain this lost ancient concord between Man and his environment?

Since Man became conscious, he has been aware that he himself is not the spiritually highest presence in the universe, and he has been seeking to communicate with this higher form of reality in order to put himself into harmony with it. His earliest avenue of approach to it was through his natural environment. He worshipped the ultimate reality through the manifestations of it in mountains, such as the beautiful and majestic Himalayas, and in forests, springs, rivers, and the ocean.

At the Western end of the Old World and in the Americas this earliest form of religion has been killed by monotheism in the forms of Judaism, Christianity, and Islam. But in India and Eastern Asia the worship of ultimate reality through the medium of Nature still survives. I have twice visited Ise, the holiest seat of Shinto. The lovely valley in which Ise lies is a meeting-place between virgin tree-clad mountains and a plain that Man has transformed, without defacing it, by turning it into an exquisite pattern of rice-paddies. At Ise, standing at the entrance to the shrine, I have felt what I felt when I was flying over the Himalayas. Through the beauty and the majesty of Nature, I found myself communicating with Nature's and Man's common source.

The Japanese people have not bulldozed Ise and have not repudiated Shinto. They have obliterated the natural beauty of the shores of the Shimonoseki Straits, which I myself saw, still unspoiled, as recently as 1929. They have almost vulgarised Nara. But Ise remains sacrosanct and intact, and Ise, like the Himalayas, has a message to give to Man in an age when he is being menaced by the backfire of his latest technological achievements. The message is one of hope. It is still possible for Man to regain his original concord with Nature, and this will bring him salvation from his present Man-made plight.

Arnold Toynbee

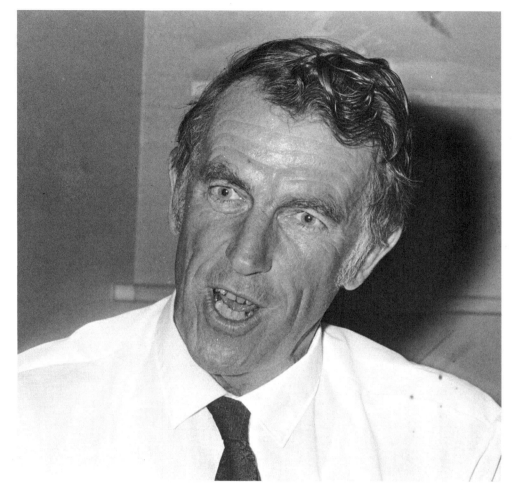

Men the world over have looked to the mountains for inspiration and refreshment. For twenty years I have walked and climbed in the Himalayas and each time has been just as exciting and stimulating as my first visit.

There is so much to see and much to do. The lack of roads and modern methods of transport force the adventurous visitor to travel on foot over the steep hill paths—but surely this is an advantage even for the city dweller who aims to cram the maximum of experience into the shortest possible space of time.

In Nepal the tempo is slower. As you walk the body gets strong; the mind has time to dwell on the beauties of nature and gain refreshment; you meet the local people, the Sherpas; and enjoy their cheerful friendliness and admire their toughness and strength; you breathe good clean air again . . . .

Above the villages the streams run clear and sparkling and their water is a delight to drink. Only in the villages and in the wake of foreign expeditions does the dirt and trash accumulate. Man, alas, is the great polluter of his environment—particularly modern industrial man—and because there are few men in the Himalayas, the great mountain slopes have been little harmed and rise in grandeur and beauty.

The summits thrust towards the sky in unbelievable fashion. Massive rock buttresses, unstable ice bulges, clinging snow slopes . . . all piled one on top of the other. Above soar knife-sharp saw-toothed ridges—the final defences before the ultimate summits. They are always changing as the moods of nature change. A bitter wind blows a plume of snow off a lofty mountain brow; sunset transforms the snow and rock to crimson and gold; a fierce storm clothes the mountains in a cloak of purest snow . . . .

As he looks at the mountains the climber's heart swells with joy and pain! It is so beautiful and yet so inaccessible. Oh! to set foot on those virgin slopes—even though death waits poised above!

Why do men want to climb mountains? George Leigh Mallory gave his answer for Mount Everest—"because it is there!" Perhaps there are no cold intellectual reasons —it is more a feeling, a wanting . . .the summit beckons . . . it is impossible, they say . . . impossible? to the spirit of man?—and so the contest is joined! The climber's skill and courage against the defences and dangers of the mountain.

The contest brings fear and joy—and a deep respect. And whatever the result of the struggle—be it success or failure—there is always the desire to go back—yes! to go back . . . .

My friend Yoshikazu Shirakawa has felt the call of the Himalayas just as I have. For three years he has returned again and again to capture on film their serenity, mysticism and grandeur. No one can doubt his love of mountains—his wonderful pictures speak for themselves—and he could not have succeeded in his objective without courage and great determination. With this great book Mr. Shirakawa has indeed reached a photographic "Everest."

Edmund Hillary

NEPAL HIMALAYAS

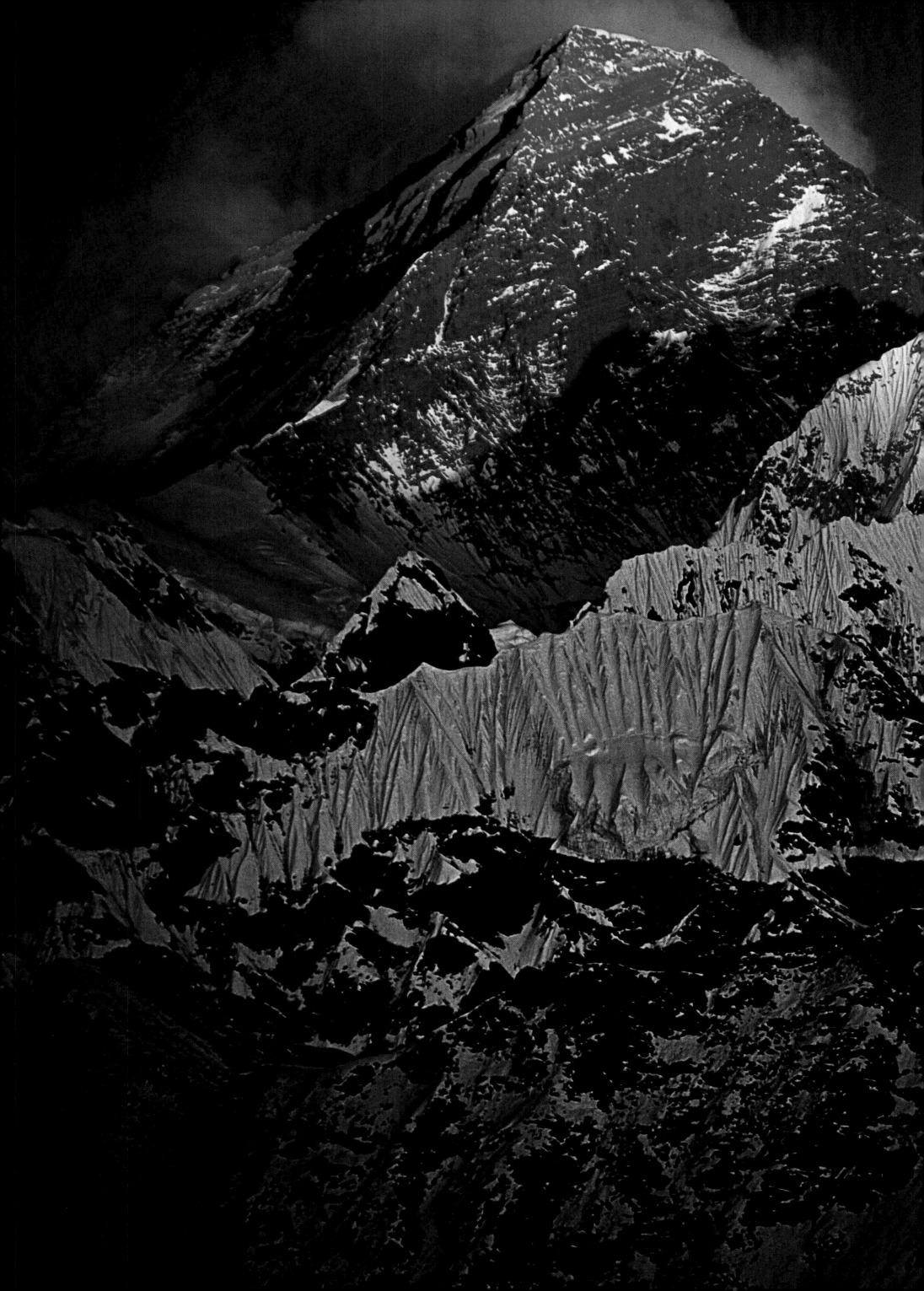

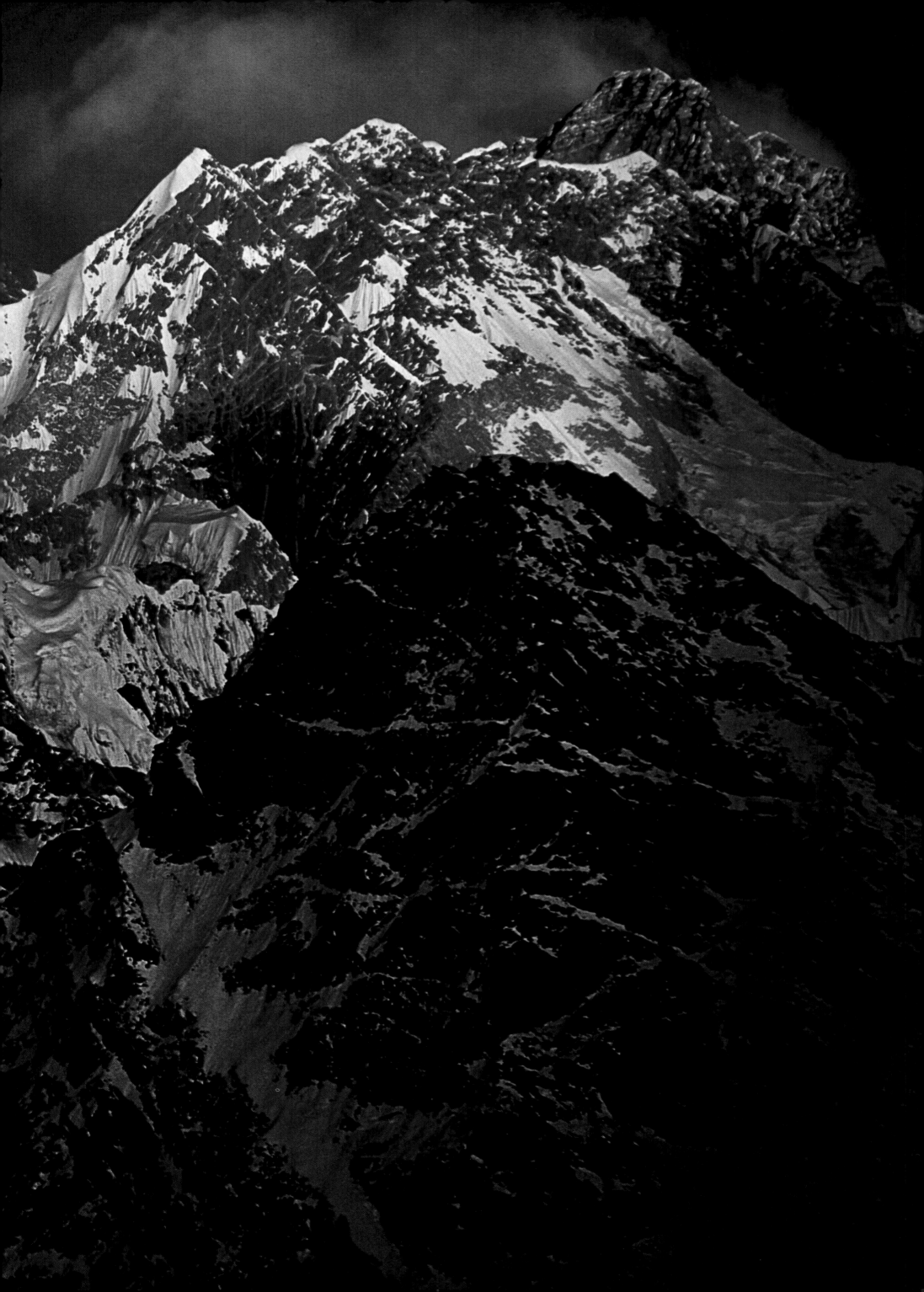

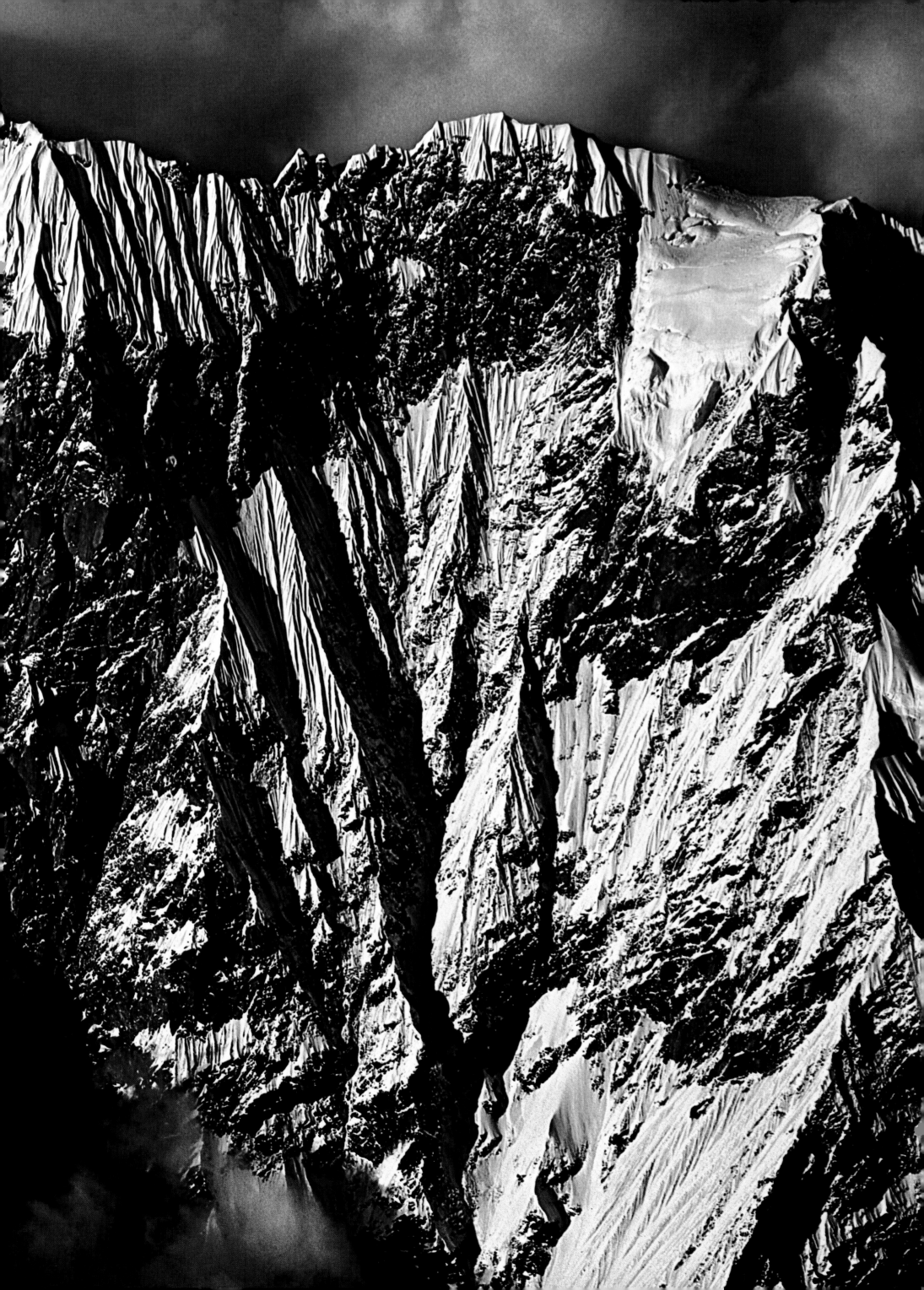

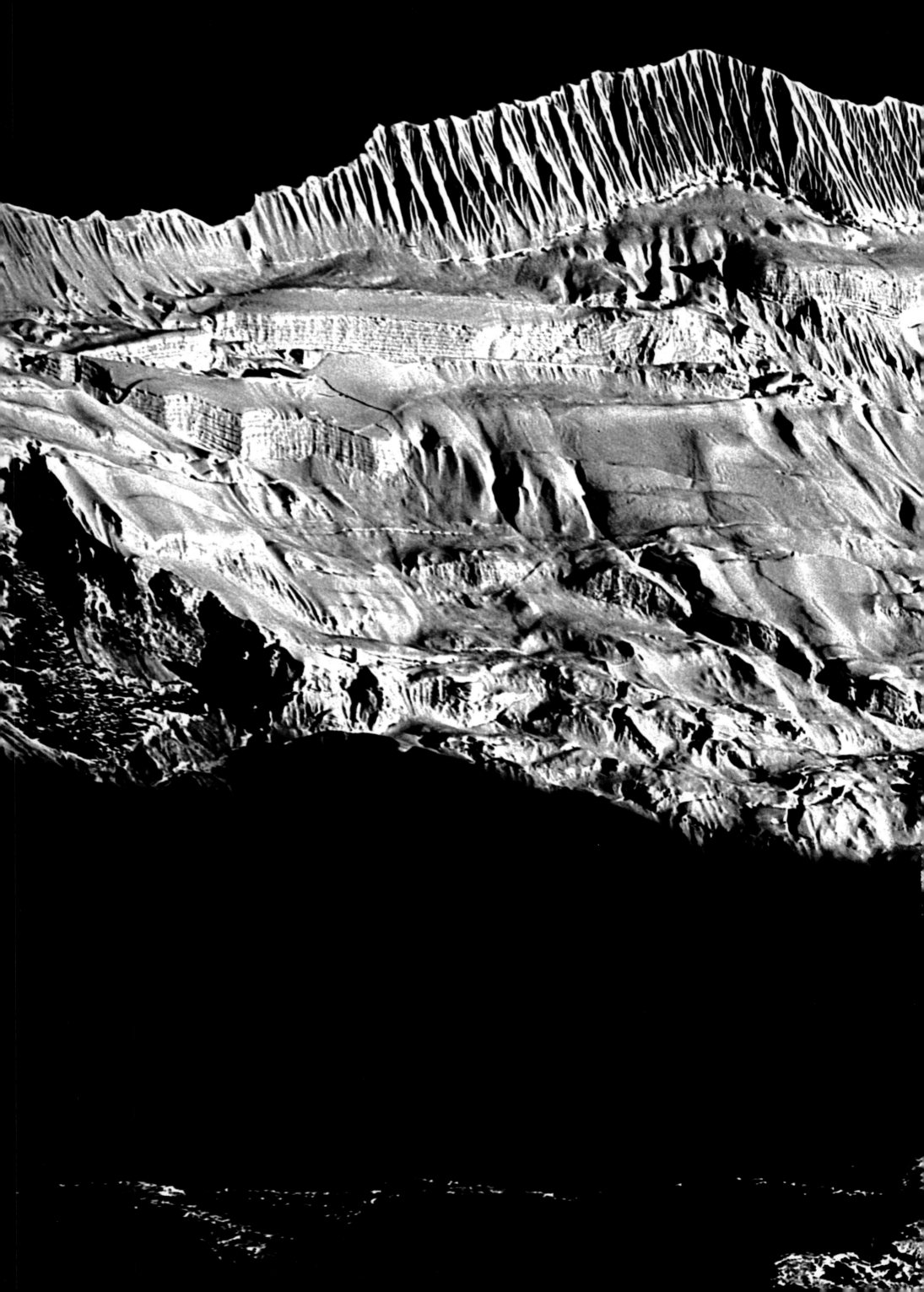

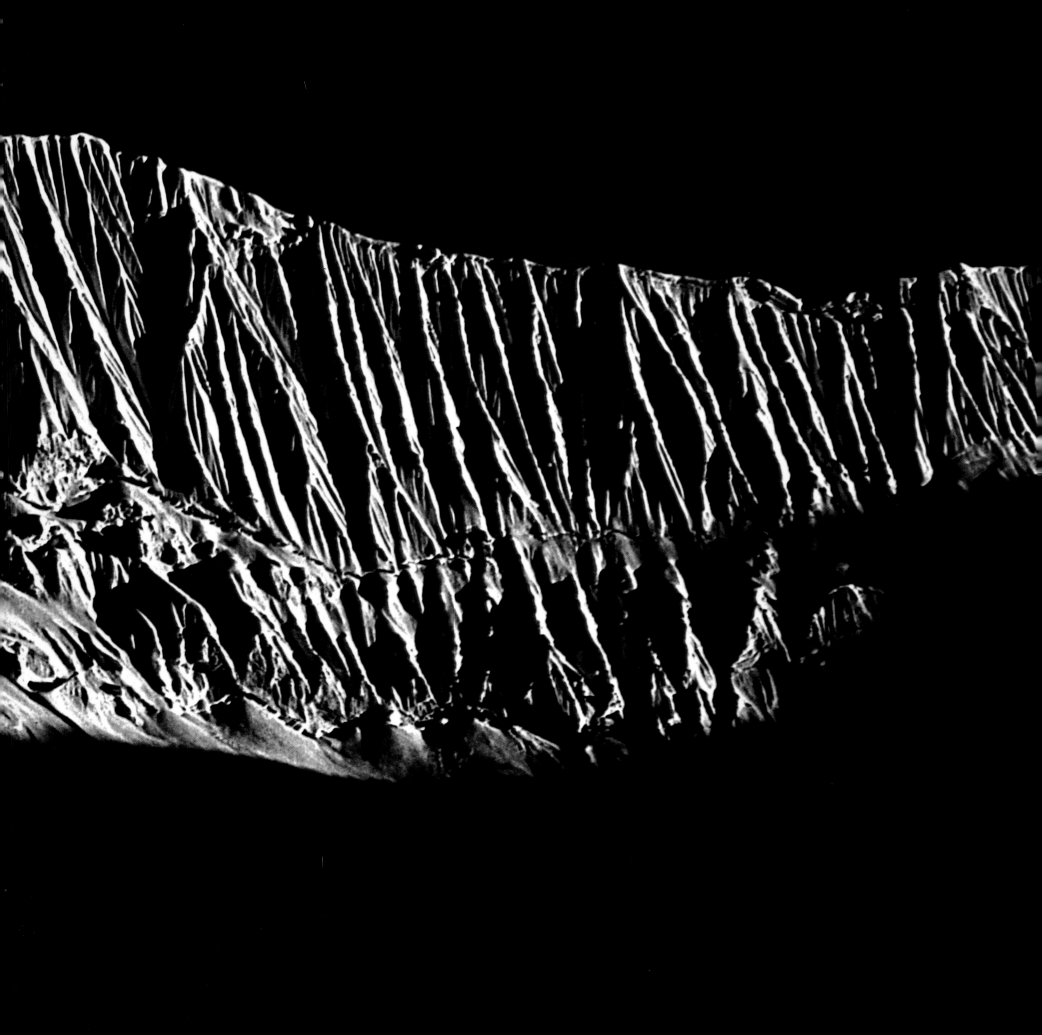

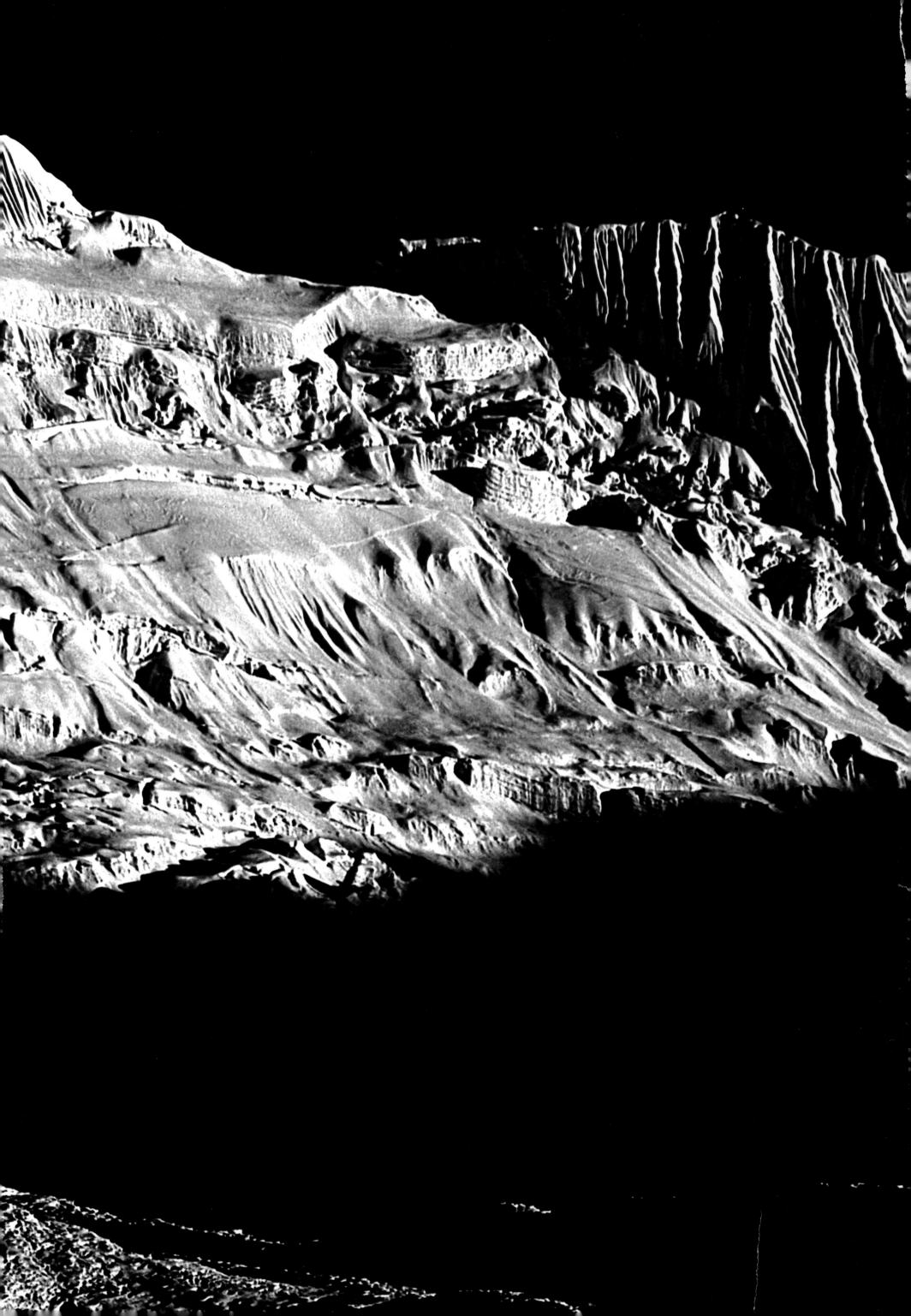

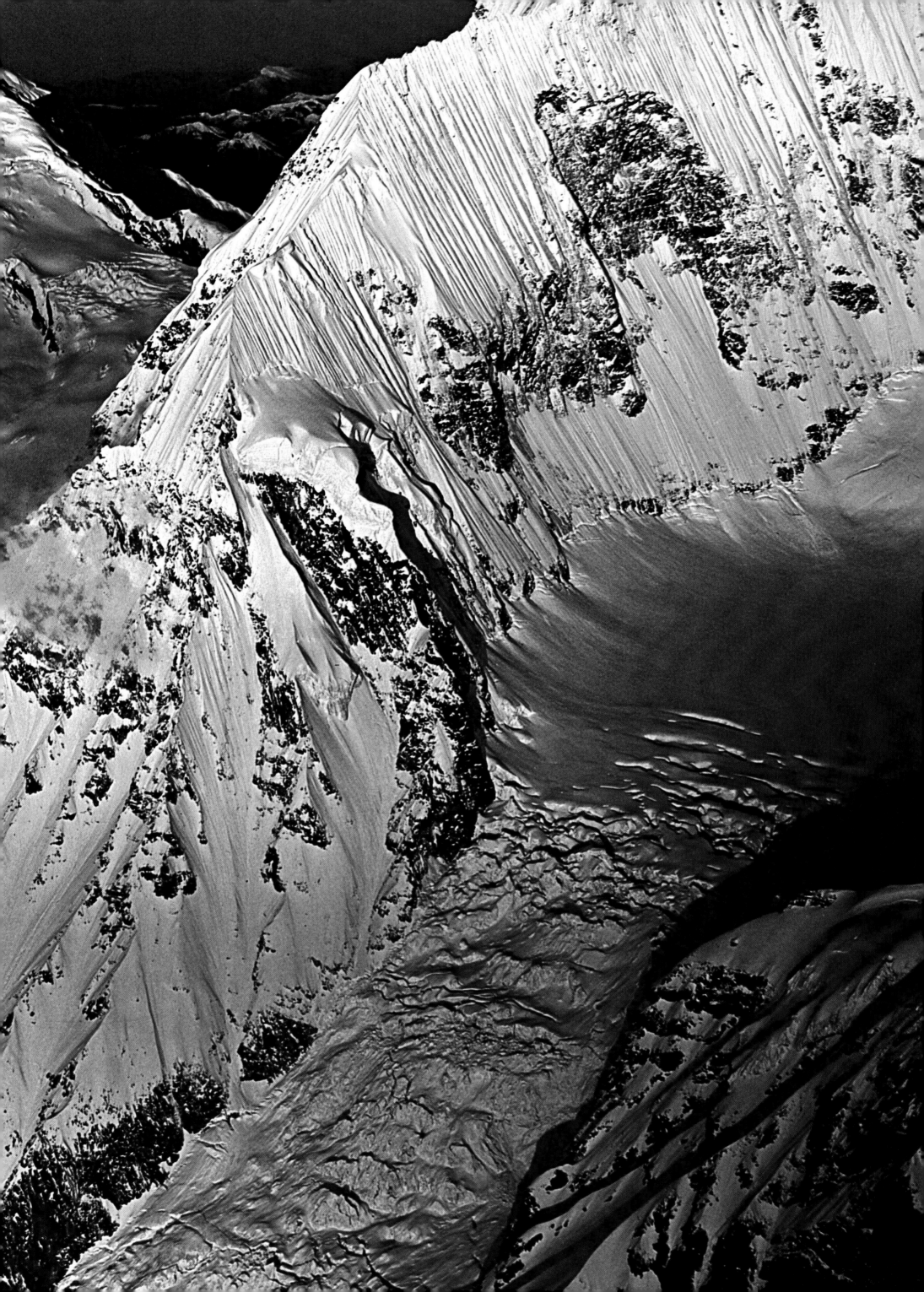

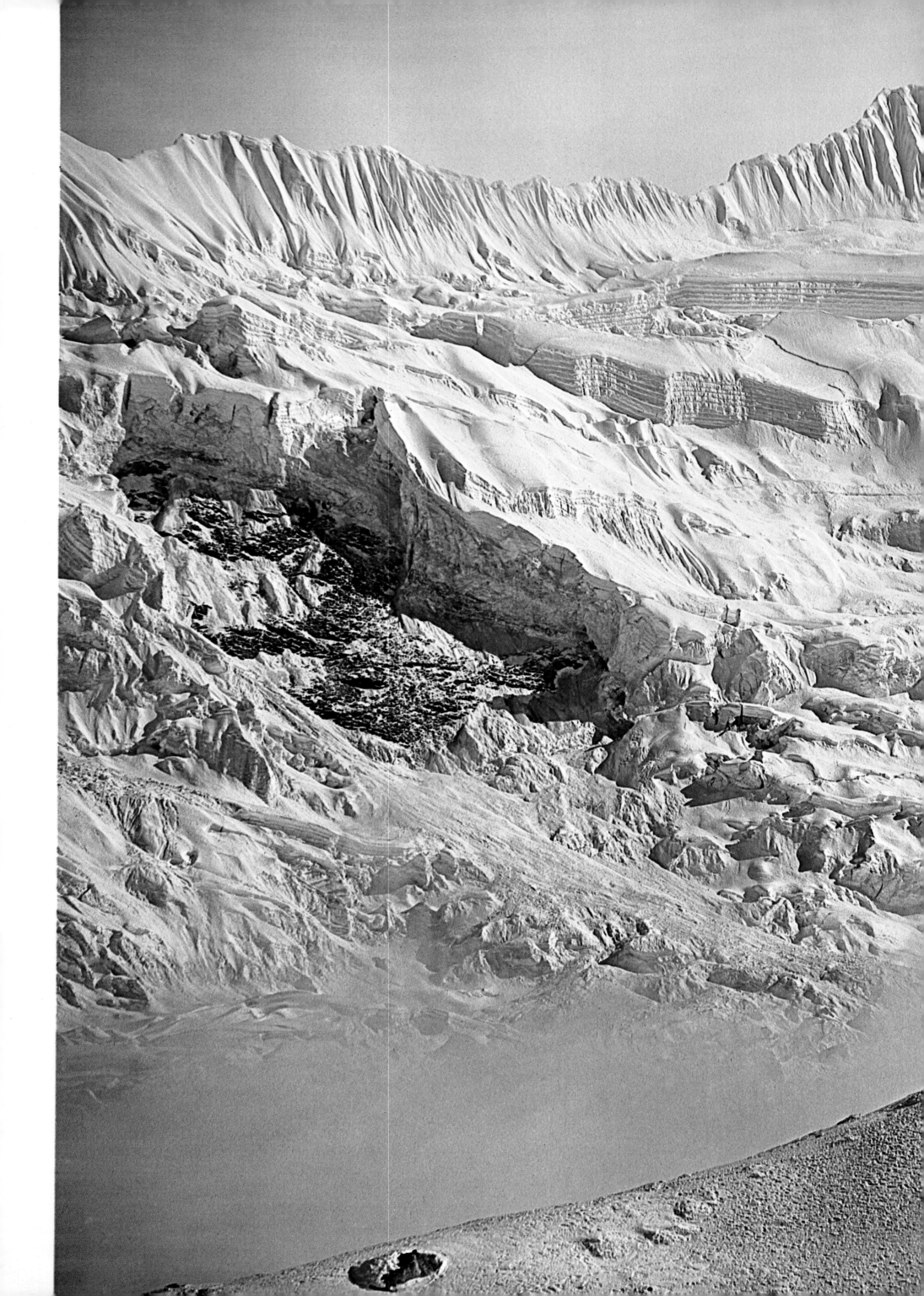

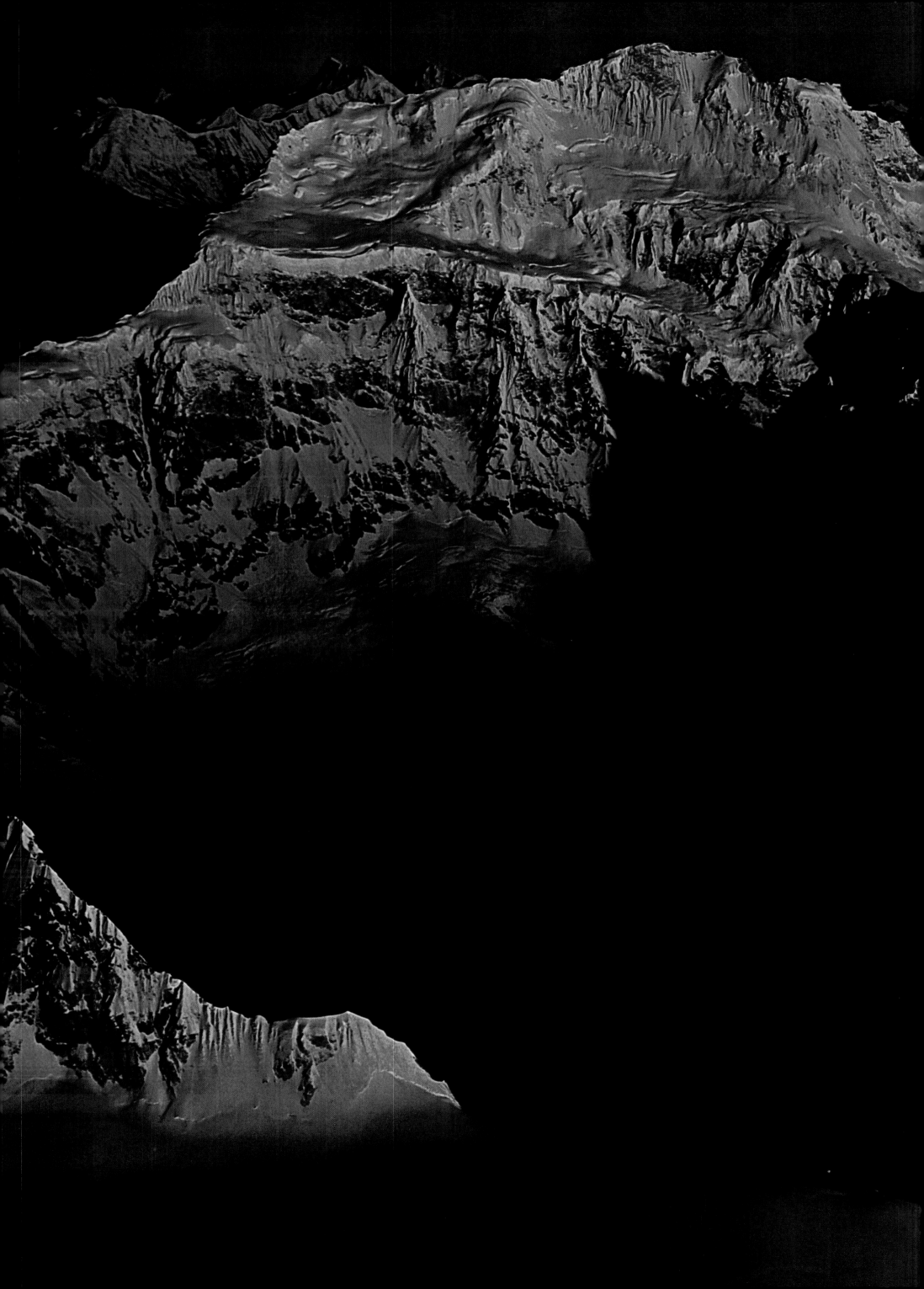

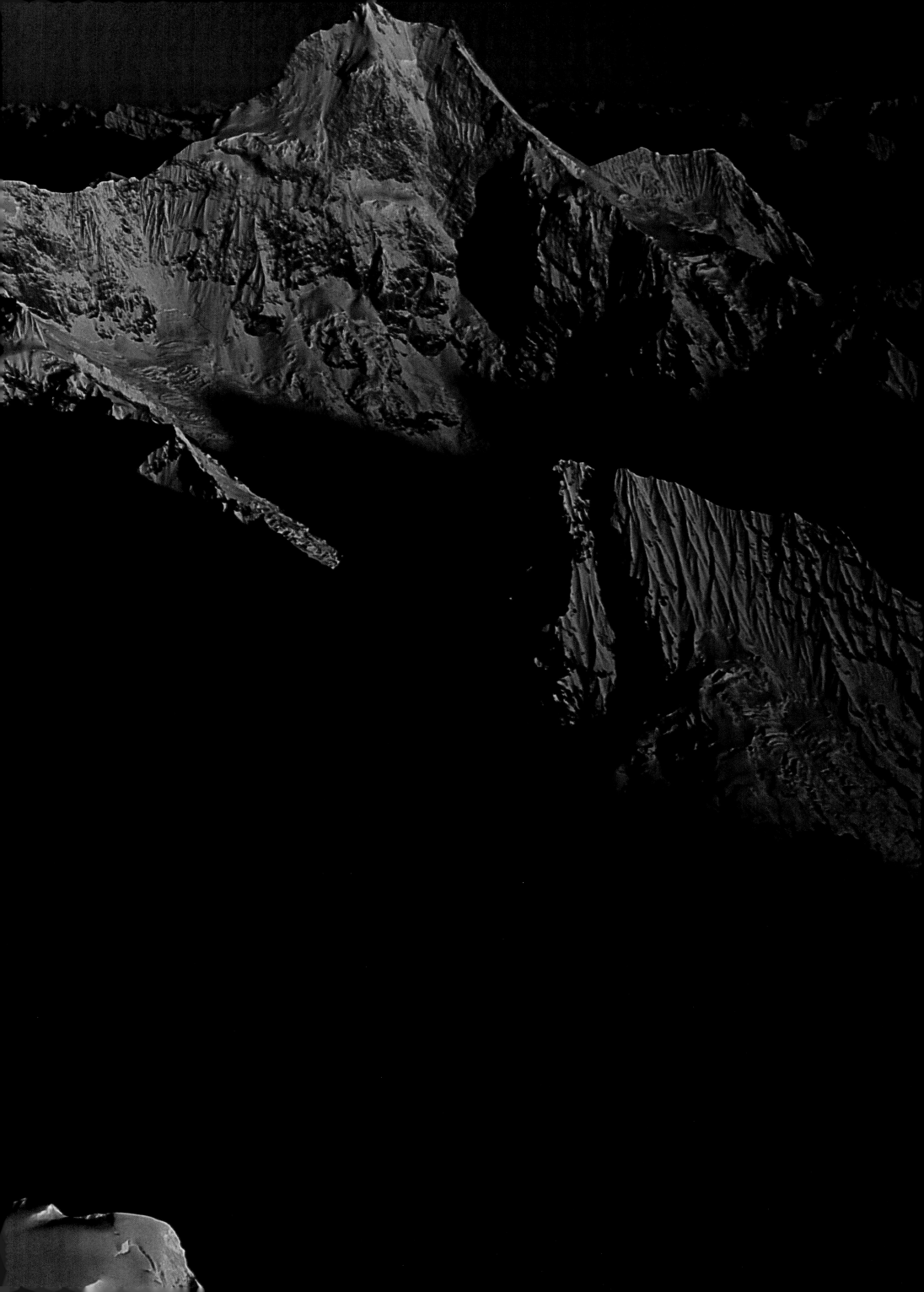

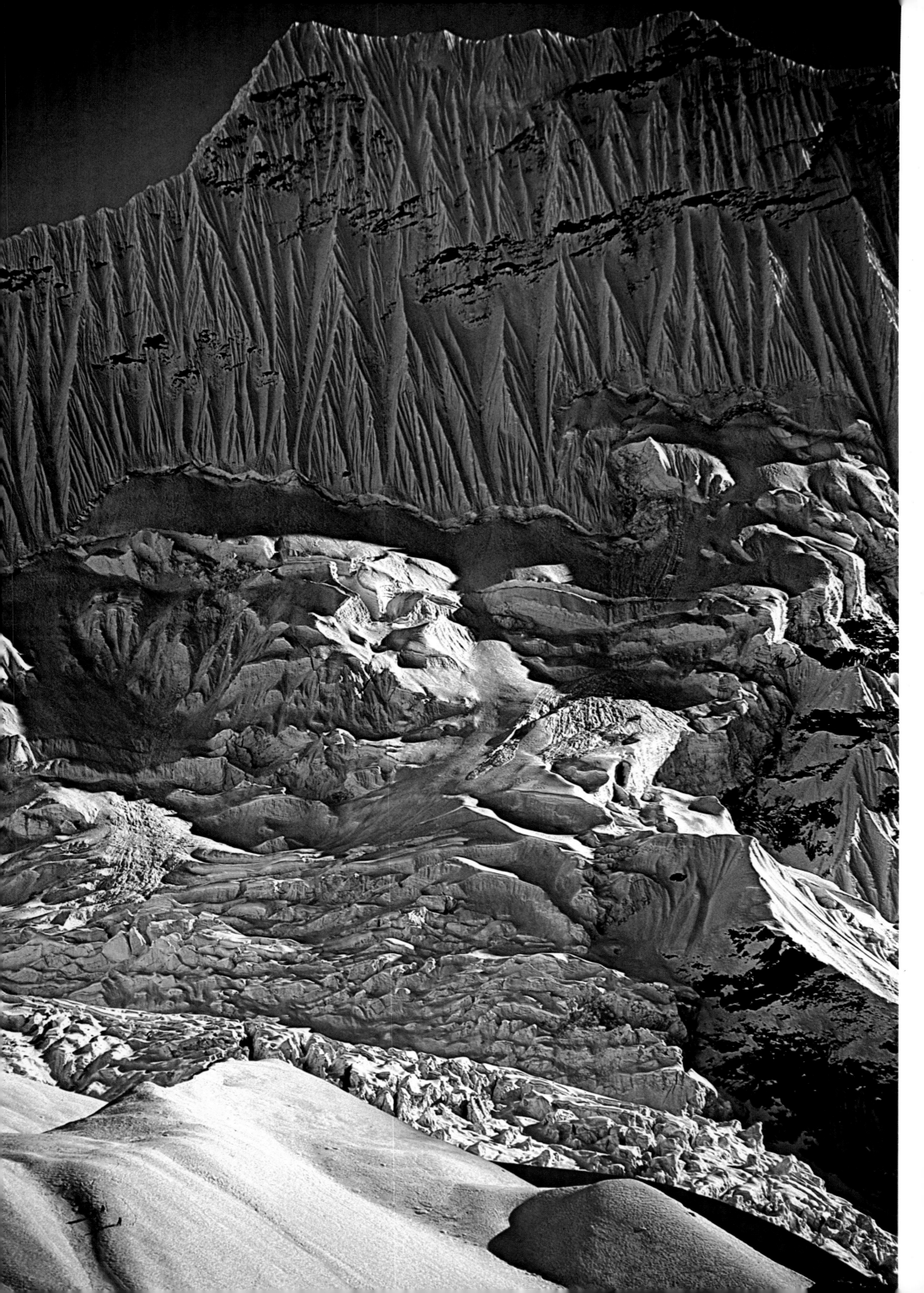

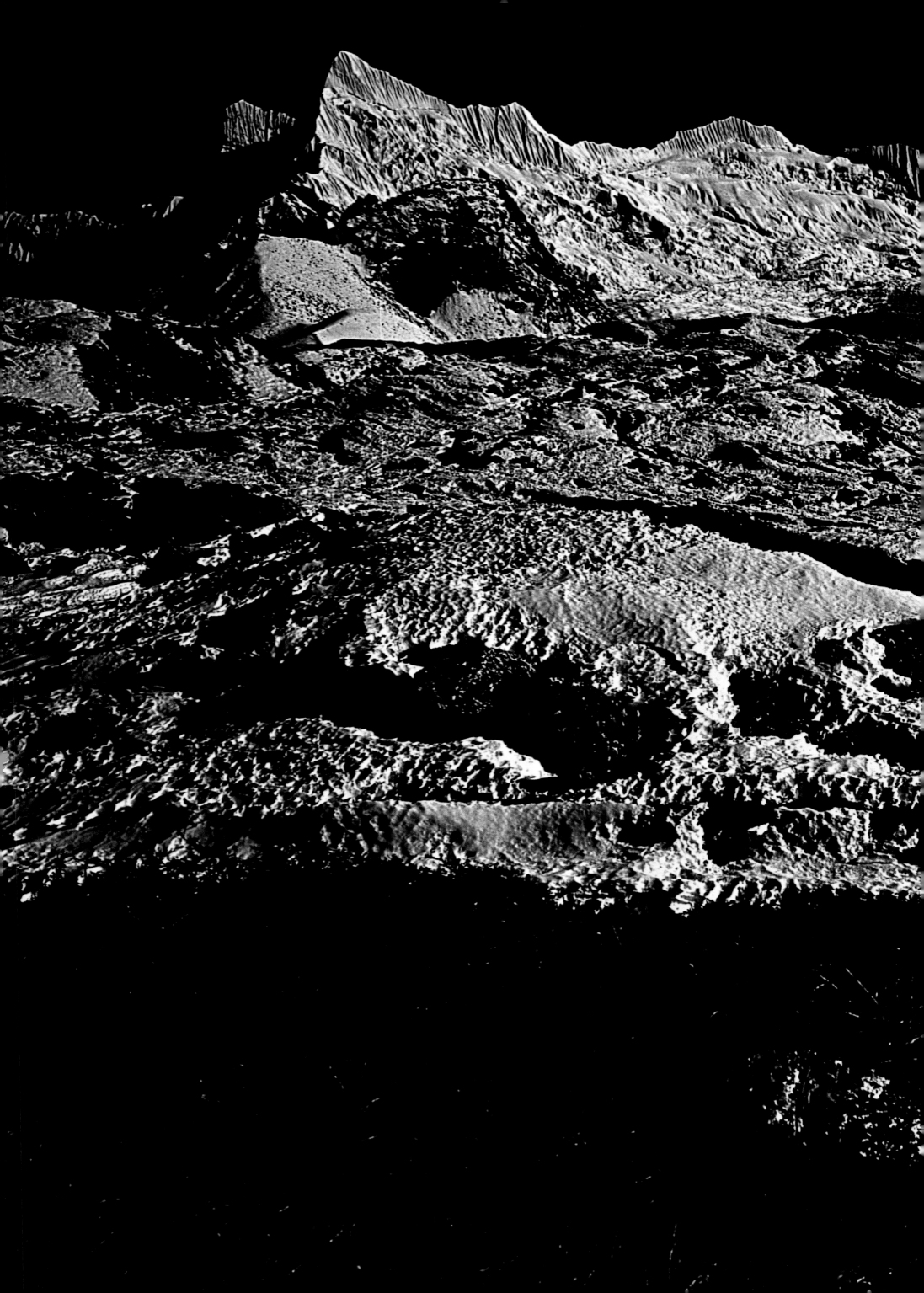

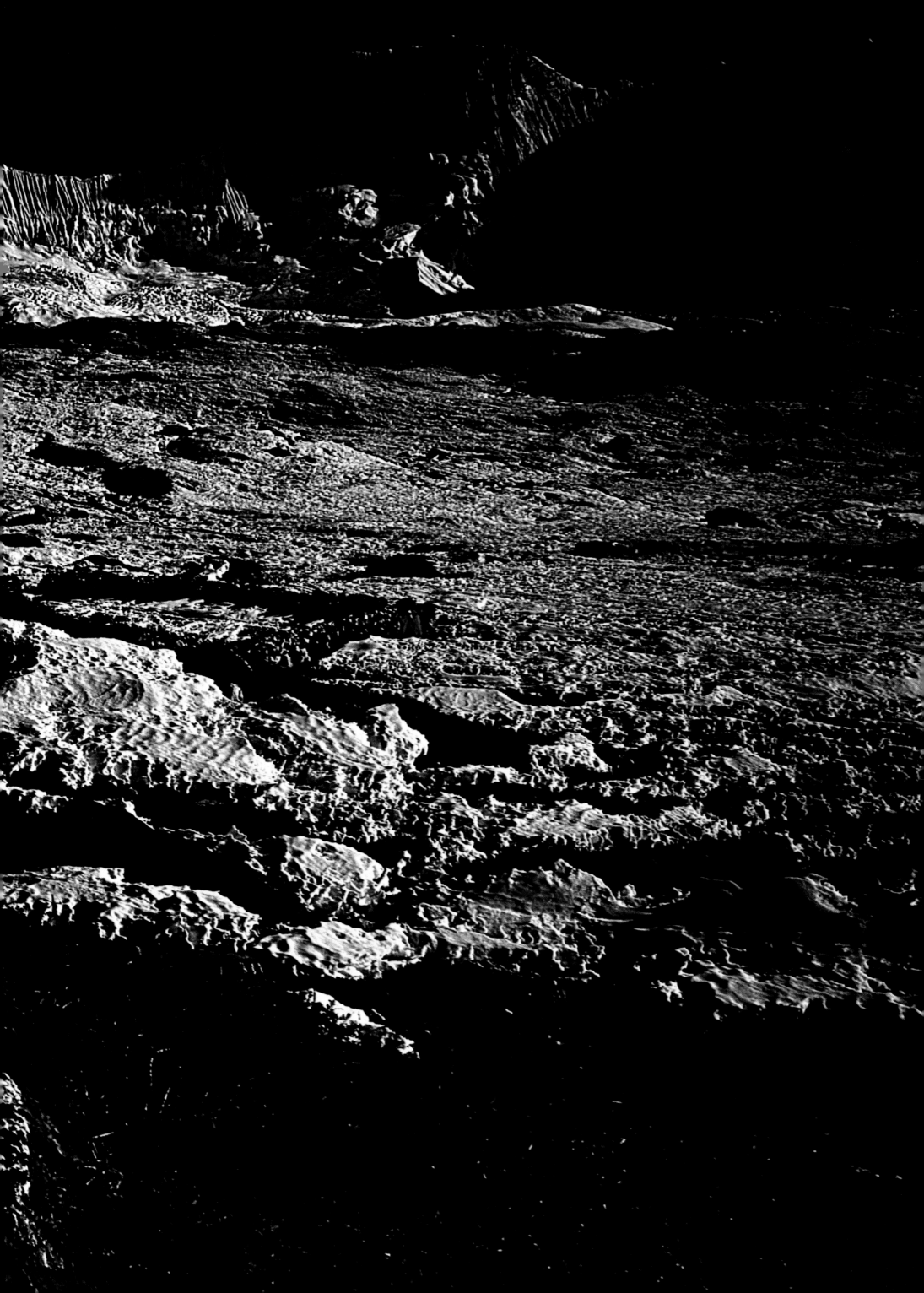

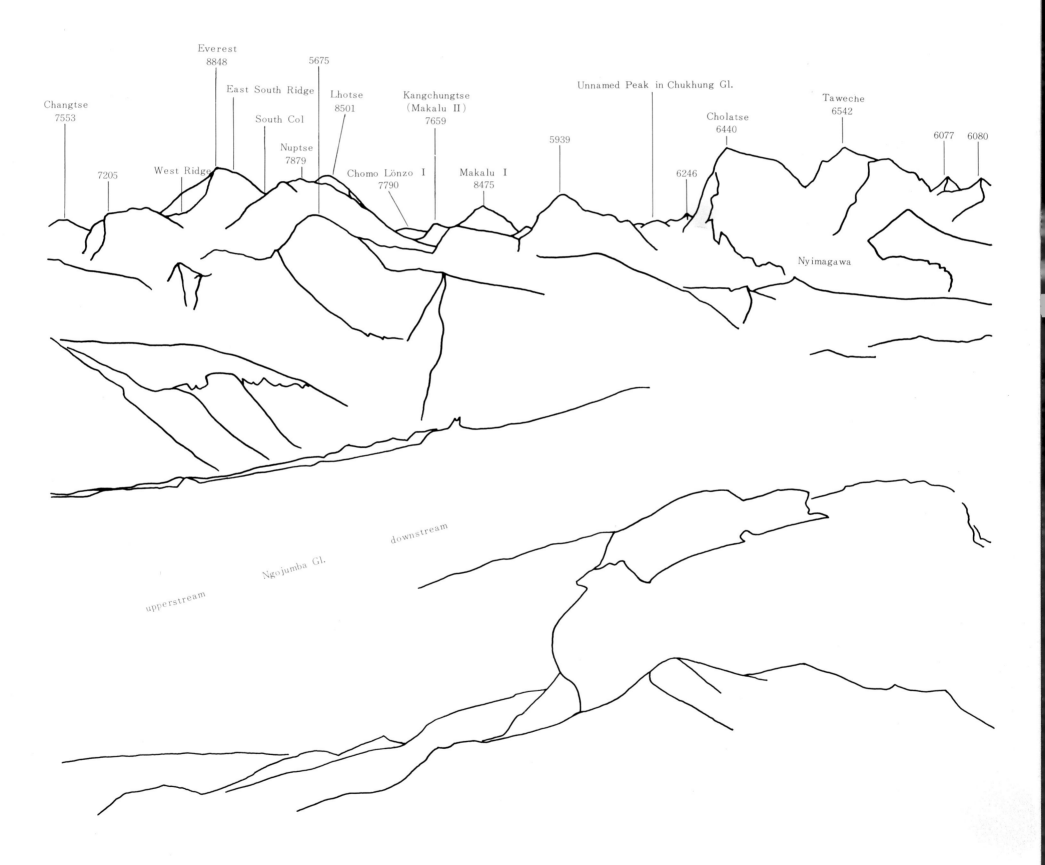

Changtse
7553

7205

West Ridge

Everest
8848

East South Ridge

South Col

Nuptse
7879

5675

Lhotse
8501

Chomo Lönzo I
7790

Kangchungtse
(Makalu II)
7659

Makalu I
8475

5939

Unnamed Peak in Chukhung Gl.

6246

Cholatse
6440

Taweche
6542

Nyimagawa

6077

6080

downstream

Ngojumba Gl.

upperstream

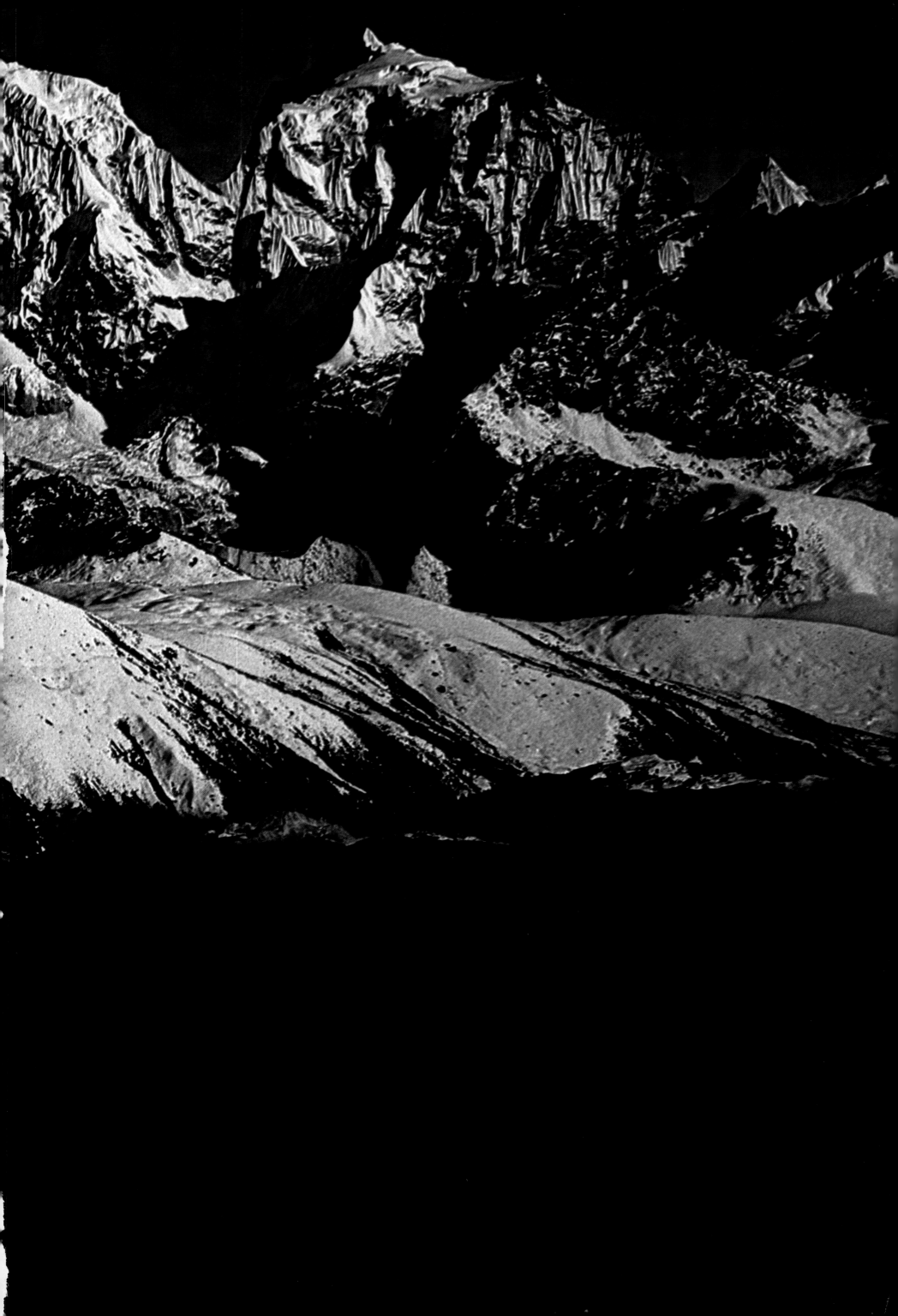

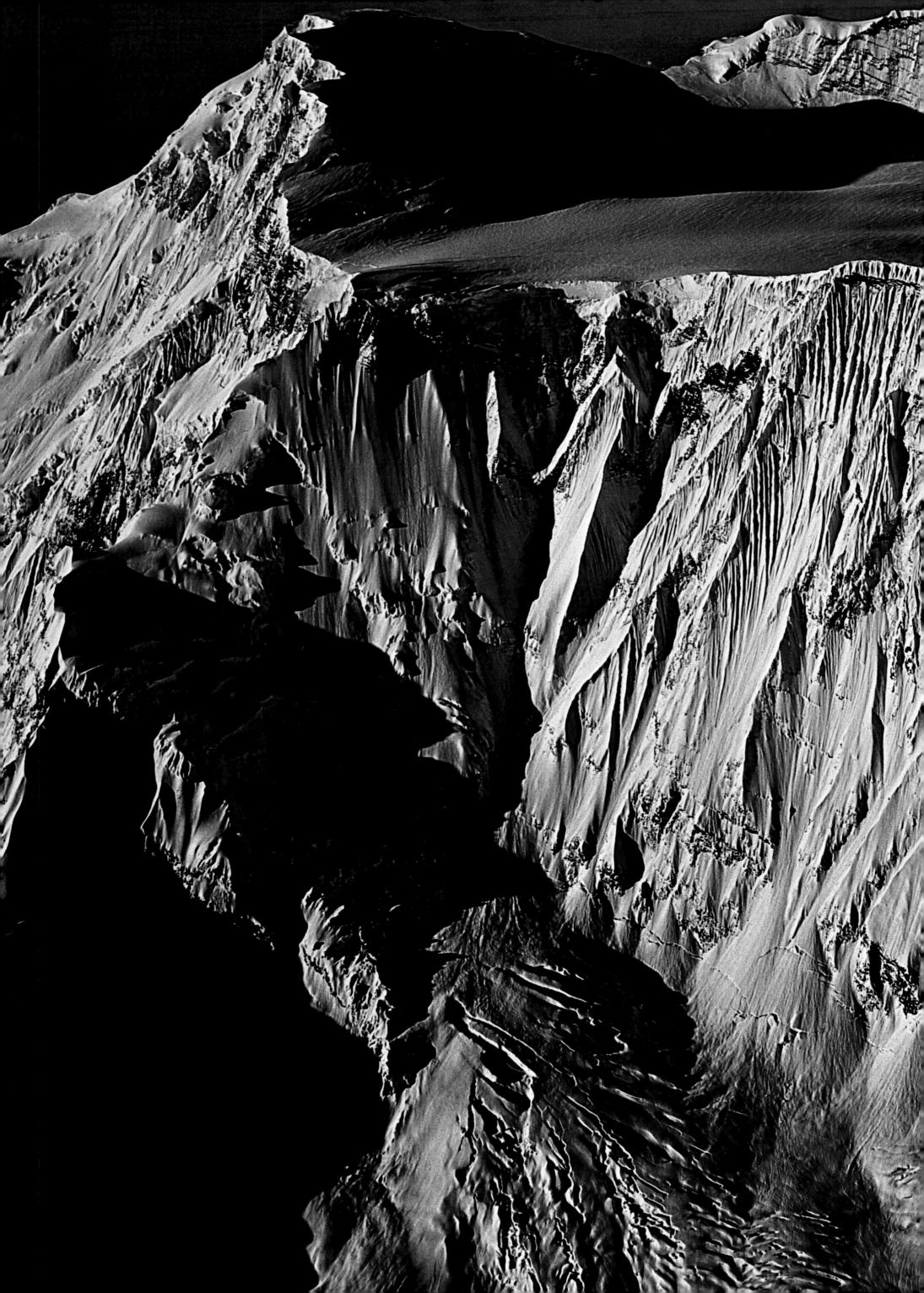

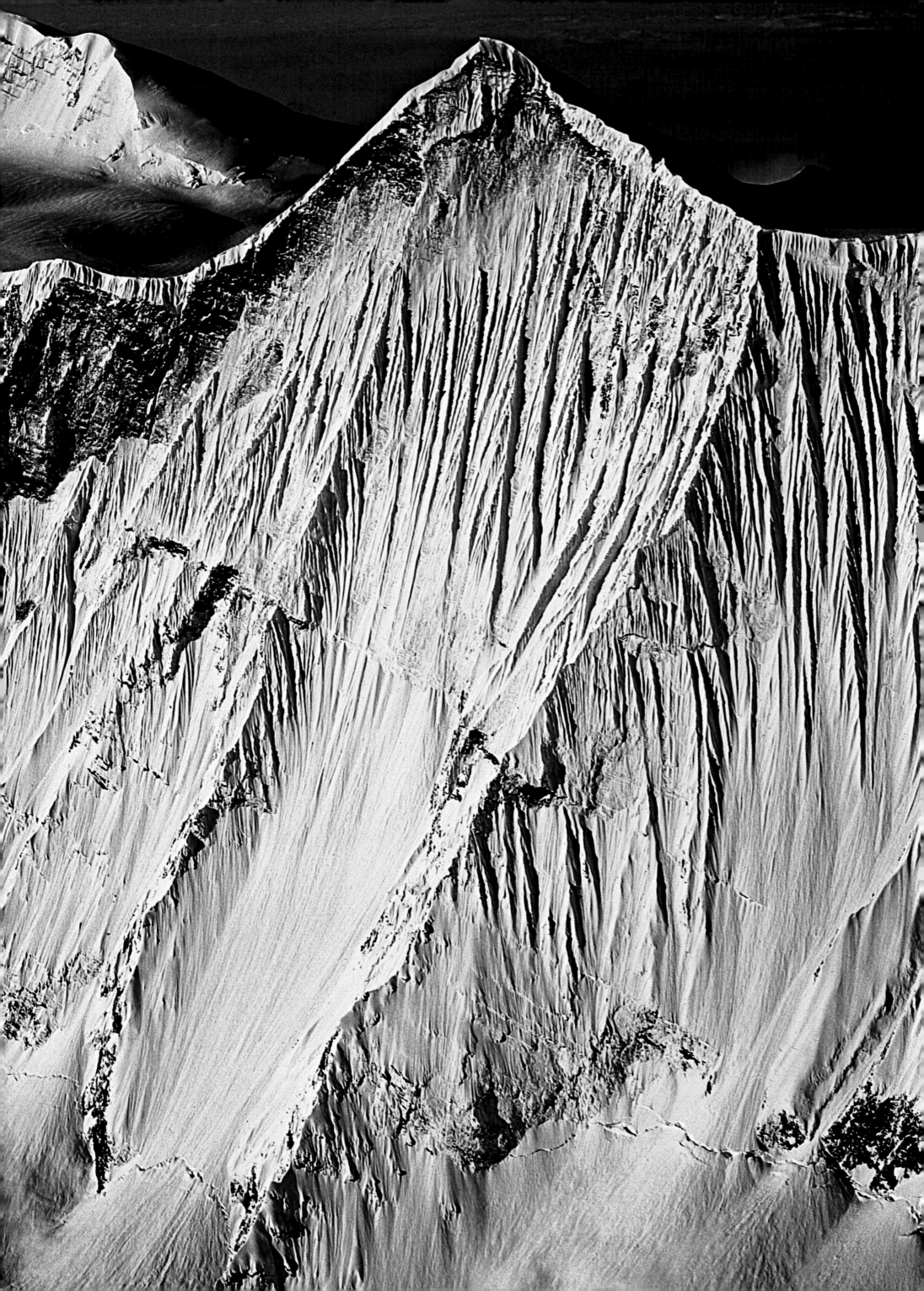

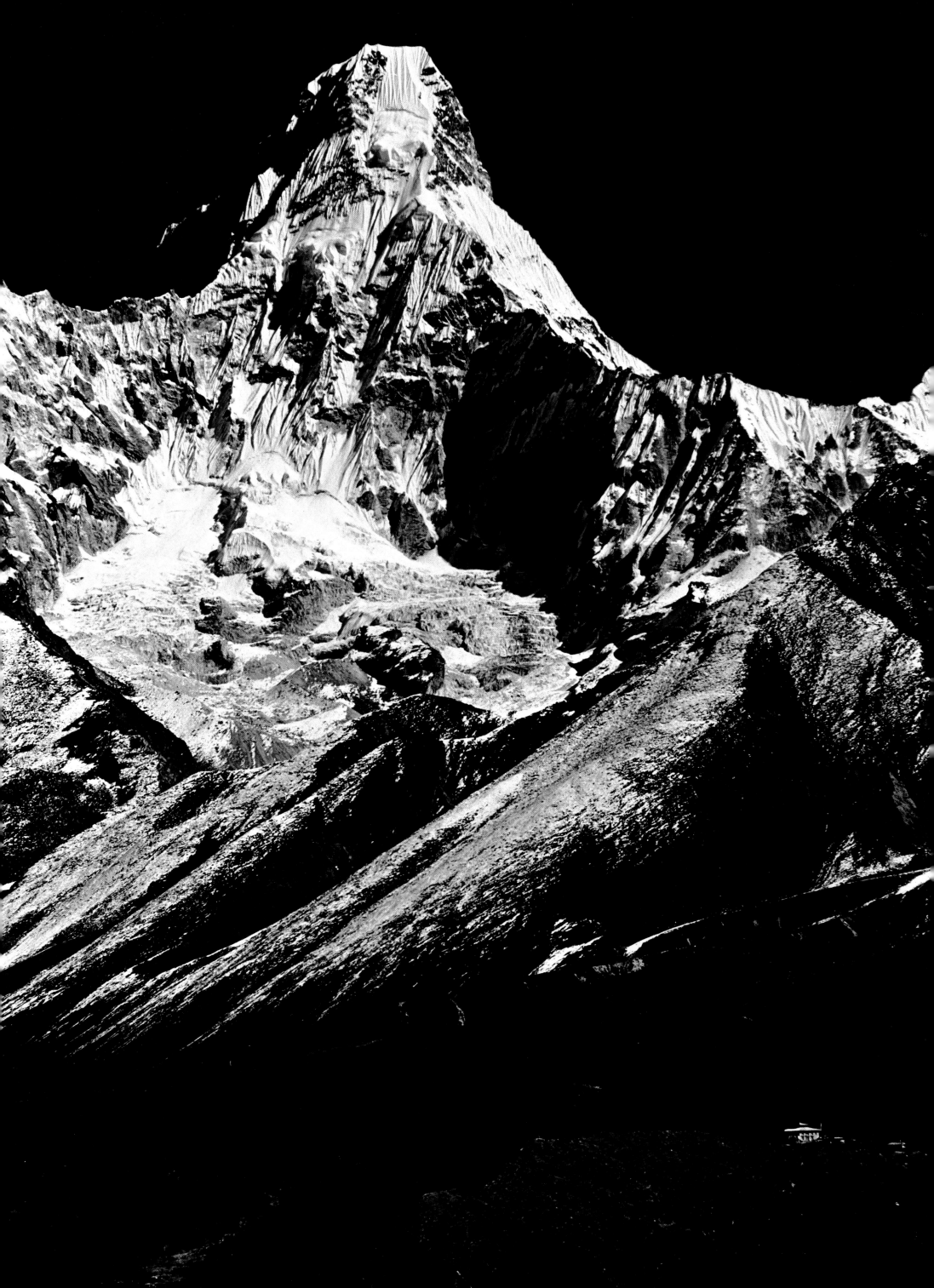

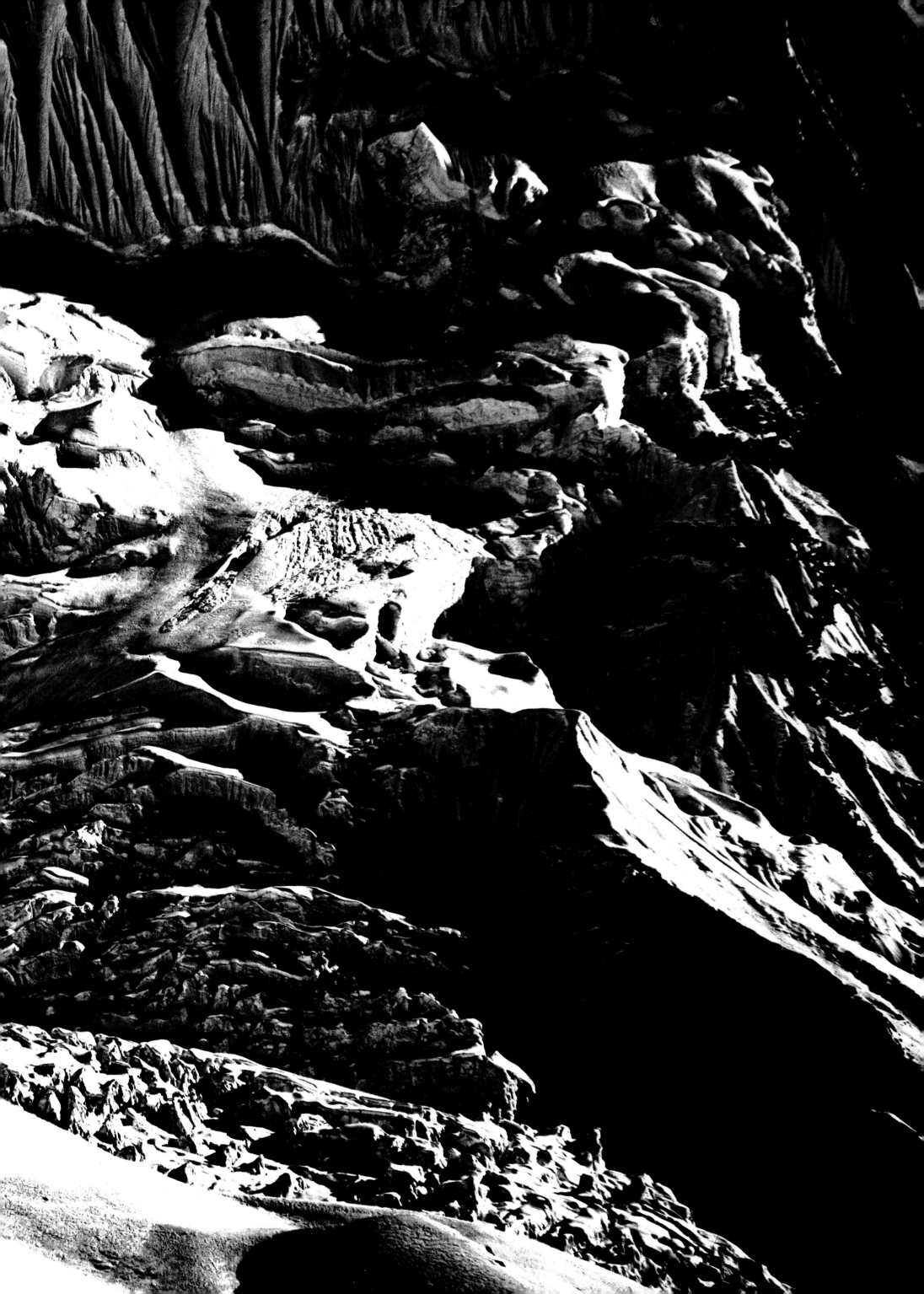

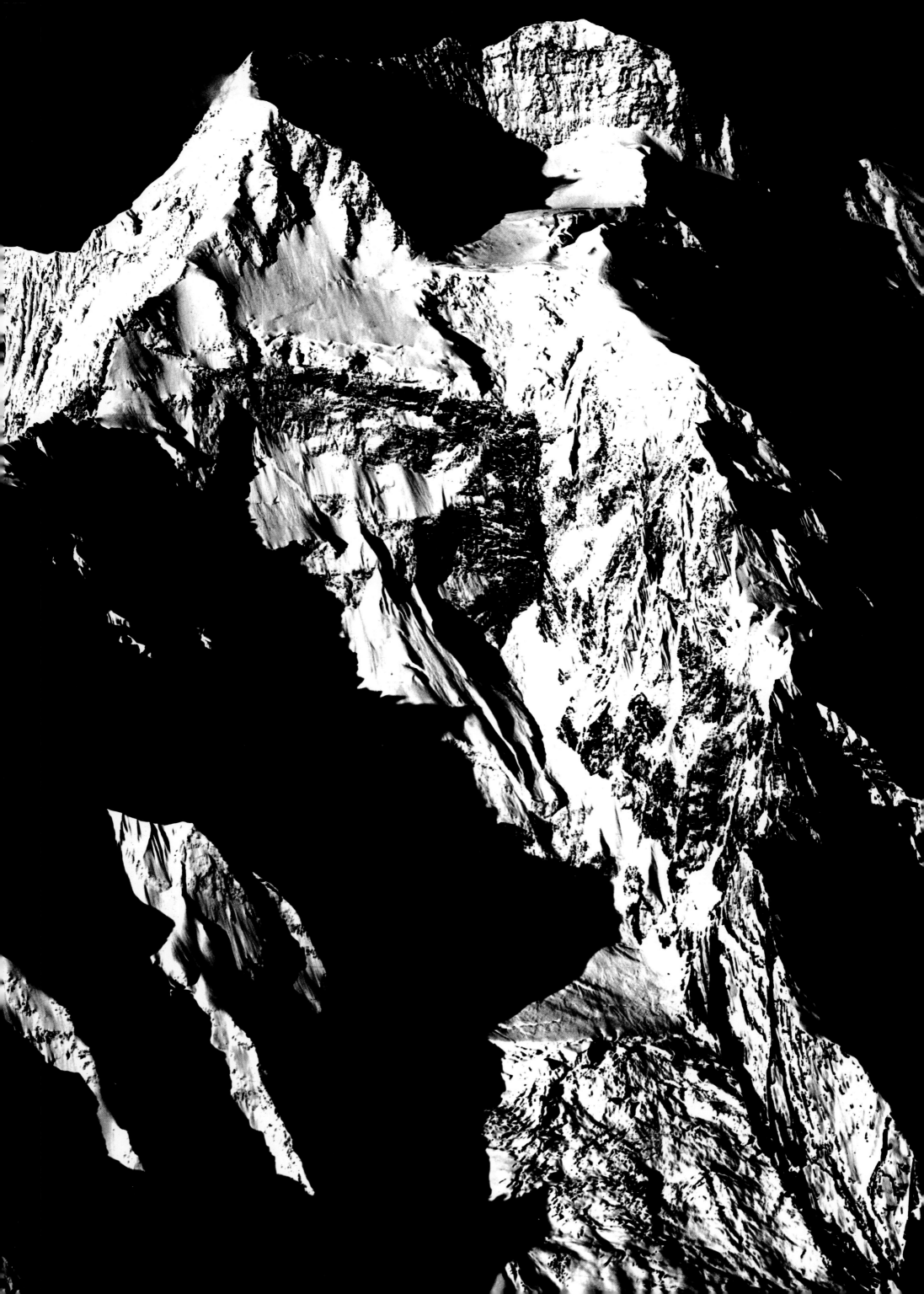

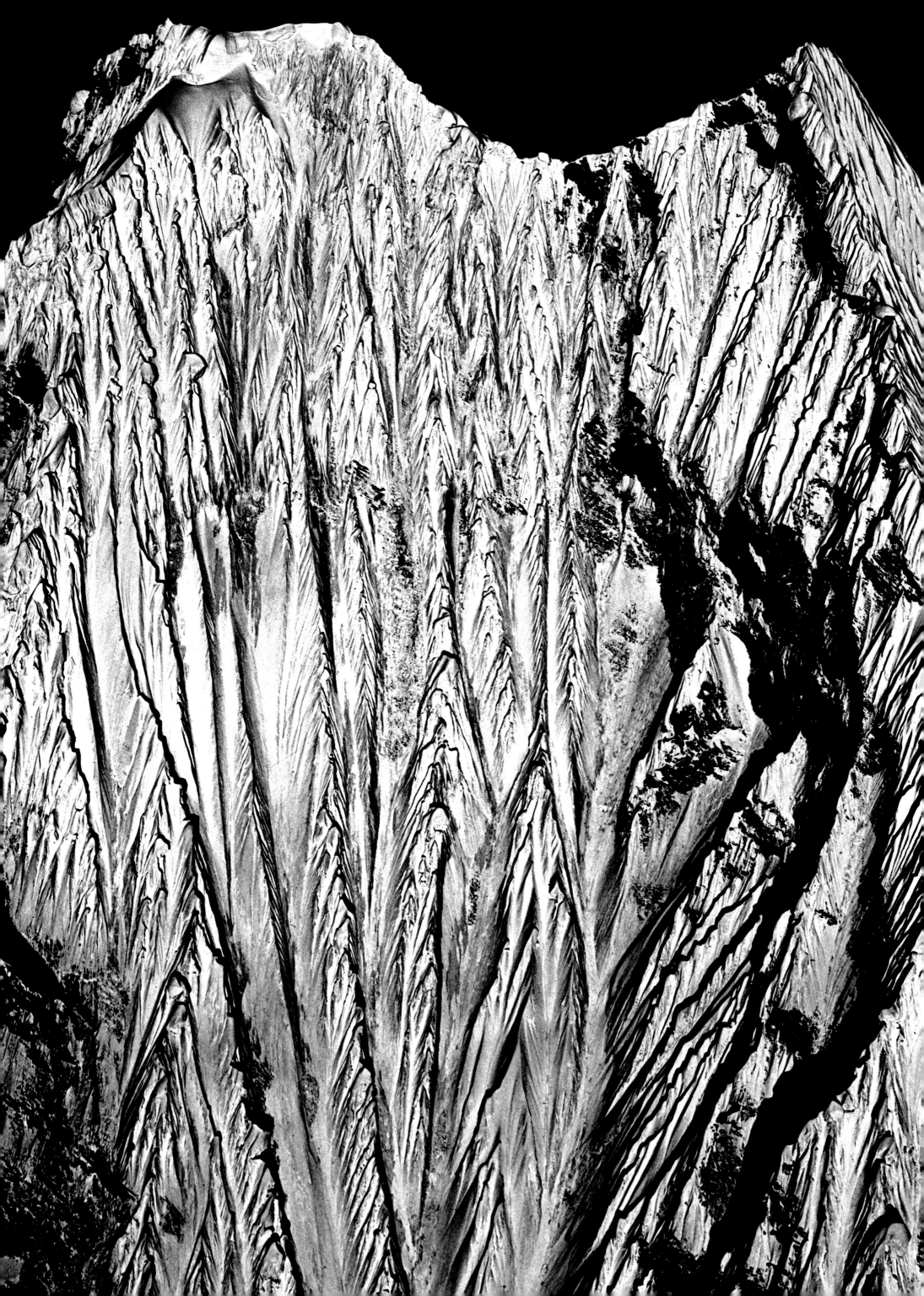

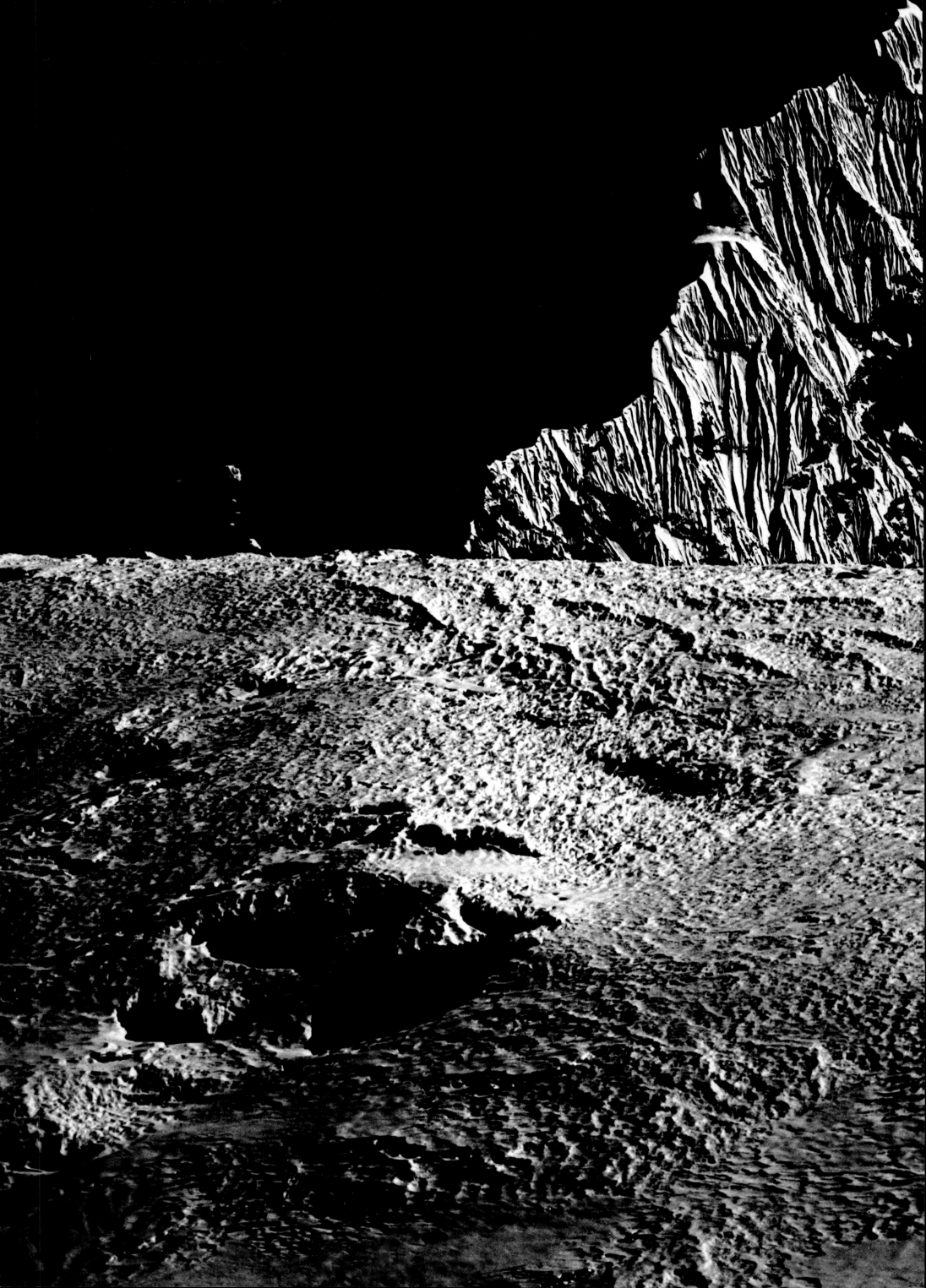

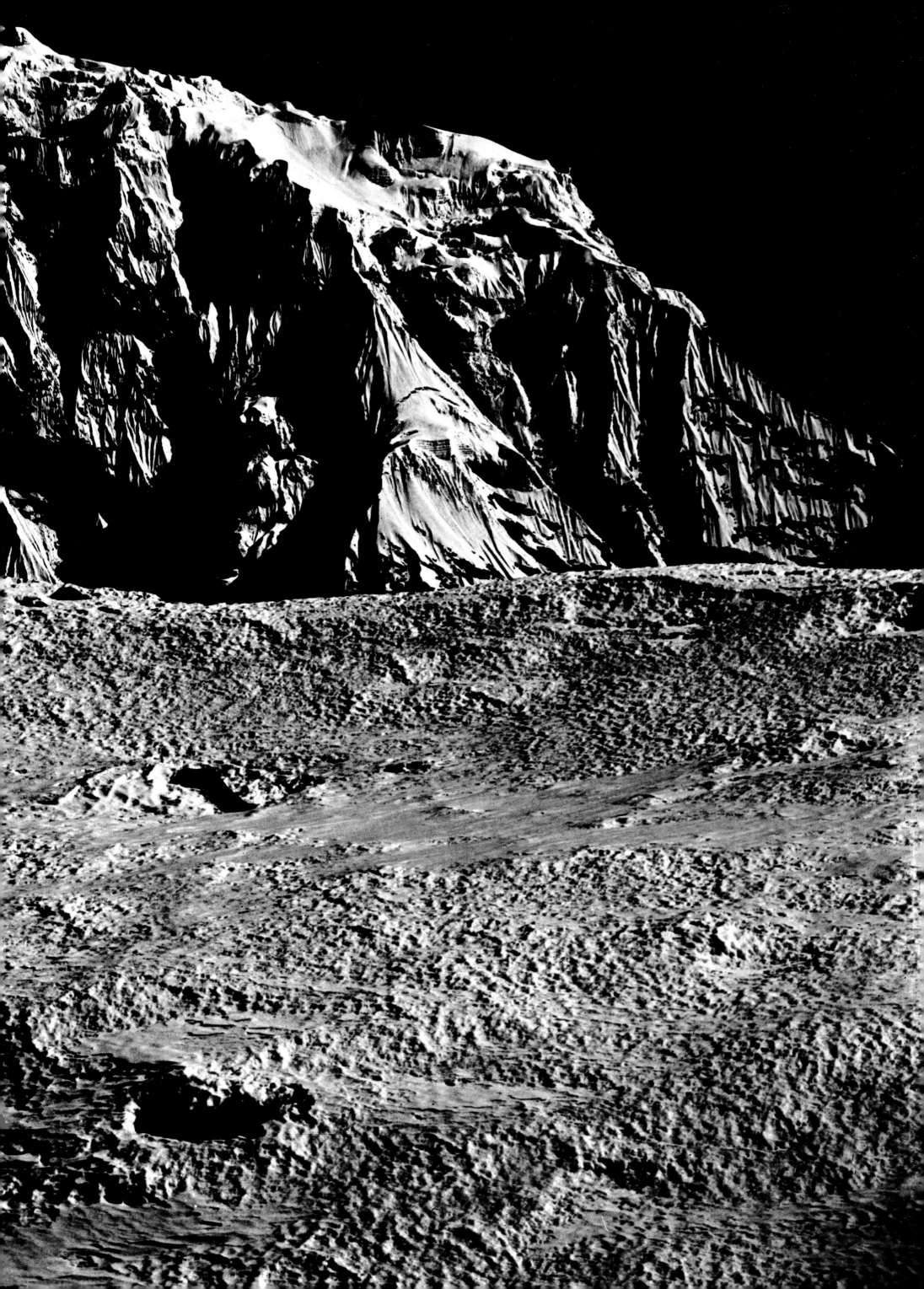

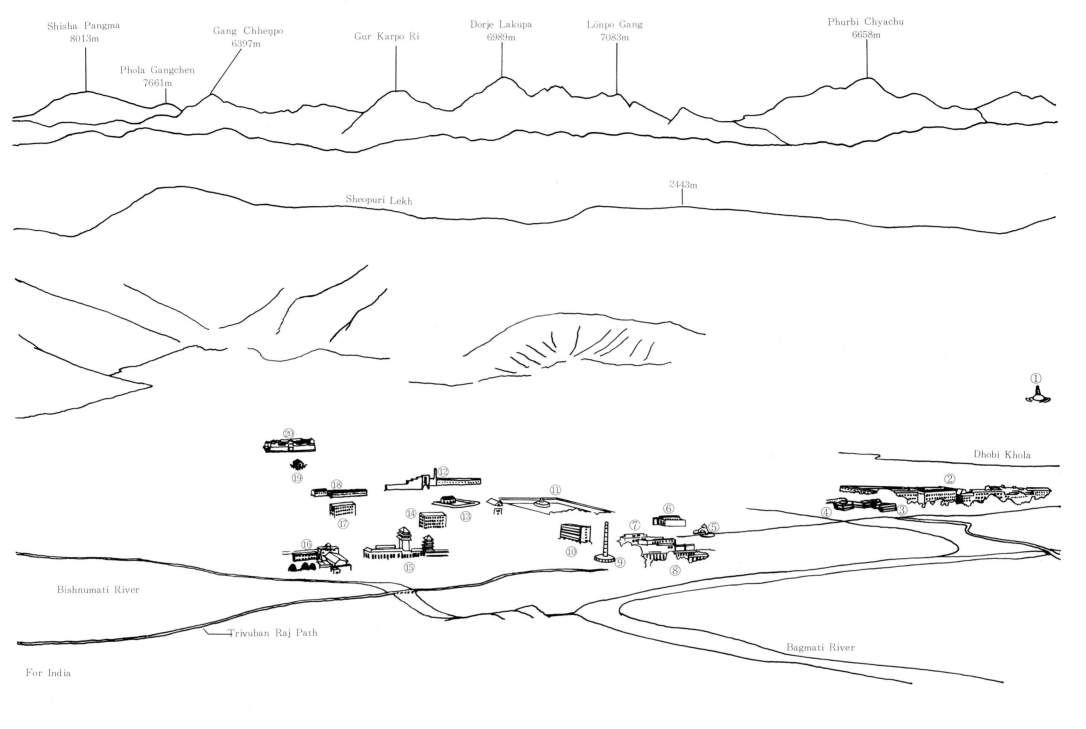

Shisha Pangma
8013m

Phola Gangchen
7661m

Gang Chhenpo
6397m

Gur Karpo Ri

Dorje Lakupa
6989m

Lönpo Gang
7083m

Phurbi Chyachu
6658m

Sheopuri Lekh

2443m

Dhobi Khola

Bishnumati River

Trivuban Raj Path

Bagmati River

For India

① Boudhnath
② Singha Durbar Secretariat
③ Department of Archaeology
④ Supreme Court
⑤ Martyrs Gate
⑥ National Theater
⑦ General Post Office
⑧ Telegraph Office
⑨ Bhimsen's Folio (Dharahara)
⑩ RNAC Head Office
⑪ Rani Pokhari
⑫ Royal Palace
⑬ Annapurna Hotel
⑭ Embassy of U.S.A.
⑮ Hanuman Dhoka
⑯ National Trading Co.
⑰ UNDP Representative Office
⑱ Shankar Hotel
⑲ Embassy of Japan
⑳ Royal Guest House

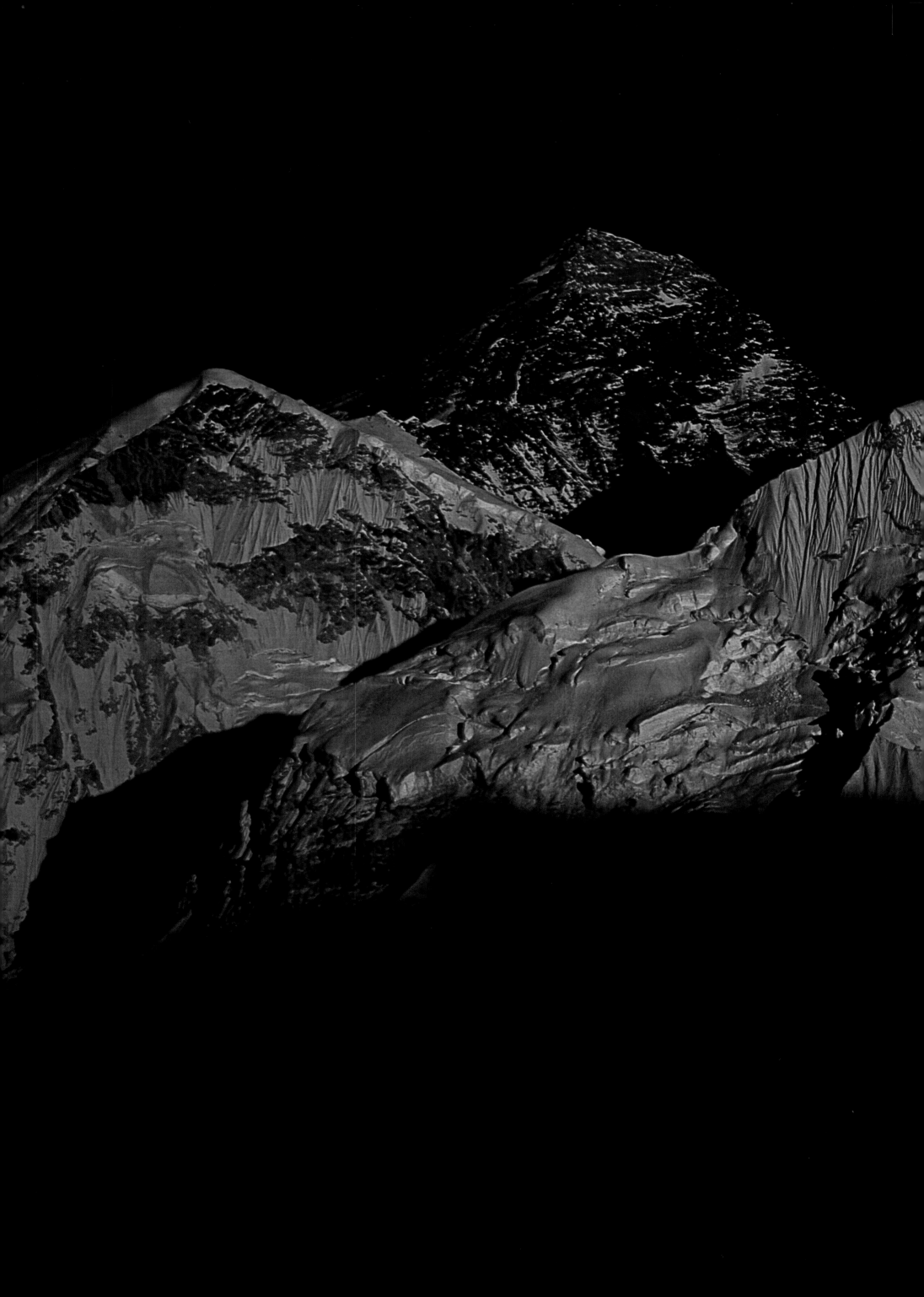

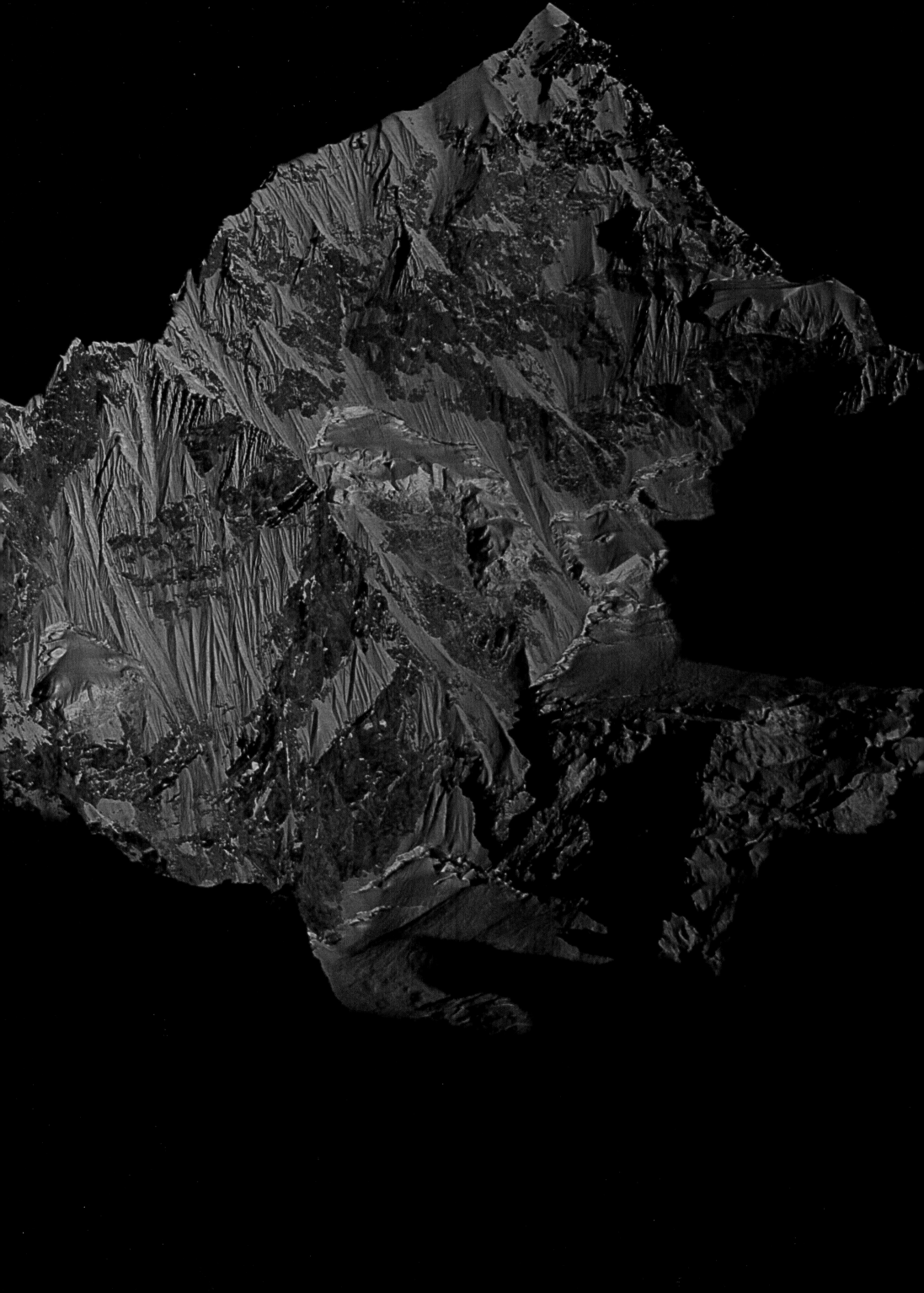

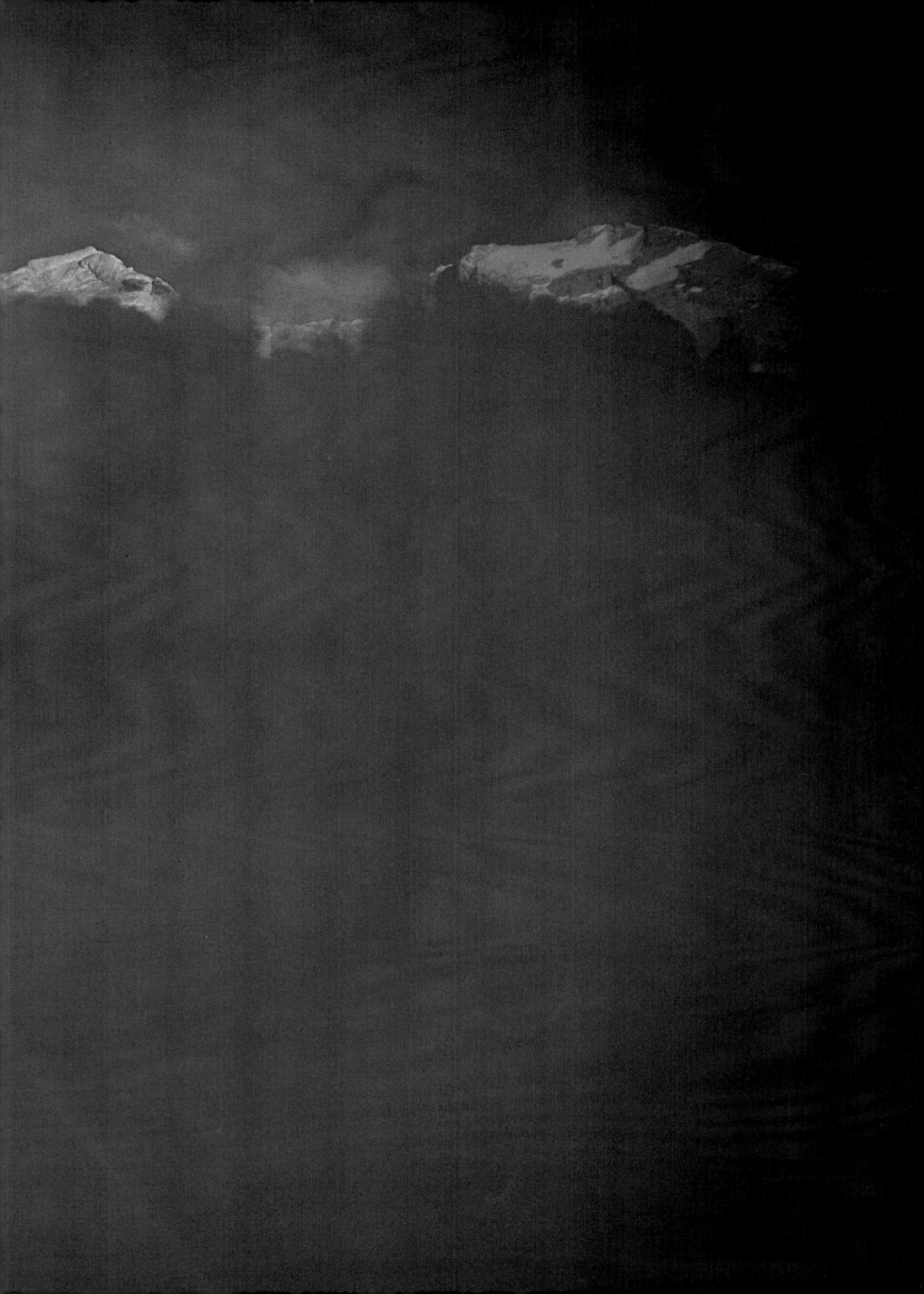

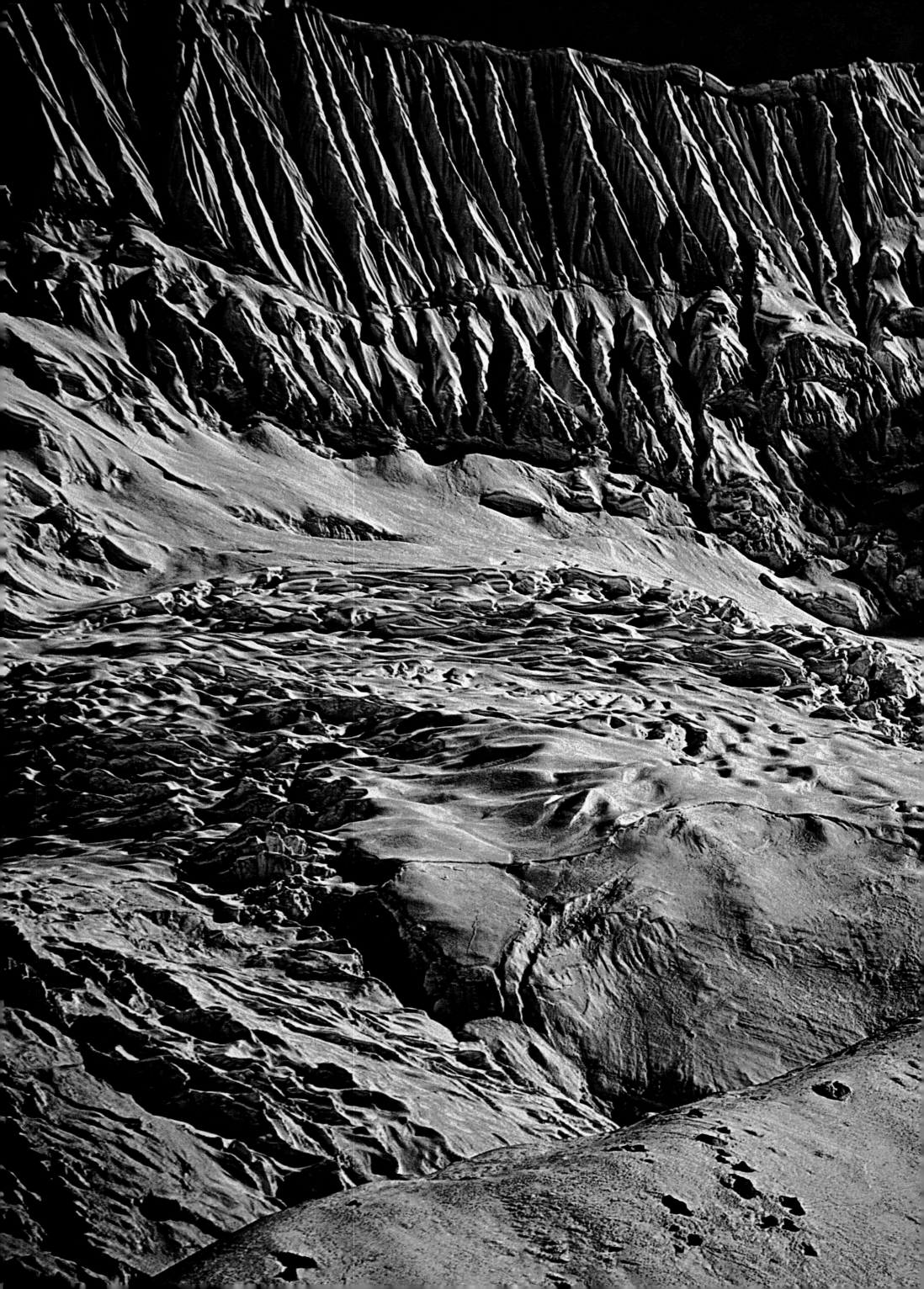

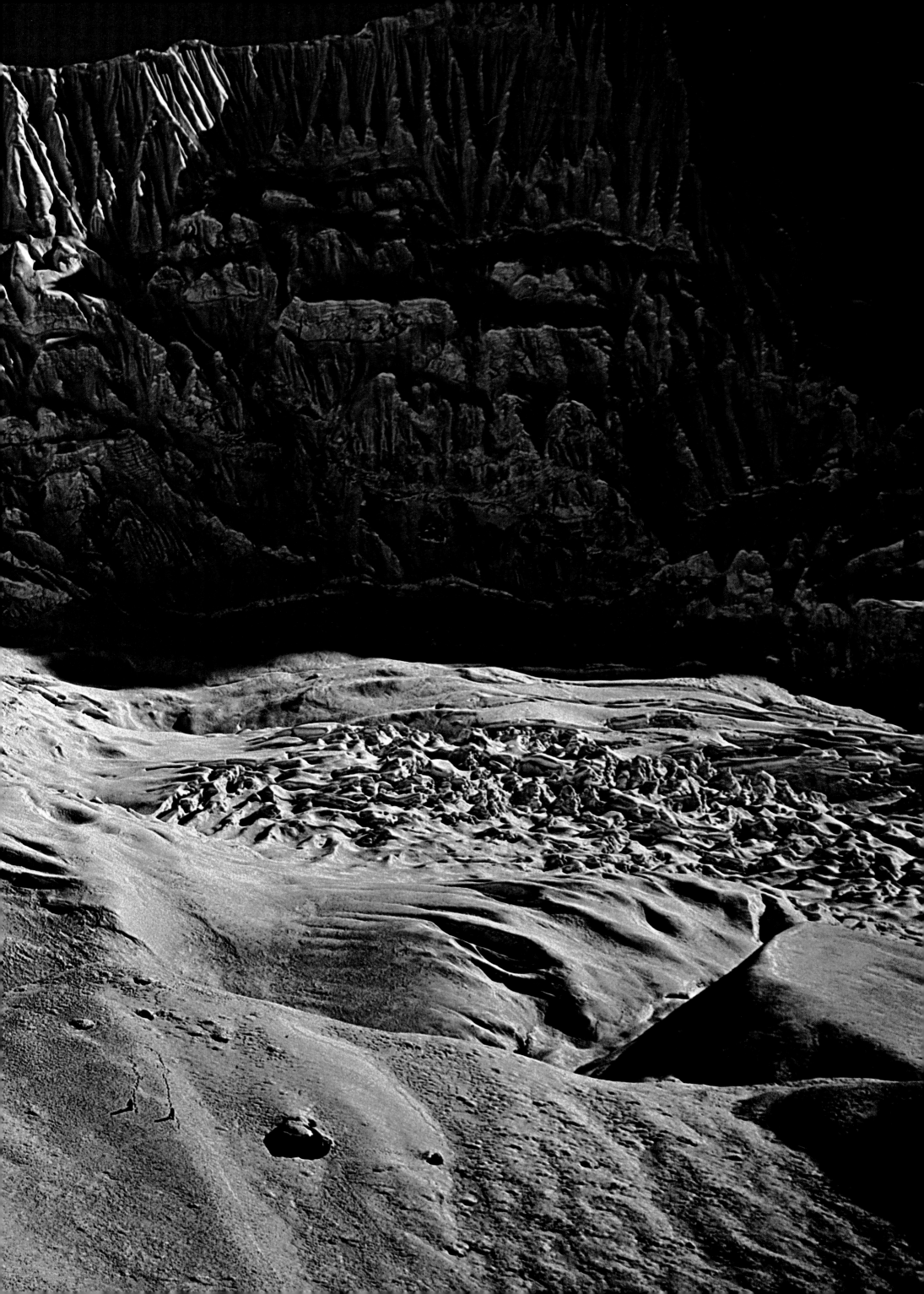

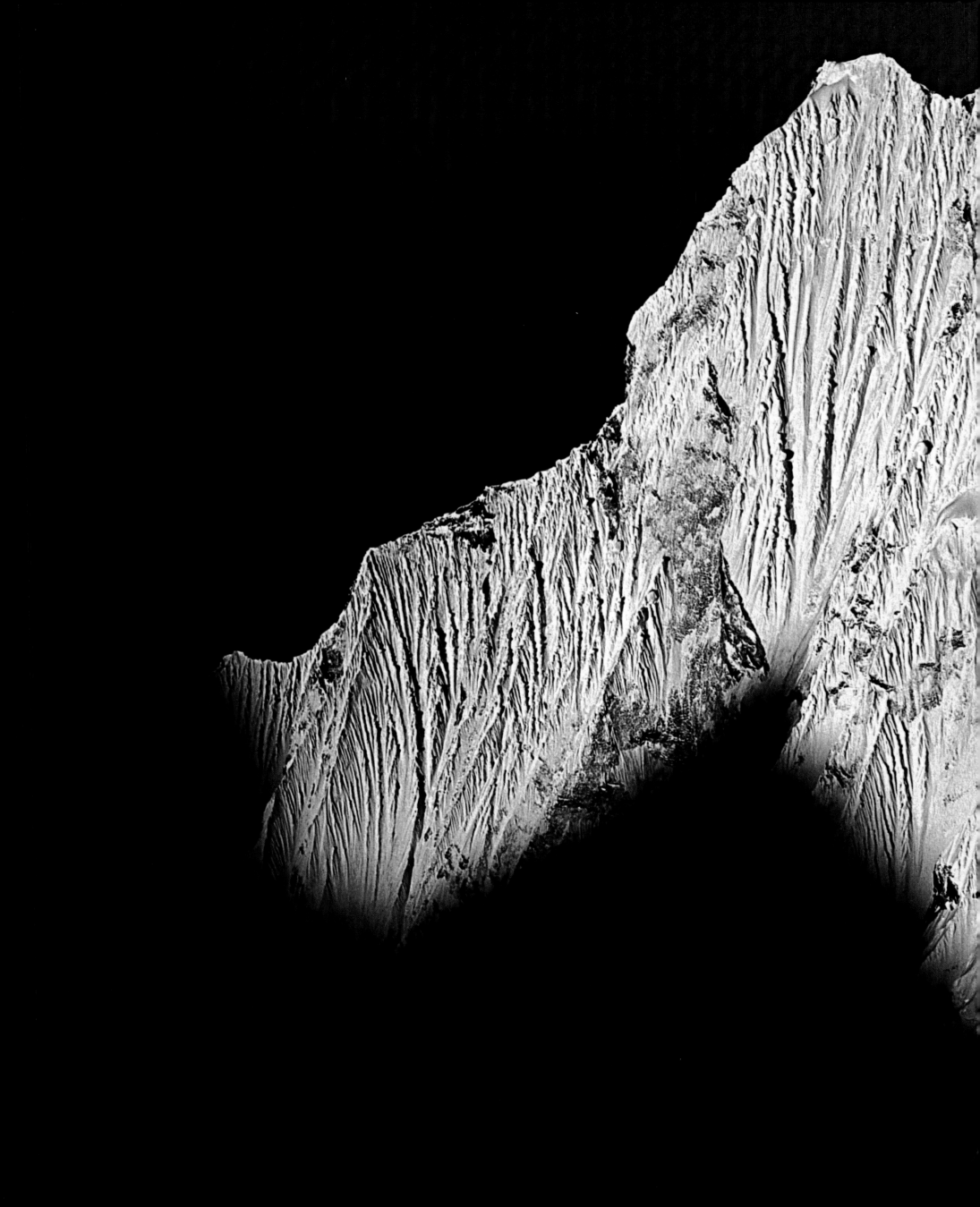

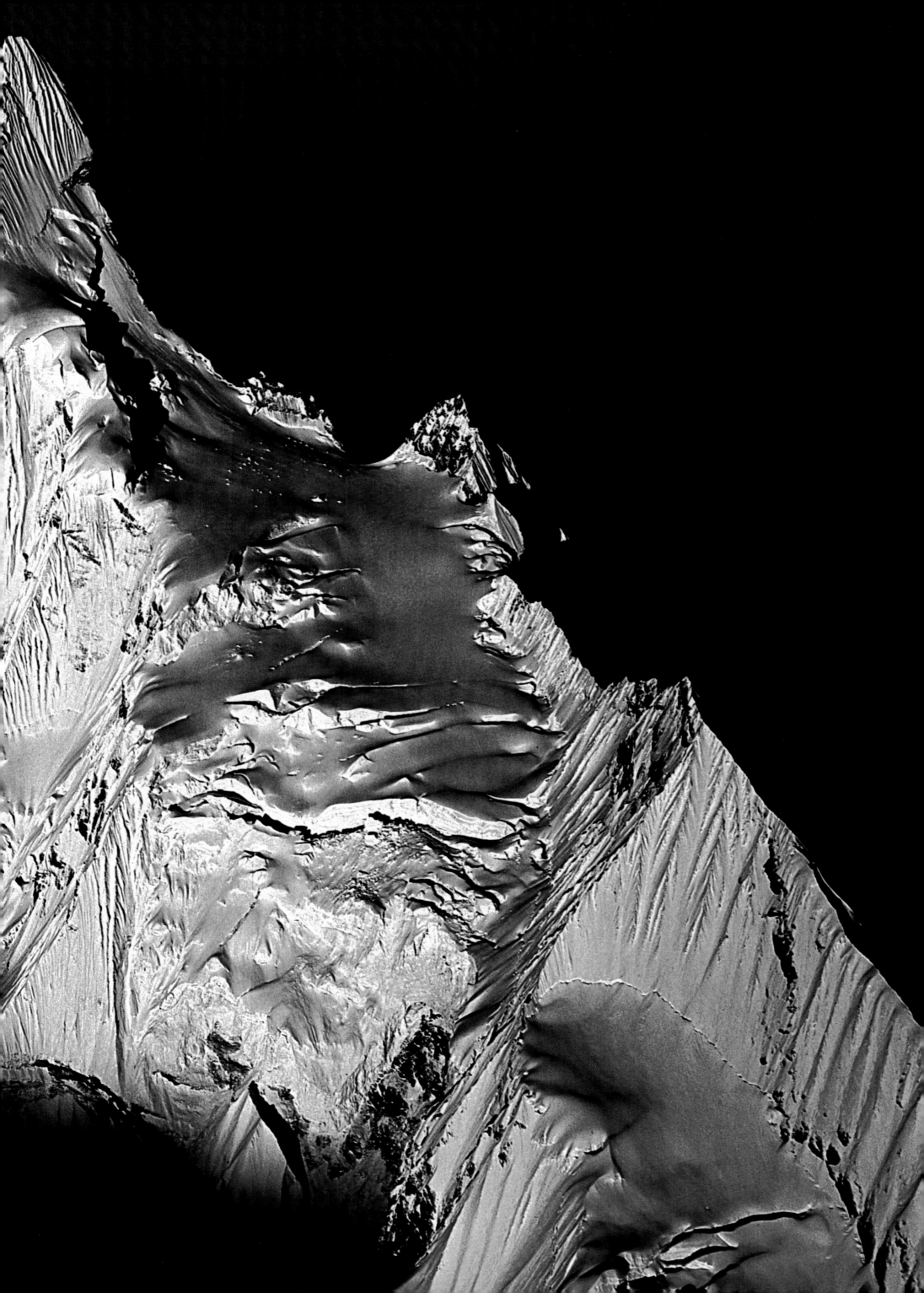

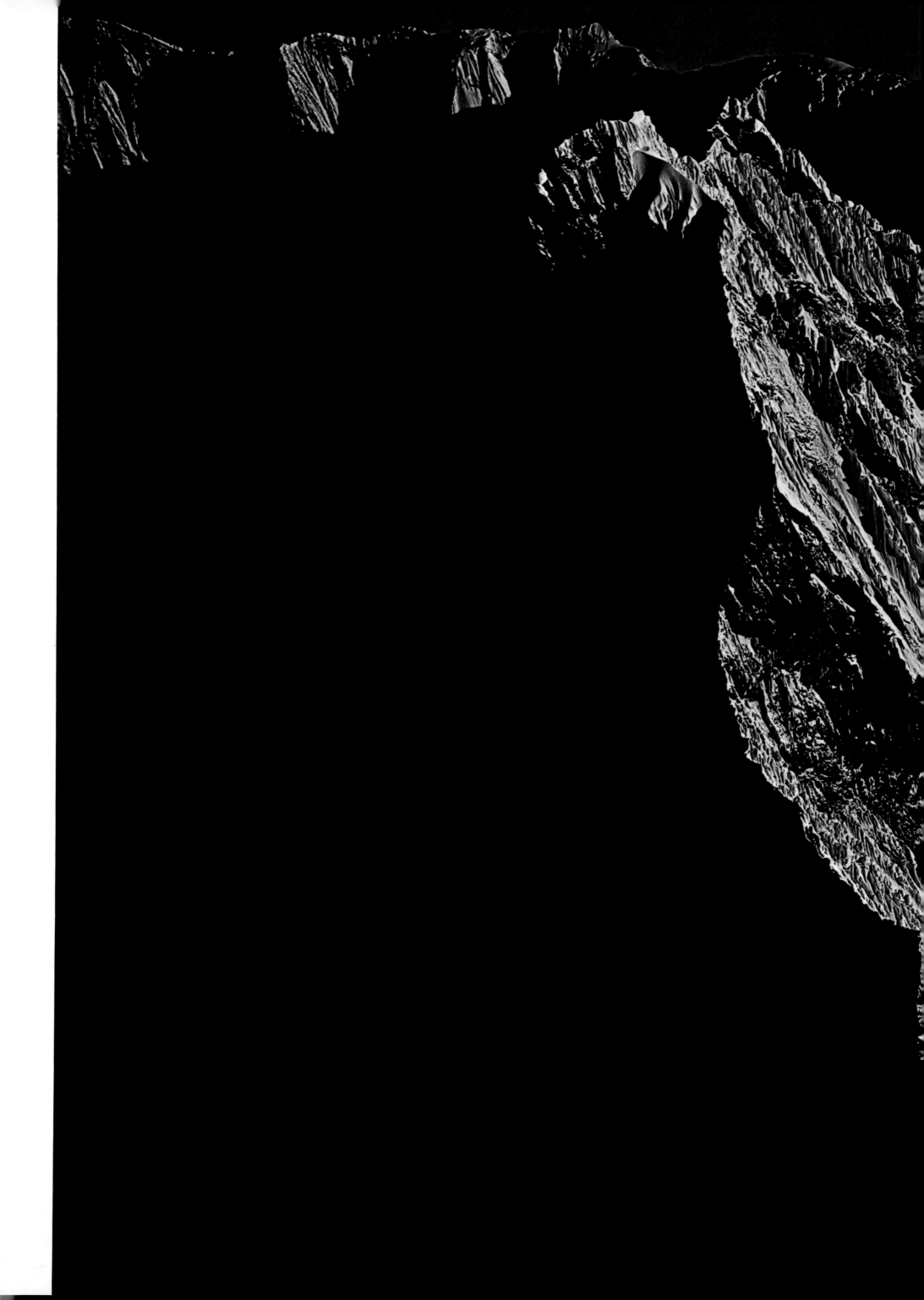

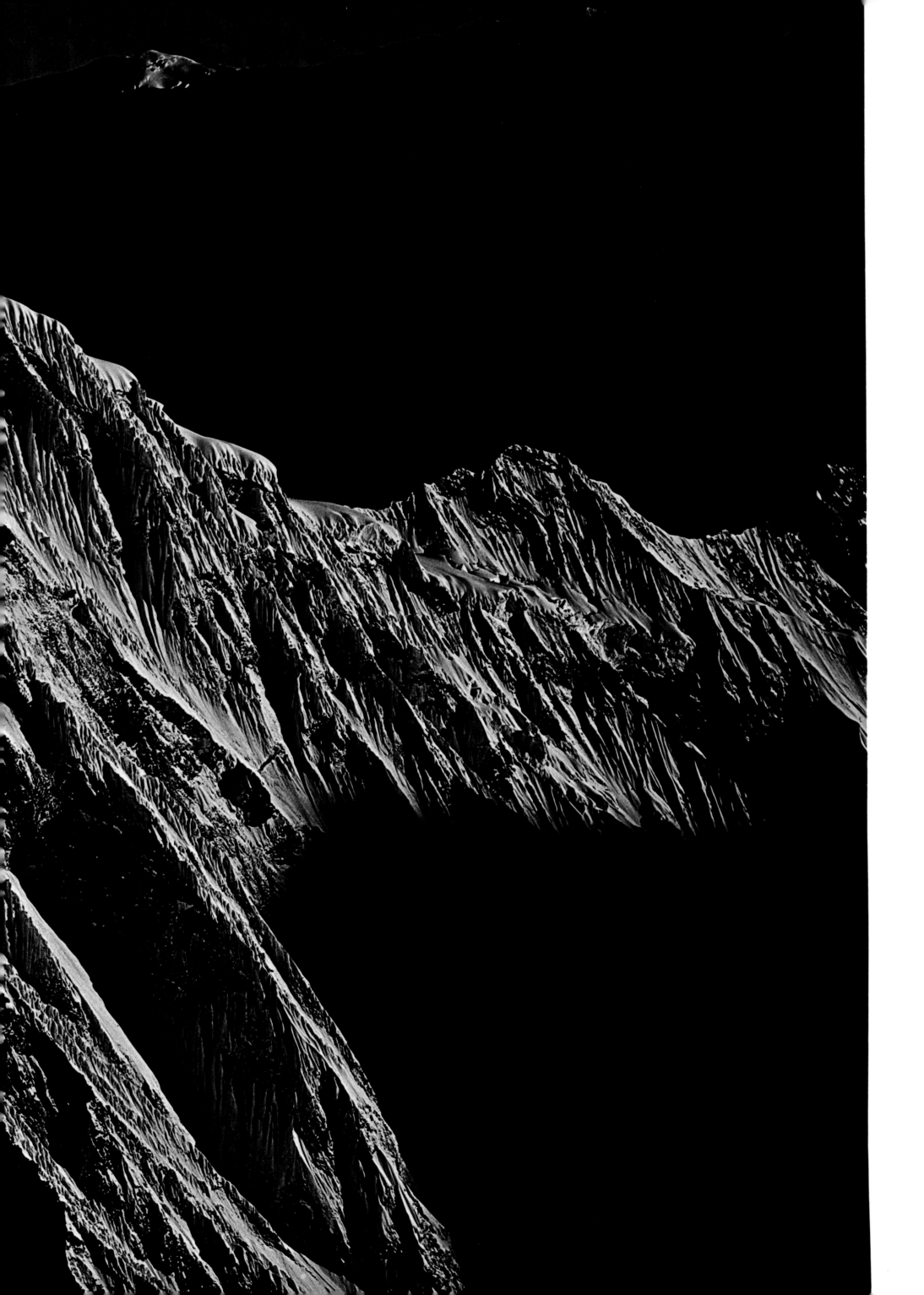

The Nepal Himalayas

EVEREST AND VICINITY

Nepal ended a long period of national isolation by opening its doors to foreign visitors in 1950. The first climbing party to enter Nepal was a French group that attacked Annapurna I. On June 3, 1950, they became the first men ever to set foot on the mountain's summit. The news of their feat, accomplished so quickly after the opening of Nepal, excited mountain climbers in many countries who dreamed of Himalayan adventure. In the next ten years, every mountain over 8,000 meters in Nepal had also fallen. The speed with which this was accomplished is truly astounding.

Nepal contains vast numbers of high peaks, more than any other section of the Himalayan Range. Near Everest rise Makalu, Lhotse and Cho Oyu, all over 8,000 meters. It seemed natural to begin my Himalayan photography expedition here.

I chartered a helicopter and flew from Kathmandu to Lukula. Traveling the same distance by foot would have taken twelve days. In retrospect, I realize that the leisurely twelve-day climb would have accustomed us gradually to the thin air at high altitudes, and prevented our later attacks of mountain sickness. Fresh from Tokyo, however, I had no patience with delay. Thinking only that "time is money" and "the sooner the better," I hurried over the mountains by helicopter.

Our party numbered six, including three sherpa porters, my two assistants, and myself. The photography equipment, climbing supplies and food we carried added up to 400 kilograms of baggage. I hired additional porters in Lukula, and we set off the same day for Namche Bazar. We arrived there two days later. It was still daytime, but as soon as the tent was set up I lay down and slept. I am not used to napping during the day and have scarcely known a day's illness in my life. Clearly, I was already showing signs of mountain sickness.

I spent the next day photographing mountains around Thamserku, and then flew to Thyangboche, the site of a large Lama monastery. Our arrival happened to coincide with their New Year, and the gay, noisy festivities were in full swing. Deep in the mountains such opportunities for merrymaking are few, and many people had traveled long distances to be there. We joined in the festivities, and even met the Head Monk of the monastery. When the devout sherpas were in his presence they prostrated themselves on the ground. They remained motionless until he left.

I photographed the festival for two days and then moved on to the village of Dingboche, the diverging point for two routes. One route leads across Khumbu Glacier to Everest's Base Camp, and the other goes over Chukhung to Lhotse Glacier.

After dinner that night, one of my assistants had still not arrived. It was growing dark, so I sent two sherpas and several porters out running to look for him. They found him collapsed in the snow, the first of our party to succumb to mountain sickness. He was so weak he could barely speak; one of the porters carried him up the rest of the way. That night was freezing cold, and a fierce wind raged until morning.

We flew deeper into the mountains by helicopter. On the third day, from tableland higher than Mt. Fuji, we again began ascending by foot. We were now aware of the danger of mountain sickness, and planned to acclimatize while climbing near Chukhung. But before reaching Dingboche, at 4,000 meters, I had already fallen sick. Nonetheless, it was imperative that we reach Base Camp while the good weather lasted. The sherpas warned me that we would have to wait for two or three weeks if an avalanche struck, since our small party could never clear away the snow alone. I decided to take the course from Gorak Shep up the southern rampart of Mt. Pumo Ri. I knew this decision meant we might all be stricken with mountain sickness, but there was no other choice.

I camped in Dingboche for three days, to acclimatize further and to impress on the sherpas the importance of my work by talking to them at length. It seemed inevitable that I would fall ill, but even in that event I could not be idle. No matter what happened, the photography work must receive first priority. Taking pictures is not only my profession, but my very life as well. For three days, I repeated the same words again and again, asking for the sherpas' assistance. I even made them promise to care for the camera equipment if I died.

On the fourth day we went up Khumbu Glacier and reached Lhotse. Even though I was already feeling weak, I forced myself on to Gorak Shep. There are no cabins or shelter at Gorak Shep; it is nothing more than a small clearing on the glacier. I have no memory of what sort of place it was. Although I can recall in detail not only the scenery, but the faces of the people at each of the other campsites I stayed in during the rest of my Himalayan explorations, Gorak Shep is a total blank in my mind. In fact, I remember very little of the events from this point on until our return to Lobutse. To view Everest from the front, we had to climb from Gorak Shep up to Kala Pattar on the south side of Pumo Ri, itself a breathtakingly beautiful mountain. The sherpas tell me I photographed Everest twice, once from Kala Pattar and once from Pumo Ri's summit, but I only remember the evening shot from the summit. Neither do I remember assigning four porters to take turns carrying me on the way back from Kala Pattar. I do remember being carried, however, from the pain of the rope cutting into my buttocks. I also remember a boulder-strewn place where I photographed Everest and Nuptse at sunset, flaming red in a cloudless sky. Half-conscious though I was, our final descent to camp made an indelible impression on my mind. I struggled slowly down a huge icy slope, leaning on the porters and sherpas and guided by flashlights. Evening had already fallen, and the lights of camp shone in the darkness ahead of us. As we approached, the porters and kitchen boys left behind came running up toward us, each carrying a flashlight or lantern. Crying ''Sahib, Sahib,'' they threw their arms around me. They had no doubt given me up for lost long ago. Exhausted as I was, their obvious relief and happiness at my safe return buoyed my spirits.

I was fortunate that my companions on this trip were sherpas. Had this been Pakistan or Afghanistan, I would no sooner have fallen ill than everything—cameras, food, and all—would have been stolen from under my nose.

That evening I had almost no appetite. I managed to swallow one cup of soup and two of rice gruel, but even that effort was exhausting. No matter how firmly I tried to grasp my cup and spoon, they fell from my fingers time and again. Two symptoms of mountain sickness are lethargy and loss of muscular control.

The next morning I realized my watch had stopped at 1:00 a.m. It was an extremely reliable watch of which I had been quite proud. I must have tossed and turned quite violently in my sleep, although I was alone in my tent and had no way of knowing for sure. I also noticed that my right thumb and forefinger were burned. Upon looking, I found many burned-out matches on the tent floor. I cannot imagine why I should have struck so many matches in the middle of the night. Possibly the intense cold made breathing difficult, and I had been trying to light a candle.

At any rate, it was plain my illness had begun to affect my ability to think clearly. In the mountains, where a leader's commands are law, there are countless times when errors in judgment have led to tragedy. Immediately, I gave orders to descend the mountain. Crossing the glacier on the way back to Lobuche, I frequently stumbled and fell. The porter who carried my baggage to Lobuche returned in the afternoon, this time to carry me. Barely conscious, I was able to take only a few pictures of the magnificent scenery I had dreamed of so long. We stopped two nights in the camp at Gorak Shep before continuing our way down.

Once we were acclimatized, the going was considerably easier. During the next three years I flew back and forth along the 3,000-kilometer length of the Himalayas many times, even climbing to a considerable height in the Sikkim Himalayas without distress. I learned later that mountain sickness is quite dangerous. If complicated by pneumonia, it proves fatal within forty-eight hours. In all, over fifty climbers have died in the Himalayas because of mountain sickness. When I returned to Dingboche I looked in a mirror for the first time since my illness, and was startled at the change in my appearance. My face was ashen, swollen twice its normal size, and carved with countless tiny wrinkles about a centimeter deep. I turned my eyes away, scarcely able to believe the face I saw was my own.

From Dingboche I went to Chukhung Glacier. The gigantic 8,501-meter crest of Lhotse rose sharply, seemingly within reach of my outstretched hand. Ice towers like glittering suits of armor rose on the front of the glacier, resplendent in the sunlight.

Several nights after we began climbing again, the sherpas sat gathered around the fire talking in whispers. Sensing something unusual, I asked what had happened. They told me the *yeti*, the Abominable Snowman, had appeared. It had been sighted, they claimed, running below an ice tower on Chukhung Glacier, headed toward Ama Dablam. They accepted its existence without question, and the tone of their conversation was quite serious. As I joined them around the fire and sat listening to their talk, I myself began to feel an eerie chill.

They said the Abominable Snowman looks like a small man but has superhuman strength, capable of felling a yak with a single blow. It reportedly rips off yaks' legs with its bare hands and disappears with them into the mountains. It usually appears in the same area, the sherpas told me—around Chukhung and Gokyo, right where we were.

For the next three days, Chukhung was hidden in a thick fog. I had heard before that the Abominable Snowman's appearance signals bad weather, and the fog somehow made the sherpas' talk more believable. The Abominable Snowman became the sole topic of conversation at camp. One day my assistant swore he had heard its voice in the night, and even imitated the sound for us. When I teased him, saying that mountain sickness had gone to his head, he grew indignant. He attached a long-distance lens to his 35mm camera and swore to photograph the Snowman the next time he saw it. He kept that camera with him even at meals. Gradually, I myself began to feel rather strange. Often, gazing at the dense fog in the evenings, I found myself half-expecting the Abominable Snowman to appear suddenly. It was all most disquieting.

When the weather improved, the sherpas and porters left en masse to try and track the Snowman down, crossing over Imja Glacier to Chukhung Glacier. Their efforts were useless. The man who had heard the Snowman's voice hunted relentlessly for a whole week, even injuring his leg in the process. But he, too, found nothing.

We went back from Chukhung to Dingboche, and entered Gokyo on the Ngojumba Glacier. There were rumors about the Abominable Snowman here, too, but no one bothered to go out looking for it.

Baths are out of the question in the mountains, and it is even impossible to sponge oneself off properly. After a while we all began to look alike, and it was hard to tell who was Japanese and who sherpa. In time, too, I grew accustomed to mountain goat meat, at first unbearably pungent. At 3,700 meters there were no more wild chickens, and goats became our only source of protein. One goat provided enough food for five days. They were small enough so that one swing of the *kukri*, a local axe, would sever the head—although more often it took two or even three swings to finish the job. At first the grisly decapitation scenes left me with no appetite for dinner, but before long I was used to them, too.

The porters skinned a goat and left it out at night to freeze. Overjoyed at the prospect of fresh meat, the porters would run around the camp holding the carcass high above their heads, yelling with delight.

At first we all stood around to watch the beheading process. One sherpa fastened a rope to the animal's horns and pulled. When the goat balked, sticking its neck out, another sherpa delivered the death blow. The *kukri* is a rather dull-edged tool, and it required a powerful swing to do the job neatly the first time. The animal's body fell to the ground with a thud: it amazed me that a little goat fell so heavily. Gradually, the beheading ceremony became a familiar part of mountain life. Often a generous portion of goat hair was mixed in with the meat at dinnertime, but I ate without grumbling. Food, water, fuel and other supplies were precious when climbing, and I was not about to complain about the meat not being washed thoroughly before cooking.

Goat soup was delicious. Our cook put a large bone with meat shreds clinging to it into a pan of salted water, and simmered it slowly. For variety he sometimes added a little curry, which was also good. Nothing could compare with the dinners where we chewed on meaty bones and drank the savory goat broth.

Passing from Pokhara through Annapurna, we were in fairly low land, and our supply of chicken meat was plentiful. One chicken supplied enough meat for one man's meal. I used to photograph the chickens strutting around the camp before mealtime, but tired of it eventually. The chickens that screeched and squawked most vigorously before their necks were wrung were firm and delicious; those that put up no struggle at all were usually less appetizing.

At Gokyo I photographed Everest, Cho Oyu, Gyachung Kang, Taweche, and Cholatse, as well as the ancient, mysterious Ngojumba Glacier. Then I returned to Lukula via Namche Bazar. When we originally left Kathmandu we arranged for a helicopter to meet us at Lukula on our return. We were happy to see the helicopter arrive right on schedule.

KATHMANDU BASIN

I photographed the Kathmandu Basin at the end of 1969, on my third trip to Nepal. My assistants preceded me to reconnaissance the area and choose the route we would later follow. The actual photographic expedition went extremely well.

Nagarkot is one of the finest spots in the Kathmandu area for photographing the Himalayas. The mountains from there look most majestic and are visible almost as an entire range. All the outstanding peaks from Dhaulagiri to Makalu are visible. One sees famous mountains like Gauri Sankar, Cho Oyu, Nuptse, Everest, Lhotse, Makalu and other giants. Gosainthan's south wall is also visible in an almost directly frontways direction. Daman Pass is also excellent for taking pictures except that the mountains are quite far away. Kakani Hill, on the other hand, disappointed me. All one could see from there were the three peaks of Ganesh.

Of all the spots for viewing the Himalayas in their entirety, however, I favor the summit of Chandra Gil, south of Darjeeling. The spot is inaccessible by jeep and requires a four-hour ascent using climbing shoes, but one is rewarded with a bird's-eye view of Kathmandu backed by all the Himalayas from Annapurna to the Everest group. Walking around the Chandra Gil area is exhilarating. We carried a portable stove to the top and cooked our afternoon meal there. All in all, the one-day trip was most enjoyable.

FROM POKHARA TO ANNAPURNA

Many people call Pokhara the most beautiful spot on earth, and it is indeed beautiful. The surroundings unfold like a screen no painting master could possibly duplicate. Machapuchare, which resembles the Matterhorn enough to be its twin, thrusts up against the sky directly in front. The Annapurna Range stretches so far to the left and right of Machapuchare that you cannot encompass the whole scene without turning your head.

I have viewed the Matterhorn and its surroundings from the Zermatt side, and really cannot say which view was finer. In majesty alone, Pokhara surpasses Zermatt, and numerous lakes in the area contribute to Pokhara's over-all beauty. ("Pokhara" itself means "lake" in the local dialect.) But if one considers the elegance of the mountains, the purity of the air and the rusticity added by the villages visible in both areas, one simply cannot distinguish between the visual splendors that are Pokhara and Zermatt.

We camped in a grassfield not far from the Royal Villa in Pokhara, on the shore of a lake a short distance from Pokhara Airport. Words fail me in trying to describe the morning and evening beauty of the Annapurna Range viewed from our camp. We made Pokhara our base of operations and travelled west through Gorapani Pass, up the Kali Gandaki as far as Jomosomba; and travelled east through Imankaluka—ahead of Thonje—as far as Namun Bhanjyang.

Pokhara is in the lowlands and in March is like summer. Agricultural products are plentiful in the area and one senses here none of the pathos felt in the Everest region where people eke out a living from frozen land. I was quite surprised on one trip from here, incidentally, to find an orange growing in the area between Tatopani and Dahna that greatly resembled mandarin oranges native to Japan.

AERIAL PHOTOGRAPHY

None of the seven countries where the Himalayas are located officially permit aerial photography. India and Pakistan, in fact, even forbid taking photographs during commercial flights over flatlands. You might charter a small plane and head for the mountains on the sly, but you stand a chance of being caught on military radar screens and chased or shot down by fighters. The mountains bordering India and Pakistan are being fortified as the frontlines in the confrontation between the two countries, and the national defense policies of both countries forbid all mountain photography. Aerial photography is unthinkable.

Nepal, meanwhile, maintains friendly relations with Communist China and does not officially permit aerial photography. If permission is granted it originates as a special consideration of His Royal Highness, the King of Nepal. Moreover, all aerial photography is from the King's private plane. I sat in the co-pilot's seat on the left side of the plane on all flights. The plane was a sixteen-passenger Twin Otter with jet-prop engines. The Twin Otter is far superior to light planes like the Piper Cub or Cessna that can only fly 4,000 or 5,000 meters at the highest, not enough to navigate Himalayan passes let alone the mountains themselves. Without a high-climbing plane like the Otter one cannot penetrate deep into the mountains. We usually flew at 6,000 to 8,000 meters, although I took most of my photographs between 7,000 and 7,500 meters. Oxygen was required at altitudes above 5,000 meters, which caused us various troubles.

The Twin Otter was not designed specifically for high-altitude flying. Its cabin was not sealed and its oxygen equipment did not meet the requirements of sustained flights at the heights I wanted to fly. All we had were two small tanks, each tank providing an hour's oxygen for one person. They were basically meant to serve the pilot. Actually, besides personally being somewhat acclimated to thin air from climbing at high altitudes, I usually was so engrossed in my work that I hardly bothered about oxygen. But sometimes I became groggy and dropped my camera. Even when I thought I held it tightly with both hands I still dropped it. And when I bent to pick it up I invariably banged my head against the cockpit window. At such times I was in a half-awake half-asleep state. If the pilot saw me like that he would yell he was going to fly lower. I yelled back for him to fly higher. The mountains around us were

8,000 meters high and if we flew any lower my photographs would be worthless. As I slowly lost consciousness I felt as though my stomach had been filled with oil and that the oil was coming up past my throat little by little. And when everything turned black and I did indeed lose consciousness my assistant jumped to feed me enough oxygen to perk me up again.

The first time we flew to Everest we bungled our oxygen allotment. We were unaccustomed to handling the equipment and used up both tanks before arriving on location to start taking pictures. There we were at 8,000 meters, and no oxygen. The pilot dropped quickly to a safe altitude and we returned to Kathmandu, hurt but wiser. After that experience I had my assistant look solely after the oxygen equipment when we flew. That equipment thereafter took priority over the cameras, the film and everything else.

A short oxygen supply was also the reason why we did not employ a co-pilot. Two men using oxygen every minute we flew above 5,000 meters would cut our photographing time in half. We thus ended up with only three men aboard: me, the pilot and one assistant. My assistant was acclimated to thin air, and even at altitudes above 7,000 meters he only required one minute of oxygen every twenty minutes. He was a life-saver for making more flying time available for photography.

We ran out of oxygen another time while flying near Makalu. My work was going well, however, and I wanted to finish it before heading back. The pilot gave me more time, even though without oxygen it was extremely dangerous for him to fly where rough air currents tossed an airplane about. While near high mountains a pilot needed a constant supply of oxygen to keep his head clear. But he kept flying. I was already groggy and sensed myself slipping toward unconsciousness, alternately seeing and then not seeing the mountains around us. When I bit the back of my right hand to wake myself up, the low air pressure caused blood to gush out of the bite and splash against the window. More than the pain the sight of the blood brought me to my senses, and I completed my photographing.

Two days after the experience near Makalu we flew to Everest again. As we went higher and higher the hand I had bitten started swelling. At about 7,000 meters blood spurted out again. My head was completely clear at the time, however, and I certainly did not want to waste valuable time tending to my hand. I tried to wrap it in a film case wrapping but could not stop the flow of blood.

Three days of flying in the Pokhara area marked the end of my aerial photography. We made two tanks of oxygen last the whole three days, but the work was the hardest of all our flying time. While we flew at 8,000 meters to photograph the sunset, the Pokhara area below was already dark. I yelled to the pilot the instant I finished and he immediately dropped down to search for Pokhara Airport. Actually, "airport" is an exaggeration, for the landing strip was a grassfield. No lights, no nothing. If we did not land quickly we might never land.

Of course we knew the field would be dark, and I planned my work so that we would be flying near Pokhara when I finished. When photographing Manaslu at sunset, for example, we headed toward Annapurna II or Machapuchare just prior to actual sunset and shot our final photos there. Even so, a descent from 8,000 meters takes time, and the landing strip was pitch dark. We had our landing lights on but still bounced three or four high bounces before settling down. The plane angled far to one side and I thought we would tip over.

One cannot really appreciate the awesomeness of the Himalayas without viewing them from the air. The mountains are tremendously high and usually you cannot see their true summits from the ground, especially while climbing. And yet their summits are the most characteristic parts of the Himalaya mountains. A mountain like Taweche, in the 6,000-meter class, looks completely nondescript from the ground. From the air, however, its 300-meter-long summit is a giant razor's edge of ice.

Numerous Himalayan mountains are impregnable. In comparison, Everest is a highly climbable mountain. Seen from the air Everest is big, very big. But it is a stocky mountain, and with oxygen one can climb it.

I took my aerial photographs between the middle of March and the middle of May. During those two months the mountains' summits changed greatly. It was obvious from the air that the climbing techniques and the energy needed to climb the Himalayas in March, when their peaks were more pointed because of ice, would differ greatly from those needed in May.

We tried to fly along the north side of the Lamjung Himal several times, but air currents chased us away every time. Our last attempt was early one morning. As we approached the area our craft began shaking as though someone were playing with it, and it rattled so loudly it sounded like machinegun firing. I saw the blood drain from the pilot's face as he navigated toward a cloudless area. We also tried twice to fly between Makelu and Kangtega, and both times were shaken violently and had to turn away. The topography evidently causes turbulence in both areas.

THE SHERPAS

One of our campsites, while we were photographing the Annapurna Himalayas, was in Gorapani Pass. Our best shots of Machapuchare and Dhaulagiri were taken from the mountaintop above that pass. For the early morning photographs taken there it was necessary to get up and complete all preparations before sunrise. We thus told the sherpas we would get up at four. Four was not early by any means, for we often rose at one or two in the morning while on expedition.

I had been asleep that night for what seemed an awfully short time when a voice outside the tent called that breakfast was ready. The surroundings were so dark I remember not believing it was early morning. My watch said nine, but I thought it had stopped and went ahead and ate breakfast. Something was not right, however, and I asked the two sherpas what time they had. It turned out that neither had a watch. They had travelled with us for two months, in other words, without ever knowing the exact time. But they had never before failed to get up at the time I set.

It seems the sherpas tell time by the stars and by changes in the color of the eastern sky. That particular night turned out to be the first time they had ever been so far off. Anyway, after eating breakfast I went to bed and slept another six hours. I know the two sherpas slept in turns the rest of that night. I could neither laugh at them nor get angry with them.

Another time, near Everest, I asked the sherpas to clean our cooking pans. I knew they would do as told and did not bother to check on them. That night, however, they were still polishing the pans. They had polished them the whole day. One could not help being impressed by their simplicity, and by their sense of responsibility. Just how strong a sense of responsibility sherpas have is preserved in history by acts they performed on Nanga Parbat and K2.

On Nanga Parbat, the sherpa Geh Reh chose to stay on a ridge and face certain death with the leader of a foreign climbing expedition rather than leave the other man and save only himself. Nothing in his work contract called for him to die for one of the climbers. His death was a human act that overcame all impersonal relationships. Pasang Kikuli was another sherpa who showed the utmost devotion and courage, this time on K2. His death also decorates the pages of Himalayan mountain-climbing history and will be related forever as a story of human devotion.

Unfortunately, visitors to the Himalayas in recent years say that some sherpas have changed considerably from their forefathers. They have become more sophisticated, and are clearly not of the same fibre.

Even now I remember all the sherpas and porters who accompanied me in my Himalayan travels. I particularly remember Gartzen, my chief porter, who was with me for eight full months. When I complimented him, I remember vividly, his face would beam with a bashful joy, and when I yelled at him he would look downcast and glance at me sideways with reproachful eyes. Sometimes while out at night drinking in Tokyo I suddenly think of Gartzen. He earned a little over one dollar a day and I still see him carrying about seventy pounds of baggage on his back, trudging silently, sweat dripping from his forehead. More than once I have left my drinking companions in Tokyo without a word and returned home because Gartzen came to my mind.

I spent three years trekking the Great Himalayas. Some of the most trying experiences I had are slipping from memory. My trials in India and Pakistan, however, I do not think I will ever forget.

If I have the chance to visit the Himalayas again I would go only to Nepal. And I would not take a camera. I would call together all the sherpas and porters who worked with me and go with them for a pleasant walk in the mountains. If they knew I was coming I know they would greet me at Kathmandu Airport. They would all be grinning, and they would all be wearing the same worn-out gym shoes.

MT. EVEREST

Everest, the earth's tallest peak, rises 8,848 meters above sea level. In this photograph, her southern face flames scarlet from the setting sun. Lhotse, 8,501 meters, is to the right of Everest. Between them stands the rugged hulk of 7,879-meter Nuptse. I climbed a hill behind my camp at Gokyo on the left bank of Ngojumba Glacier and spent an entire day photographing Everest from various angles. At sunset she revealed her splendor. I took this picture as 1969's first day was about to relinquish its light to the year's first night.

DHAULAGIRI

Sand and snow storms battered us every day of our trek through Kali Gandaki, "Black River." At one point we were forced to stop for two days waiting for the weather to improve. On the day the weather cleared I used a telescopic lens to photograph Dhaulagiri, 8,167 meters high. In the foreground is the Eastern Glacier. The sharp rise on the left is not a peak but a slope. I had taken some air photographs of these mountains, but to me the view from this angle is the best.

MACHAPUCHARE

Macha means "fish" and *puchare* "tail." The name was perhaps selected because the crest of this mountain sometimes resembles a fish's tail. We were flying past Annapurna III when I snapped this photo from a height of 7,300 meters. As the horizon swallowed the last edge of the sun the entire Annapurna Himal range was quickly obscured by darkness. The sky took on a pale blue transparency, and in this light Machapuchare took on an unexpected beauty.

FAR VIEW OF WESTERN WALL OF MANASLU

This photograph of Manaslu high above Marsyandi Valley was taken from a spot between Namun Bhanjyang Pass, 5,785 meters, and Imankaluka, a village of only two houses. I tried to catch the western wall lighted by the red of sunset, but mist-like clouds always rose from the valley in late afternoon to obscure the view. I tried for a week without success to get the photo I wanted.

UNNAMED PEAK

Lukula Airport was one of the air bases for my expedition. Plane crashes are frequent in the area, and when I was told that a small strip of land on a high plateau was Lukula and we were going to land there, I felt a cold chill run down my spine. The expedition was quite exciting. The high mountains can create treacherous masses of clear air turbulence. Should an aircraft enter one of these pockets between the mountains, luck, rather than the pilot, guides the plane into calm air and safety. The photograph shows an unnamed peak near Thamserku.

UNNAMED PEAK ON CHUKHUNG GLACIER

I left camp early in the morning to climb this ice tower and photograph the entire Chukhung Glacier, but it took me three times as long as I had expected to reach its foot. Evening was approaching as I climbed. The rock far below is as big as a large building; the mountains are enormous. The only reference point is the surrounding mountain range. Since everything in sight is unbelievably large it was impossible to get any perspective. The men in the picture are my assistants.

ANNAPURNA HIMAL

Some say the view of the Annapurna Range is the most beautiful on earth. I took this photograph from the monastery of Nadara, located fairly close to the mountains. On the left is Annapurna South Peak, 7,219 meters above sea level. The smaller peak to the right is Annapurna I, 8,091 meters. The peak in the center of the picture is Machapuchare, 6,993 meters. Annapurna III, 7,555 meters, is partially visible on the right of Annapurna I. Annapurna II, 7,937 meters, is seen on the far right. To its left is Annapurna IV, 7,525 meters.

GANESH HIMAL

It was 5:30 p.m. when I left Kathmandu Airport to photograph Ganesh Himal in the evening glow. We flew fairly high, but clouds in the western sky spoiled the otherwise perfect setting. This photo was taken during a cloud break and shows the southern side of Ganesh Himal in the fading sunlight. We were flying not too far from the border between China and Nepal. Tibet is roughly under the clouds in the distance.

HIMALAYA RANGE

This photo, taken from an altitude of 7,000 meters, shows Taweche (6,542 meters) on the left and Cholatse (6,440 meters) on the right. Gaurisankar (7,150 meters) is in the far left background, and left of it are the two peaks of Menlungtse (7,181 meters). Partially visible on the far right is an unnamed peak, 7,352 meters high. Famous Cho Oyu is to the right of this mountain, out of the photograph. Mountains sticking above the clouds and those in the distance are part of the Tibetan range.

LHOTSE

The view from Chukhung Glacier is one of the most picturesque in the Himalayas. Lhotse stands on the left, and ice towers on the right are like frozen suits of armor. Here Lhotse (8,501 meters) is about to be wrapped in darkness. The peak on the left is Nuptse, 7,879 meters; Lhotse Shar, 8,383 meters, is on the right. One never wearies of the majesty of this area. It was especially impressive when, as the sun set, the first star appeared over the peak of Lhotse Shar.

ICE WALL OF CHUKHUNG GLACIER

This was also taken from our camp at Chukhung. The face of Lhotse towering on the left contrasts sharply with the white ice wall extending to the right out of sight. Few flutes as splendid and large as this can be seen anywhere in the Himalaya Range. As the sun slowly moved westward, the icy blue of the frozen wall gradually changed color. I stayed in this area for ten days photographing only the icy walls.

MOON OVER MACHAPUCHARE

Machapuchare viewed from Gorapani Pass. *Gora* means "horse" and *pani* "water." Lone travellers and countless caravans stop here to water their horses since the pass is on the main route between Pokhara and Tibet. From here to either Modi Khola or Miristi Khola at the entrances to the pass takes an entire day.

SOUTHEAST SIDE OF DHAULAGIRI I

This aerial photograph was taken over Kali Gandaki. The southeast side of Dhaulagiri I extends from the upper right to the lower left. In the lower right is the Eastern Glacier. On the right-hand side of the page can be seen about two-thirds of the sharp peak that appears in the photograph of Dhaulagiri (second plate in the book). The southeast side of Dhaulagiri I is just a simple, flat Himal line when seen from the air, but it looks like a needle from the ground. The mountains in the background are the Manapati. I photographed this view thirty minutes after sunrise; due to atmospheric conditions, the color turned out very strange.

ANNAPURNA SOUTH

Annapurna South (on the left), 7,219 meters high, viewed from Gorapani Pass. The trip from Pokhara to Jomosomba through the western foothills of Annapurna Himal is extremely monotonous. A traveller might walk the valley path all day and see nothing but the sky ringed by a chain of mountain walls. The view from Gorapani Pass was a most refreshing change, and it was there that we pitched our tent, both coming and going.

UNNAMED PEAK ON HIMALAYA FLUTE

We left our camp at Chukhung to photograph the part of the Chukhung Glacier which lay beyond Imja Glacier. This photograph was snapped from Chukhung Glacier. A few days after we had made camp at Chukhung one of the sherpas reported that he had seen *yeti*, the abominable snowman, running over the glacier. With this news the whole camp became excited and we formed a search party. For a few days the camp at Chukhung was wrapped in a thick fog from which the *yeti* might appear any time. The thought kept us in suspense for days.

MANASLU AND PEAK 29

Manaslu, 8,156 meters high, is lighted by the morning glow of sunrise (right). The eastern face of 7,835-meter-high Peak 29 is on the left. When we took off from Pokhara the air was still wet with night dew. At 7,500 meters the sky was so bright I thought it incredible that the airport could have been so dark. Waiting for sunrise we flew around to the eastern side of the three great mountains of Manaslu. At this height the morning arrived in startling brightness.

CHUKHUNG GLACIER

This photograph was taken by a member of the party who searched for the *yeti*. Even after the mist cleared the camp was still lively with talk of the snowman. But our search for him was in vain. The peak standing over Ama Dablam Glacier, right, is Ama Dablam, 6,856 meters. The sherpa said he had seen the snowman run across it at mid-slope. It did not sound at all improbable. Days are monotonous in the Himalayas and sometimes this sort of excitement is a welcome change.

MACHAPUCHARE AT DAWN

The night sky had been so clear that not one cloud dimmed the overwhelming brilliance of the stars. But when daylight started peeking over the eastern horizon, clouds gradually formed. Making a turn above Lamjung Himal, the airplane flew up to 5,500 meters and I shot the southeast face of Machapuchare. The sun's rays created an unexpectedly welcome effect by shading part of the mountain in an unnatural color. By flying too low and taking pictures too close I present a rather misshapen mountain.

IMJA GLACIER

This photograph was taken from the campsite at Chukhung. The wide-angle lens caught Imja Glacier and an unnamed peak next to Chukhung Glacier. It looks as if it might be easy to reach, yet even a fast-walking person needs half a day just to reach the edge of the glacier at the foot of the wall of the Himalaya flute. That glacier meets Lhotse Glacier. Whichever path one might take to the foot of the glacier it is a one-day journey and the subject material for photographs is always the same.

AMA DABLAM WITH MOON

Ama Dablam, 6,856 meters above sea level, viewed from Thyangboche Monastery. As I photographed this beautiful mountain after sunset, I had just realized the sky above the mountain was unusually bright when the moon appeared. The disks of the moon overlap in this picture because a cloud hid the moon for ten seconds of the three-minute time exposure. The monastery here is the largest in the area. The view from the monastery was particularly magnificent.

ANNAPURNA I

Annapurna I, 8,091 meters, viewed from 7,300 meters. The mountain in the foreground is Machapuchare, 6,993 meters. The clouds blowing off the peak into the northern sky vaguely resemble an erupting volcano. Dhaulagiri I, 8,167 meters, is in the far left background. The peak on the near side of Dhaulagiri I is Annapurna South, 7,219 meters. Although this mountain looked enormous from the ground, from above it looked like a hill compared to the surrounding giants.

THAMSERKU

Thamserku, 6,608 meters high, as seen from Namche Bazar. One does not have to travel as far as Namche Bazar to see beautiful ice-covered mountains such as Everest and Lhotse. However, if one wants to take impressive pictures it is necessary to climb some height. There are not many places at lower elevations where one can capture the true splendor of the Himalayas. It is from Thamserku that one begins to explore the mountains in earnest.

HIGH PEAKS IN THE HIMALAYA CHAIN

The position of each mountain is shown in the plate on the previous page. Note that three of the earth's tallest peaks are included: Everest (8,848 meters), Lhotse (8,501 meters) and Makalu (8,475 meters). The latter two are the fourth and fifth highest mountains in the world. I took this picture with a wide lens from the top of a hill in the Gokyo area. As the sun began to sink, the shadows on Ngojumba Glacier rapidly lengthened and it became colder and colder. My frozen camera stuck to my gloves.

DHAULAGIRI HIMAL

The approaching morning sun, reflected upwards, splashed the western sky with red, while the moon was about to disappear behind Churen Himal. It was dawn in Gorapani Pass. From right to left are Tukche Peak, 6,920 meters above sea level; Dhaulagiri I, 8,167 meters; Dhaulagiri II, 7,751 meters; and, in the lower left, Manapati, 6,030 meters. On the upper left is Gurja Himal, 7,193 meters.

NORTH SIDE OF LAMJUNG HIMAL

This is the north side of Lamjung Himal, 6,931 meters above sea level, photographed from an altitude of 7,000 meters. When viewed from the south, from Pokhara, for instance, one can see only one peak. From the northern side, however, two gently sloping peaks can be distinguished. The triangular-shaped mountain on the right, framed by a ridge, is merely a part of one of the slopes. Not only this particular photograph, but all photos in this book taken from the Tibetan side of the Annapurna Himal are probably the first ever published.

THAMSERKU AND MOON

The sun sank in the western sky and the surrounding area became dark immediately. Since early morning I had been photographing Thamserku's changing features from the top of a hill. I was about to return to camp when I looked back. On seeing the faint, icy tower of Thamserku in the evening sky, I reset my camera and went back to work. Although the earth below had lost all color, the peak at 6,608 meters still held the glow of the sun.

AMA DABLAM AND THYANGBOCHE MONASTERY

This is the largest Lamaist monastery in the Thyangboche district. Erected on a huge plateau above the Imja Glacier, the monastery affords a panoramic view of the entire region. Nearby Ama Dablam stands at 6,856 meters. I had photographed the same area from the sky, but the view from this angle was far better. The contrast of the splendidly white mountain and the brick-colored monastery leaves a sharp impression on the viewer.

WALL OF THAMSERKU

From the ground Thamserku's sculptured outline is extremely beautiful. I had great hopes of taking a good picture from the air too, and tried to take a close-up directly from the front. I worked from various angles at different altitudes, but the view was far from what I had expected. The mountain's highest point is 6,608 meters above sea level. Thamserku seen from the ground is the sharp peak in the bottom right hidden in the shadow of the mountain's higher part.

STRANGENESS OF CHUKHUNG GLACIER

This is a telephoto of Chukhung Glacier taken from above the moraine on the side of the Imja Glacier opposite our camp. The flute and serac in this photograph make the scene peculiarly Himalayan. In black and white, the image suggests the intestines of some kind of monster. My assistants are seen returning from a scouting expedition.

ANNAPURNA II, NORTH SIDE

From Pokhara the south side of this mountain appears gigantic. One huge piece of rock leads up to the summit. It is hard to imagine that the same mountain could look so different from another side. I flew at 7,500 meters past the north side of the peak. Annapurna II (7,937 meters) towers above the other mountains in the area. Far on the horizon, on the other side of the plane, was Tibetan territory.

EAST WALL OF MACHAPUCHARE SUMMIT

The Gurungs who worship Machapuchare say that their Goddess lives in a hollow just below the summit. I flew in close to the summit many times but did not see the Goddess. I did feel that I might possibly be guilty of profaning the guardian of the Gurungs for taking such a clear photograph. This picture shows the entire east wall of Machapuchare.

MOUNTAINS AROUND GANESH HIMAL

An aerial photograph of the mountains around Ganesh Himal viewed from the north. Ganesh Himal, at 7,406 meters, stands on the left at the Tibet-Nepal border. The wind-blown clouds in the center of the photograph mark a 7,130-meter unnamed peak. I checked with many people to see if my altitude figure was reliable, but I could not get a definite answer. Another high mountain is Pabil Peak on the right, 7,102 meters.

CHOLATSE

On the way from Gokyo I was constantly in sight of Cholatse, 6,440 meters high. In this photo, the base of Cholatse is hidden by the snow-covered moraine bank of Ngojumba Glacier. As can be seen in this picture, the moraine lies all along the edge of the glacier in a succession of low hills. The white dots on the left are piles of rock covered with snow. The frozen scenery made me feel as if the entire world were made of iron and ice.

SUB-MOUNTAINS OF GANESH HIMAL

As the sun declined, the clouds in midsky were swept away toward the horizon. Flying at 7,000 meters, one can see all the sub-mountains of Ganesh Himal. I estimated them to be as high as 6,000 meters. None of these mountains have names. Although there are many beautiful mountains among them, no attention is paid to peaks in the Himalayas only five or six thousand meters high.

PANORAMIC VIEW OF KATHMANDU

Kathmandu as seen from a spot near the summit of Chandra Gil, 2,831 meters above sea level. Mountains and buildings are identified in the illustration on the previous page. Only during November and December can the town of Kathmandu and the surrounding Himalayas be seen this clearly. On the left are Ganesh Himal and Annapurna Himal. To the right the mountains around Everest are clearly visible.

EVEREST AND NUPTSE

Everest, center, and Nuptse, right, viewed before sunset from Kala Pattar. Immediately after arriving at Lukula I climbed the summit of Kala Pattar. I was careless and did not acclimatize myself to the high altitude properly. Mountain sickness soon overcame me and I had to be carried down by a sherpa. Though I do not clearly remember doing so, it seems that while I was lying sick I shot 10 or 15 photos. The fact that I could unknowingly take fairly good pictures gave me much confidence. After this experience I never again considered photography as difficult as I formerly had.

MAKALU

Makalu, 8,475 meters above sea level, photographed from an altitude of 7,700 meters. As our plane approached Makalu we ran into a powerful flow of air from the north, possibly the Jet Stream. Our twin-engine Otter, which seats twenty passengers, was shaken up and down in a violent, machinegun-like motion. I could barely support myself, and taking pictures was out of the question. For the rest of the day we dared not approach the mountain walls too closely for fear of the violent turbulence. The peak rising above the others on the left is Everest, and the rocky mountain to the left of Everest is Lhotse. I took this photo around 5:00 a.m., just after the sun rose.

MANASLU IN CLOUDS

From the foot of Namun Bhanjyang on its west, I got a good view of Manaslu. Later, clouds rose from the valley of Marshyandi and engulfed us. Manaslu is visible on the left here, beautifully rimmed by a triangle of clouds. Those clouds probably were blown eastward as they rose from below and were forced to the other side of the mountain.

GOKYO

This small village on the left bank of Ngojumba Glacier is inhabited only during the monsoon season, and is the upper limit of habitation in the area. The moraine rises to a height of fifty meters behind the village, and beyond it flows Ngojumba Glacier. In the winter, snow blowing off the moraine looks like smoke. In front of the village are three frozen lakes.

TUKCHE PEAK AND KOBANG

Snow is shooting off the summit of Tukche Peak, 6,920 meters high. At the base of the mountain is Kobang, a village near the border on the highway between Pokhara and Tibet. Kobang is famous from days when women here entertained travellers. Under the dusty cloud in the foreground lies the vast dry bed of the Kali Gandaki, "Black River." Sandstorms are frequent here in winter.

DISTANT VIEW OF SIKKIM HIMALAYAS

From an altitude of 7,500 meters, near Makalu, I had a good panoramic view of the Sikkim Himalayas. The peaks of Kangchenjunga and other high mountains are hidden in the clouds. This photograph shows the entire range that divides Nepal and Sikkim. Waves of clouds spread as far as I could see. Massive clouds began to close in on us and we headed back to Kathmandu.

FACE OF ICE WALL IN CHUKHUNG GLACIER

One might think that flutes this size would be seen often in the Himalayas. Actually, they are rare. Rocks are scattered here and there in the flute, and the scenery is generally uninteresting. But the rarity of the flute alone would make Chukhung a bustling tourist attraction. In the bottom foreground my assistants are returning from reconnaissance.

EASTERN WALL OF MACHAPUCHARE

In looking at this photograph one might immediately think of the Matterhorn in the Pennine Alps. The two mountains so strongly resemble each other that one can hardly tell them apart. In this album I have included photographs of Machapuchare's east, west, and south faces. The east wall provides the best photographs. We circled at 7,000 meters until the shadows gave me this shot.

MACHAPUCHARE IN CLOUDS

Leaving Pokhara, I hiked west for one day until I could get a partial view of the western wall and summit of Machapuchare. I photographed the mountain from the path on the Nadara ridge at evening time. I had taken another shot from there of Annapurna's peak protruding from the clouds. It was difficult to decide which of the two to include in this album, but I finally chose this view of Machapuchare. Its ridge is sharply defined and the red, striped pattern on the clouds creates an interesting photographic effect.

ANNAPURNA HIMAL AT SUNSET

Our plane was flying at approximately 7,300 meters on the way back from photographing Manaslu's three great peaks when I photographed Annapurna South, which is on the left. Annapurna I is among the clouds directly under the sun and Machapuchare is in the foreground with its peak reflecting the sun's rays. The line formed by these mountains is fairly sharp. Pokhara is to the left. It was evening and darkness crept over Pokhara as we flew back.

SOUTHEAST RIDGE OF MACHAPUCHARE

Machapuchare is one of the most graceful mountains in the Himalayas; one look is enough to understand why the Gurungs regard it as a fortress of beauty. Making Pokhara my base, I flew reconnaissance flights to the vicinity of Machapuchare every day. I photographed every detail of the mountain from the sky and from the ground. Here the south (left) and east (right) faces reflect the early morning sun. The southeast ridge forms a sharp line.

NGOJUMBA GLACIER

Ngojumba is one of the largest glaciers in the Nepal Himalayas. Left of center is the white hill from which I photographed Everest for this book's front page. Gokyo Lake is partly seen below the hill. Although the hill and lake look close, they are actually a four-hour climb apart. The high mountain on the left of the picture is Cho Oyu, 8,153 meters above sea level. On the right, Gyachung Kang (7,752 meters), a peak that fell to Japan's Nagano Prefecture Alpine Society, looks like the hull of an upside-down boat.

WOMAN SHEPHERD

Pokhara was our base camp for numerous trips into the Annapurna Himal. Tired from climbing, we returned to Pokhara for a few days of rest. We pitched our tents there in a field close to the Royal Villa, not far from the local airport. We were near a lake, and from our vantage point Annapurna was in plain sight. In these pleasant surroundings we watched a young woman tending her sheep.

AFTERGLOW OF THAMSERKU

Thamserku, 6,608 meters high, viewed from Thyangboche Monastery. The afterglow of the western sky is reflected red on the Thamserku ice wall. The direct rays of the evening sun, I learned, do not turn a mountain red. The light must be indirect. The high pinnacle is the front peak. The summit of the main peak is on the left. It was already dark where I was standing and I worked using a flashlight.

CHILDREN AT GHANSA

Ghansa is a day's hike from Tatopani. There is an azure blue lake on the village outskirts and camping there was quite pleasant. North from there, however, sand storms whip across Kali Gandaki Glacier. These children were at a rest house near Ghansa where we stopped for a short time. The eyes of infants in this area are all marked with strong pencil lines. I supposed these children to be Nepal Hindu. There are sixteen different ethnic groups in Nepal, and it is difficult to tell them apart.

CHOLATSE AND TAWECHE

A view of Cholatse (6,440 meters) on the left, and Taweche (6,542 meters), on the right. I took this looking across Ngojumba Glacier from above the moraine behind Gokyo. When I came to the Everest base camp after crossing over Khumbu Glacier and looked back I felt a strange sensation. The left-right relationship of the two mountains was reversed. I thought I was looking at a picture drawn backwards. The high winds blowing across the Ngojumba Glacier seemed like they might carry away my camera, my tripod, and me with them.

WOMAN AT TATOPANI

I took a one-day excursion to Tatopani. Going through Gorapani Pass I went by Sikha. Travel was not tiring, since there was no climbing involved. Towering Dhaulagiri provided a breathtaking contrast to the gradual descent of the slope we crossed. At the bottom of the slope is Kali Gandaki. The name Tatopani ("hot water") refers to the two hot springs here on the banks of Kali Gandaki. I snapped this photograph there. From the woman's make-up and dress I concluded that she was Nepal Hindu rather than sherpa or Bhotiya.

CARAVAN

Traders travel between Tibet and Pokhara, bringing salt to Pokhara and returning with rice and lamp oil. They cross through the Gorapani Pass and follow the Kali Gandaki northward. I met this caravan near Kalopani. Some caravans take with them as many as one hundred head of cattle. There are almost no trees from here to Tibet and the runoff feeding the river causes turbidity. Although the river appears white in this photograph its banks and bottom are actually black.

STREET SINGER

Itinerant street singers like the man in this photograph might be called strolling musicians, street performers or even minstrels. No single term seems to fit them. Caravans always stop at the same places, and these minstrels wait there for them. The compensation for singing four or five selections is fifty Paisas, or about $.05. This photograph, taken in Siswa, shows a singer with a fish he got as payment. He is happy because fish is a rare delicacy in Nepal. The singer had a delicate, melancholy voice.

PUNJAB HIMALAYAS

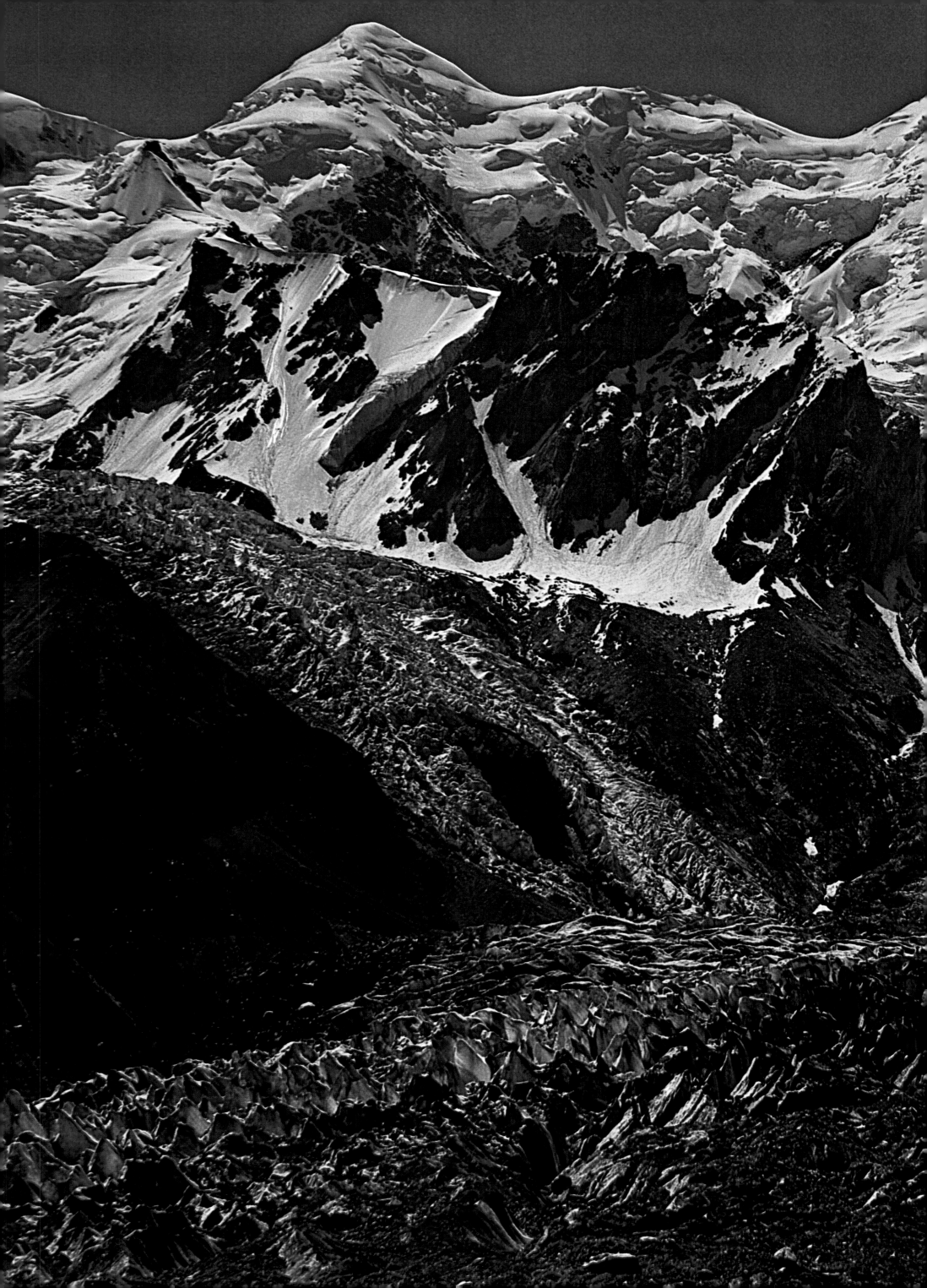

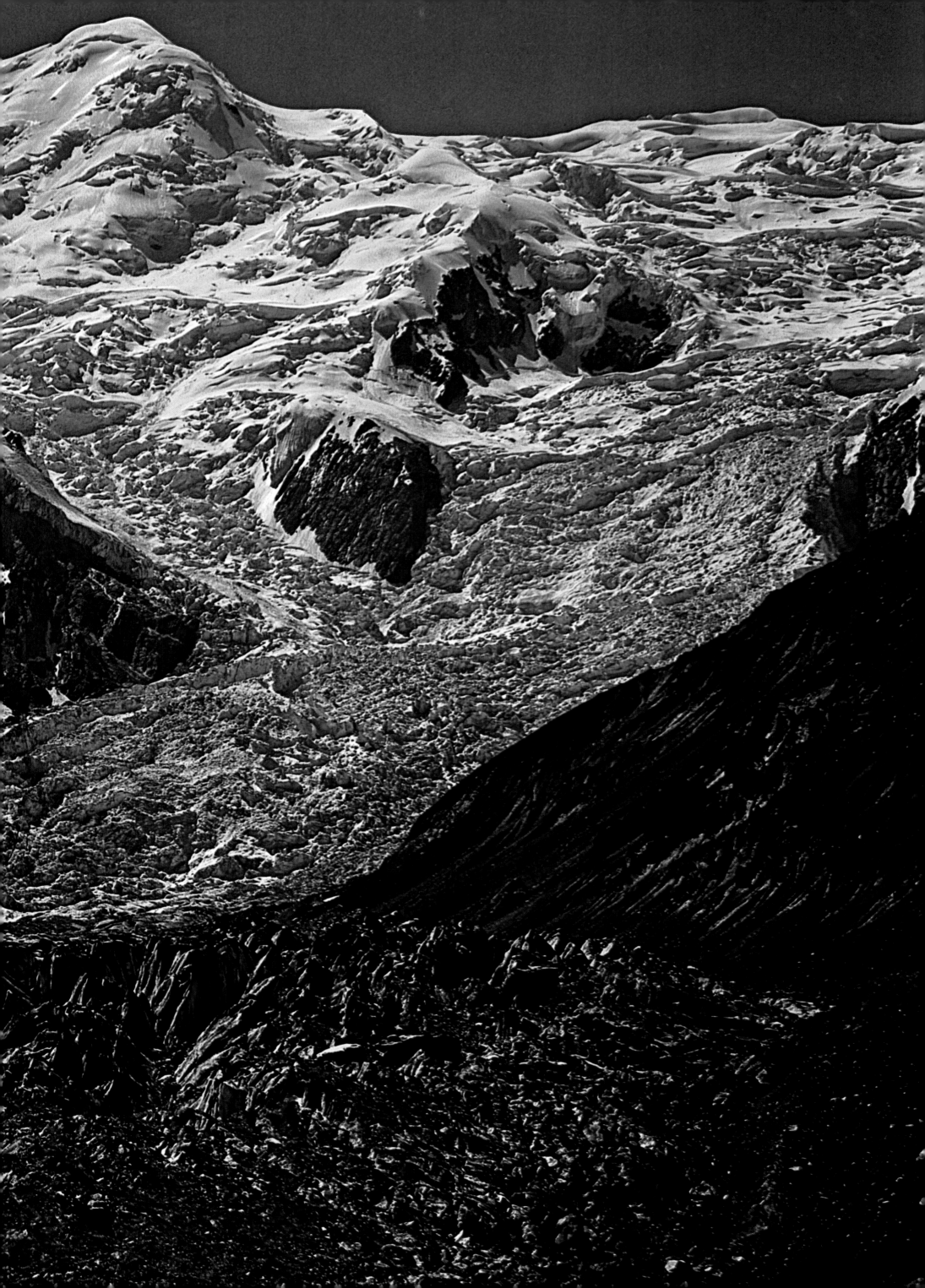

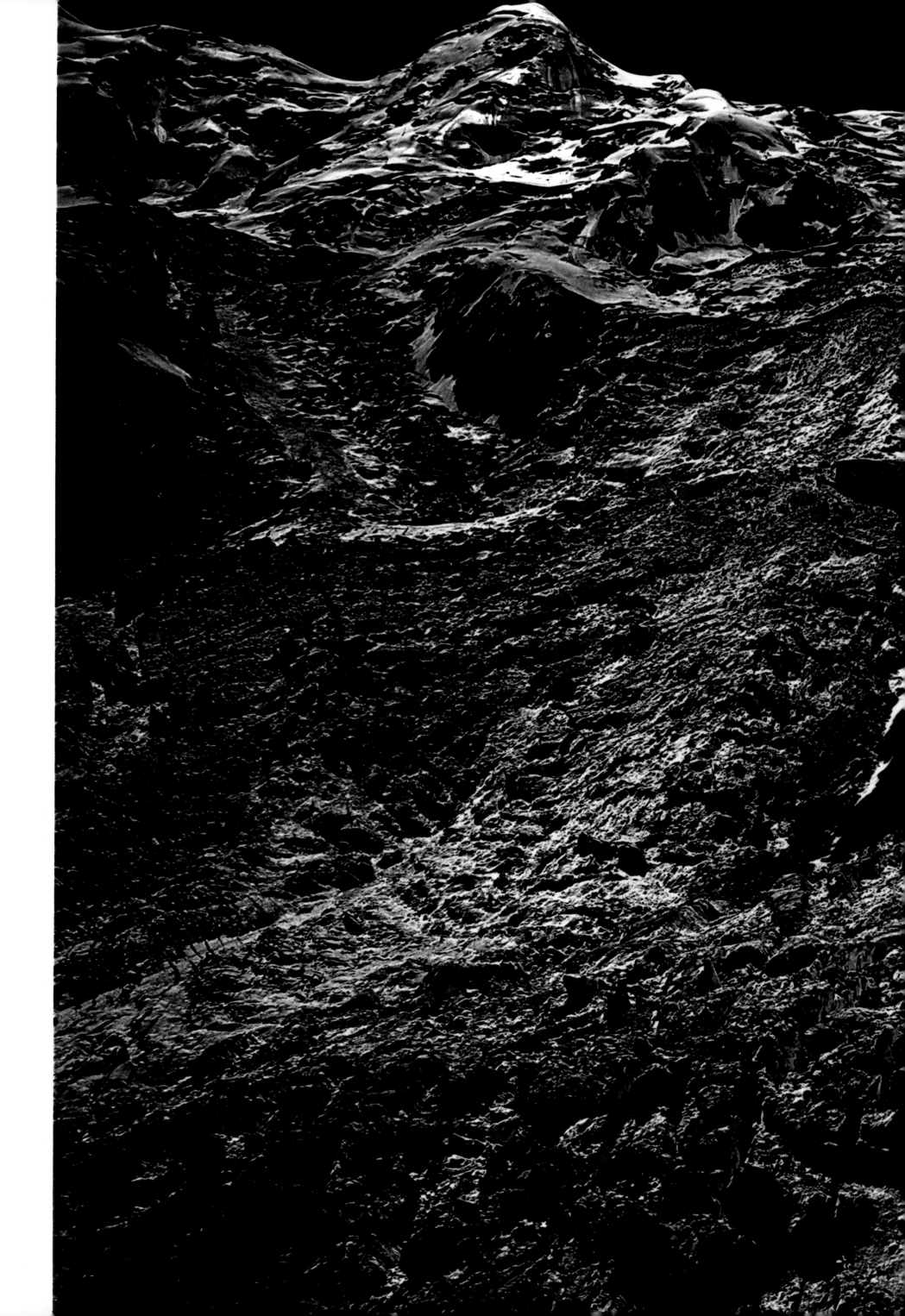

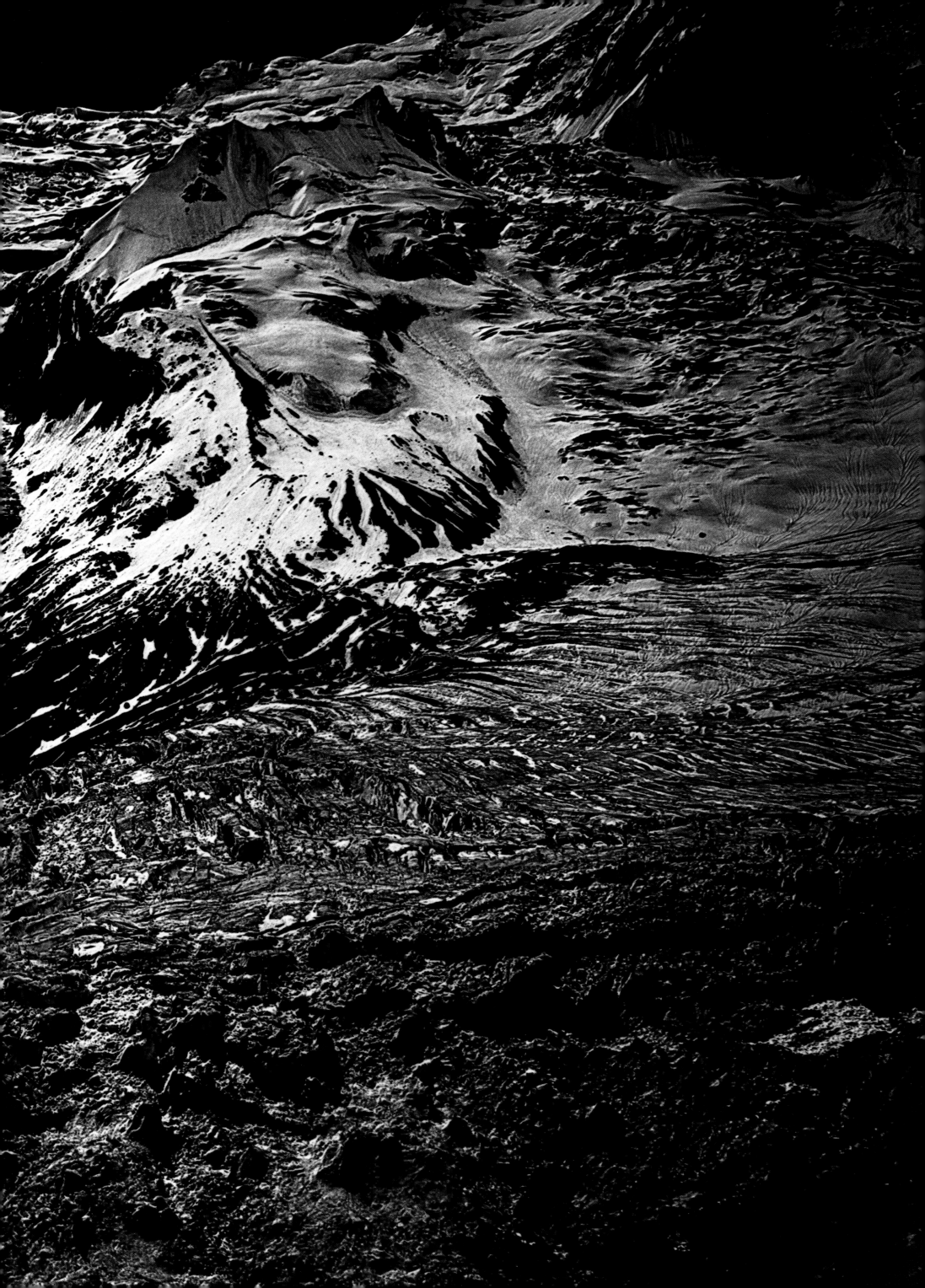

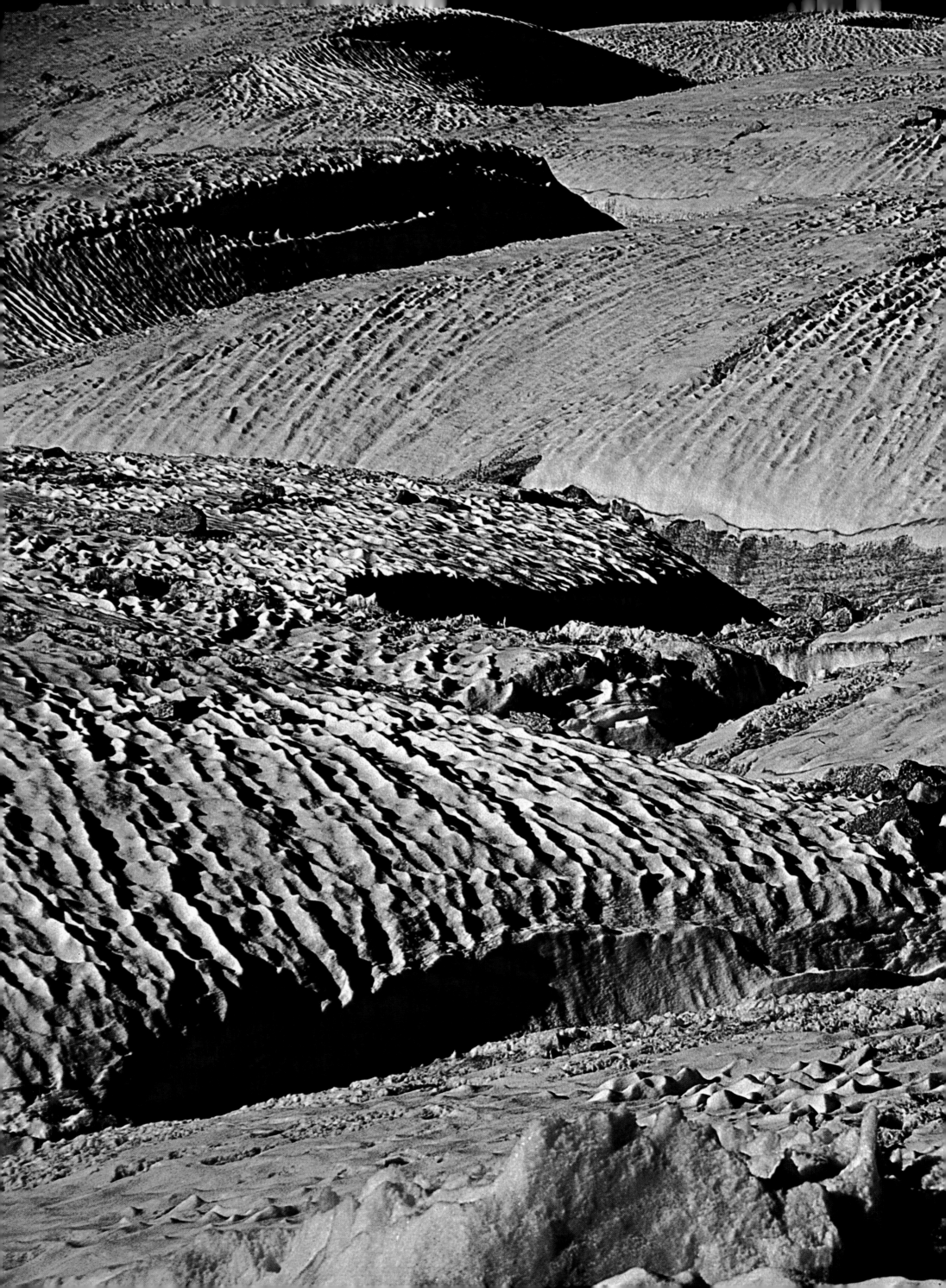

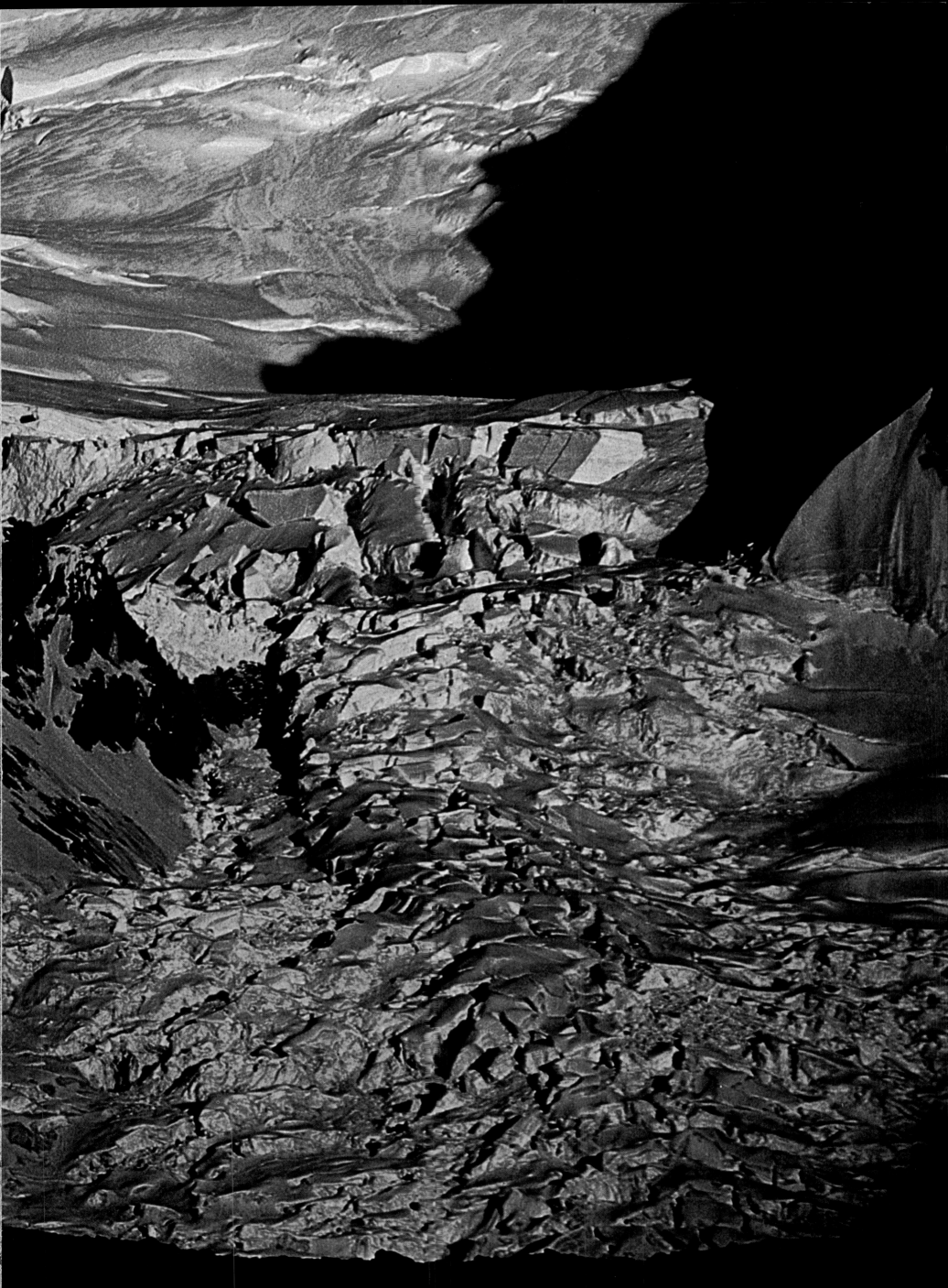

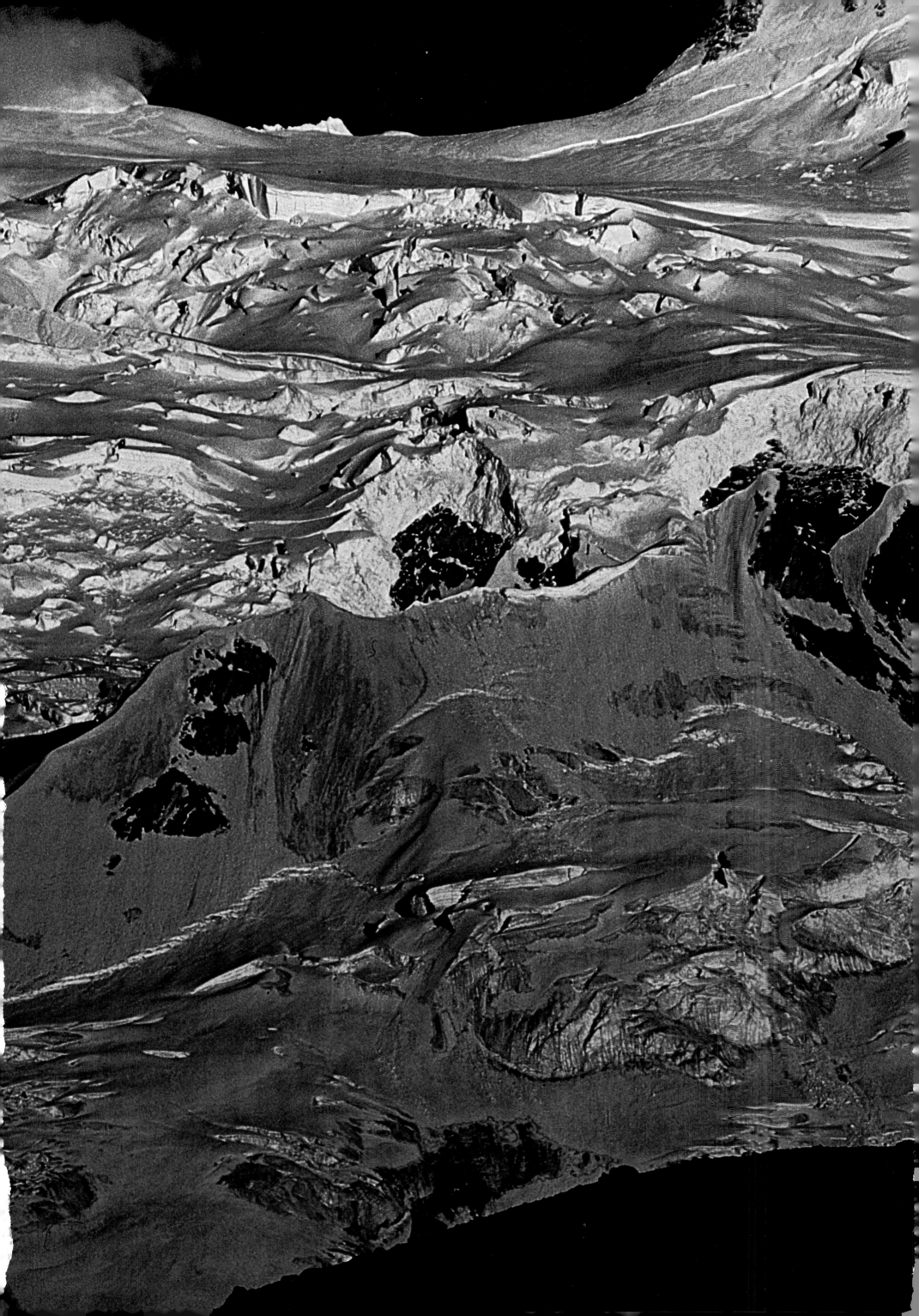

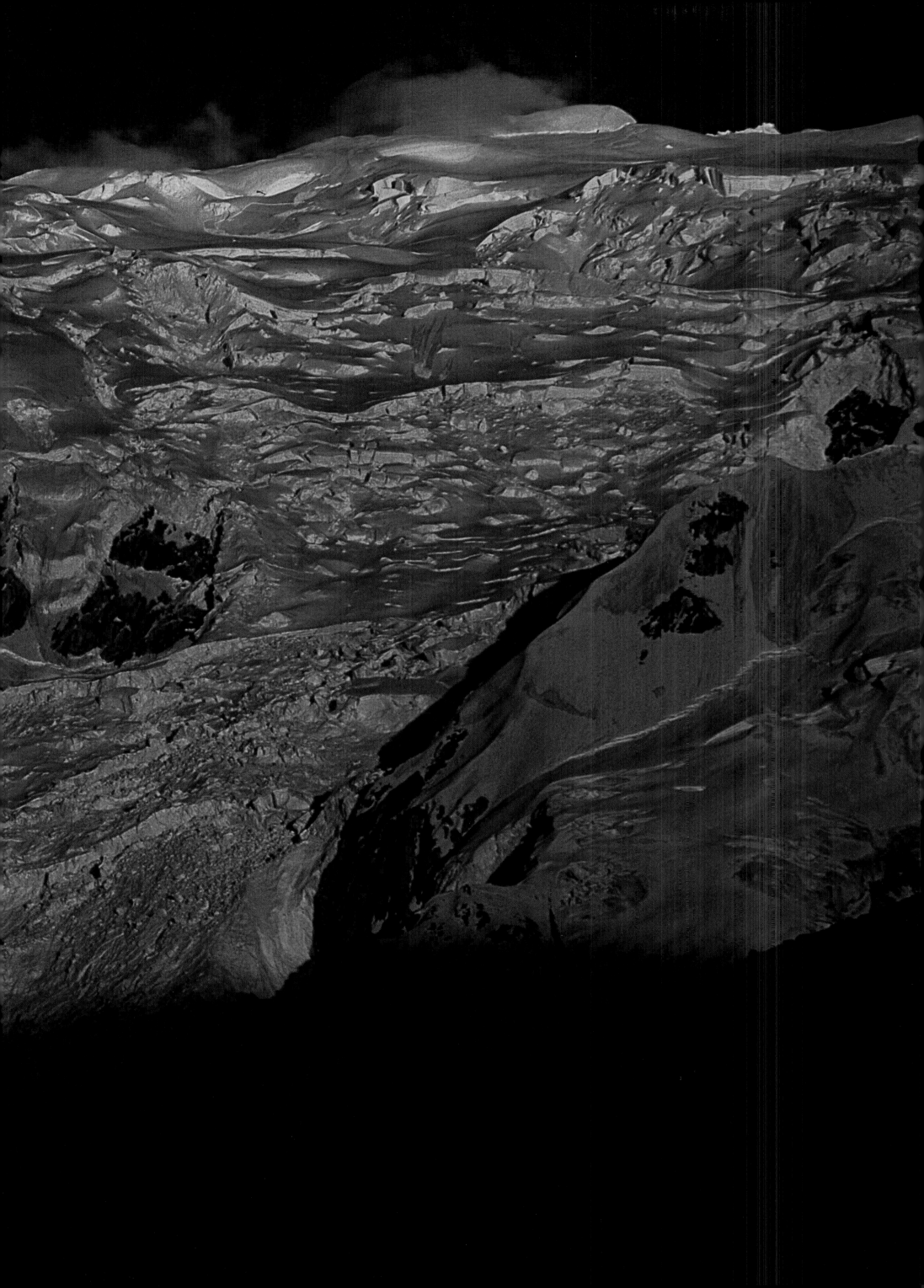

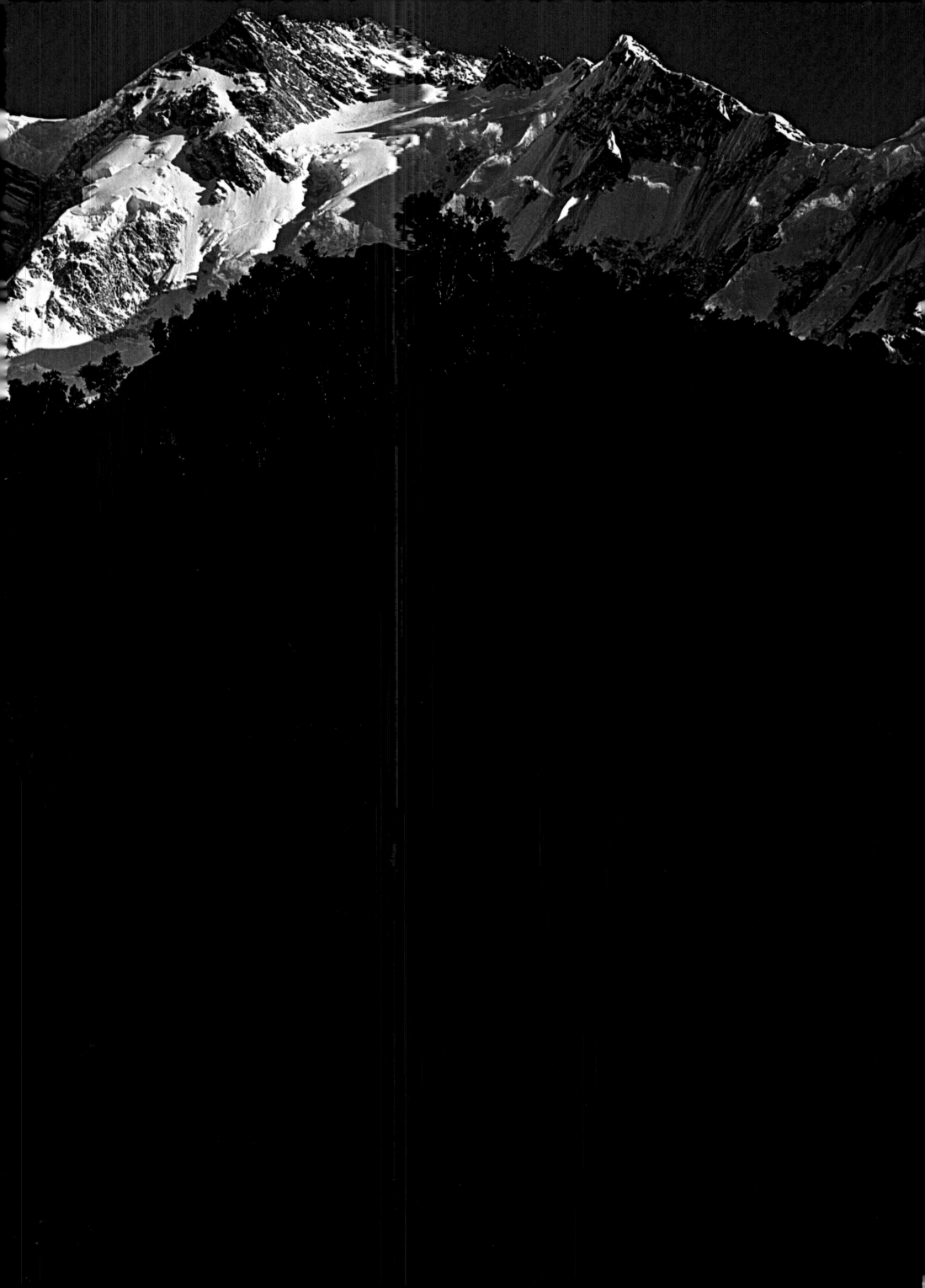

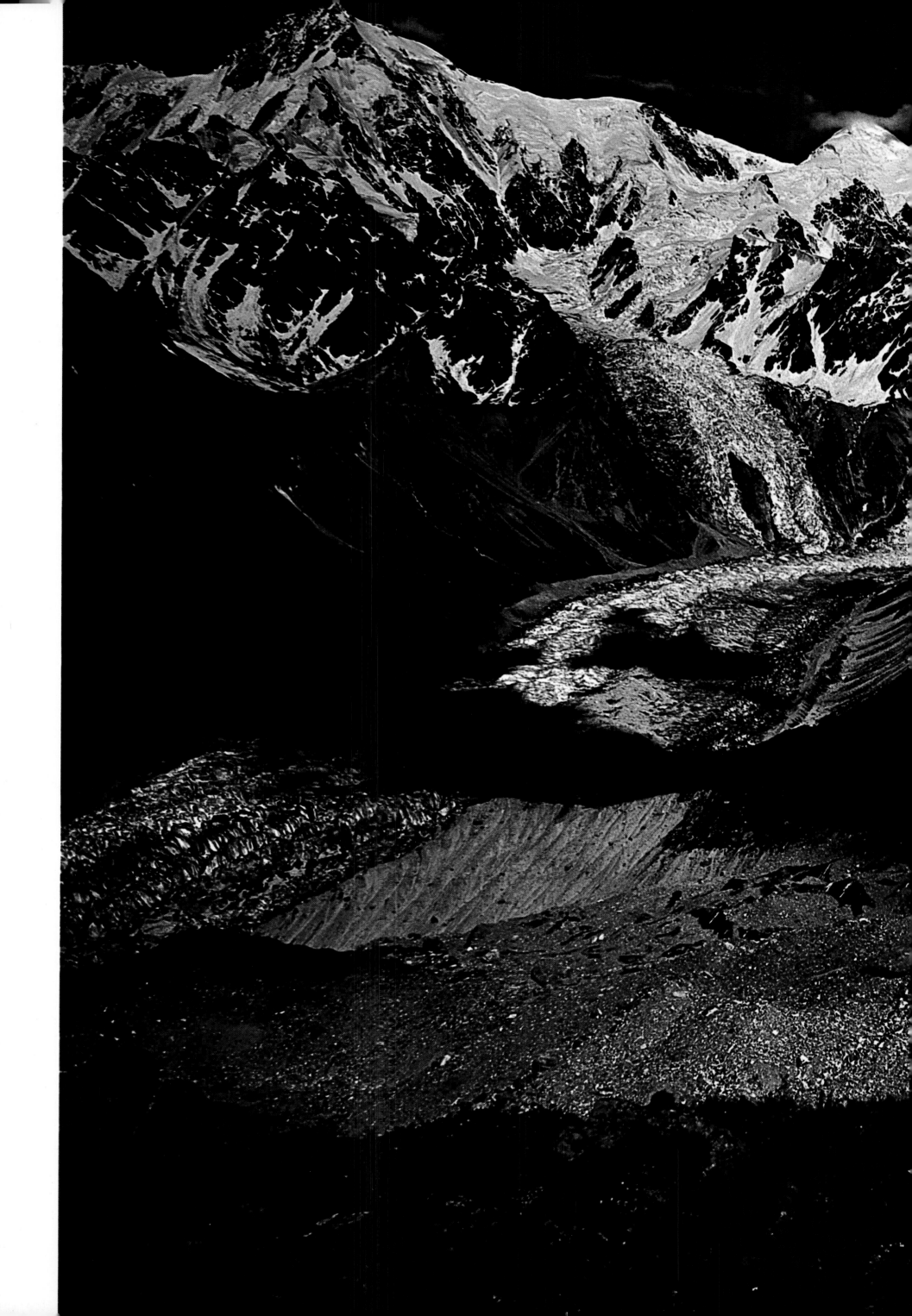

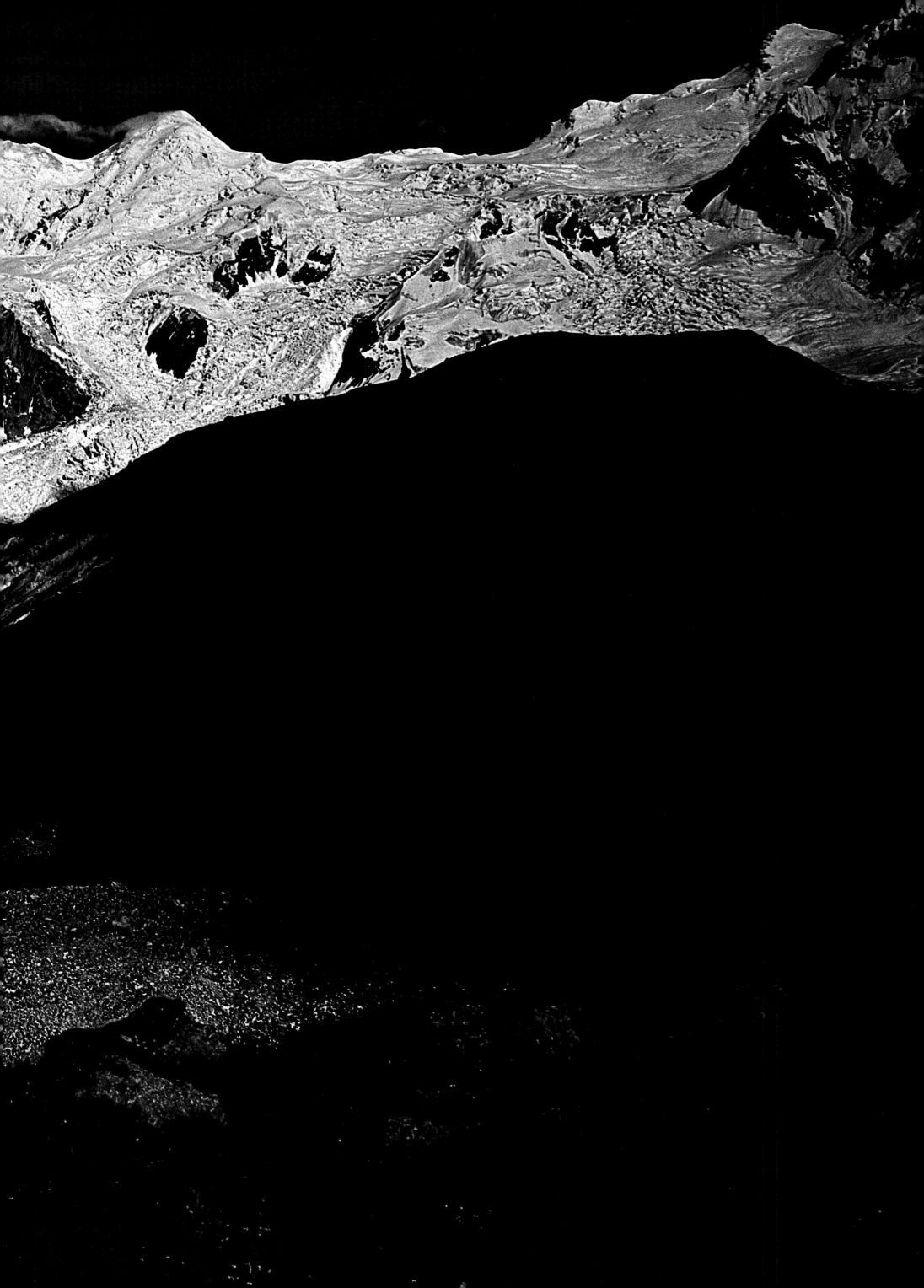

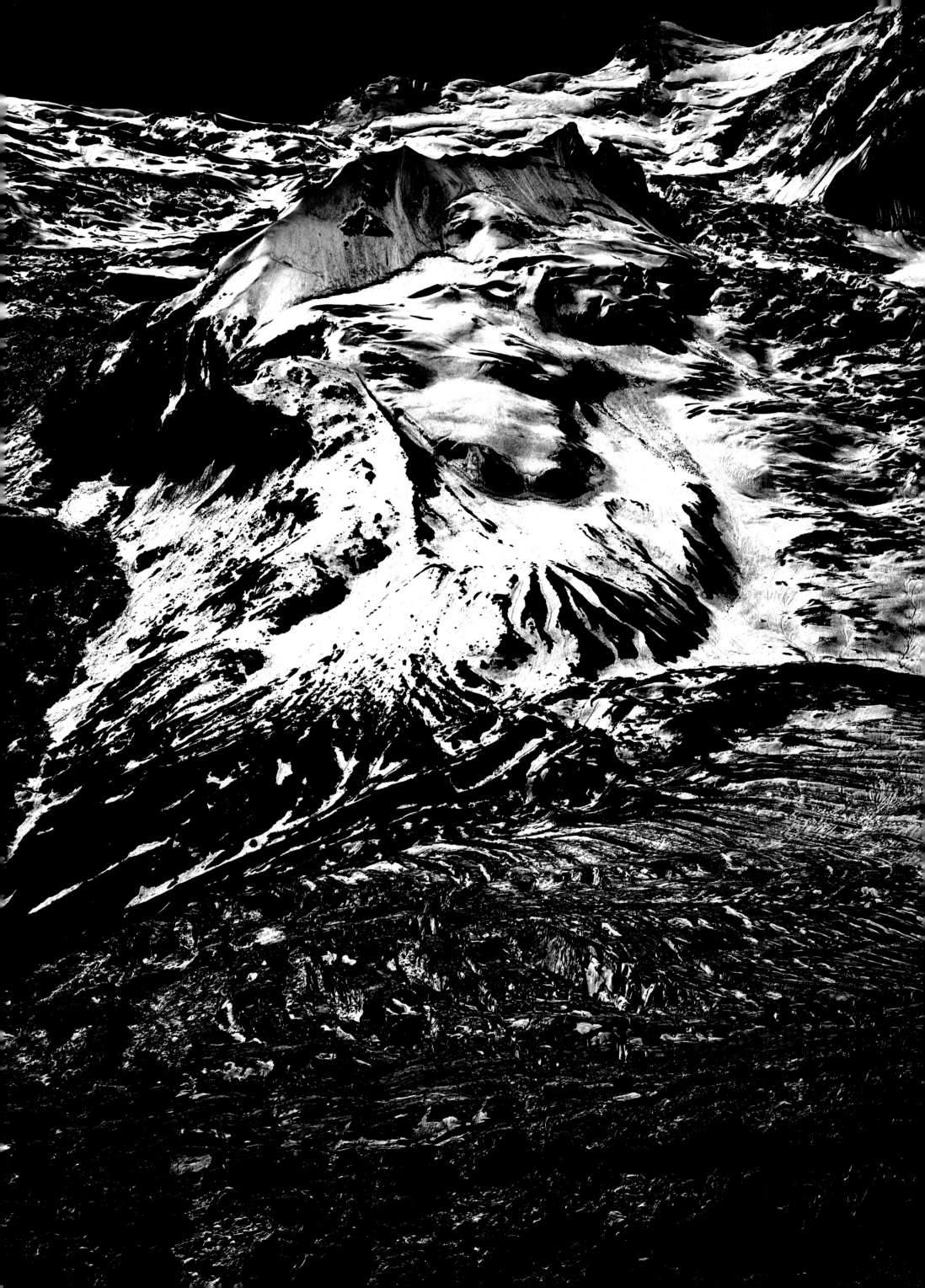

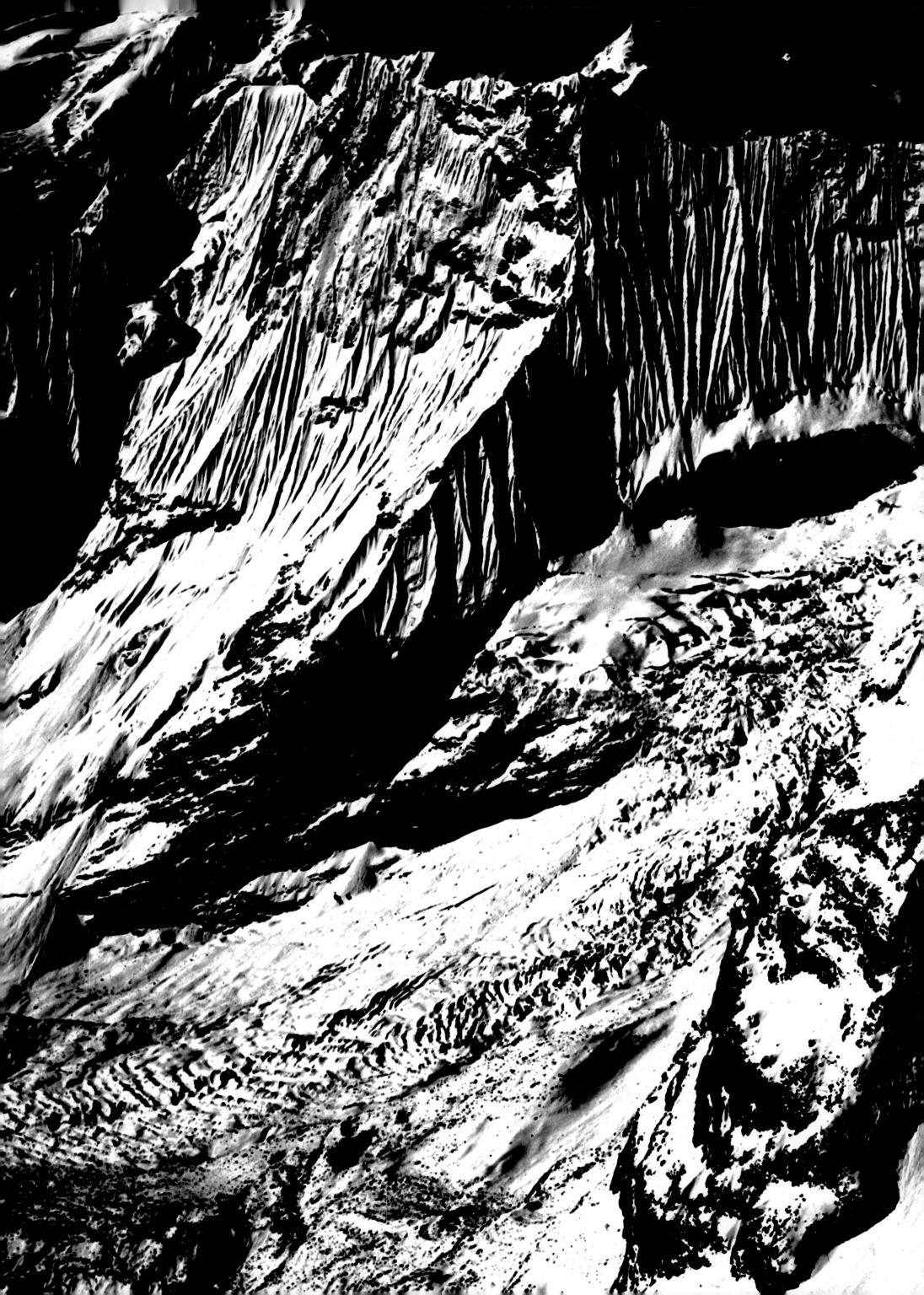

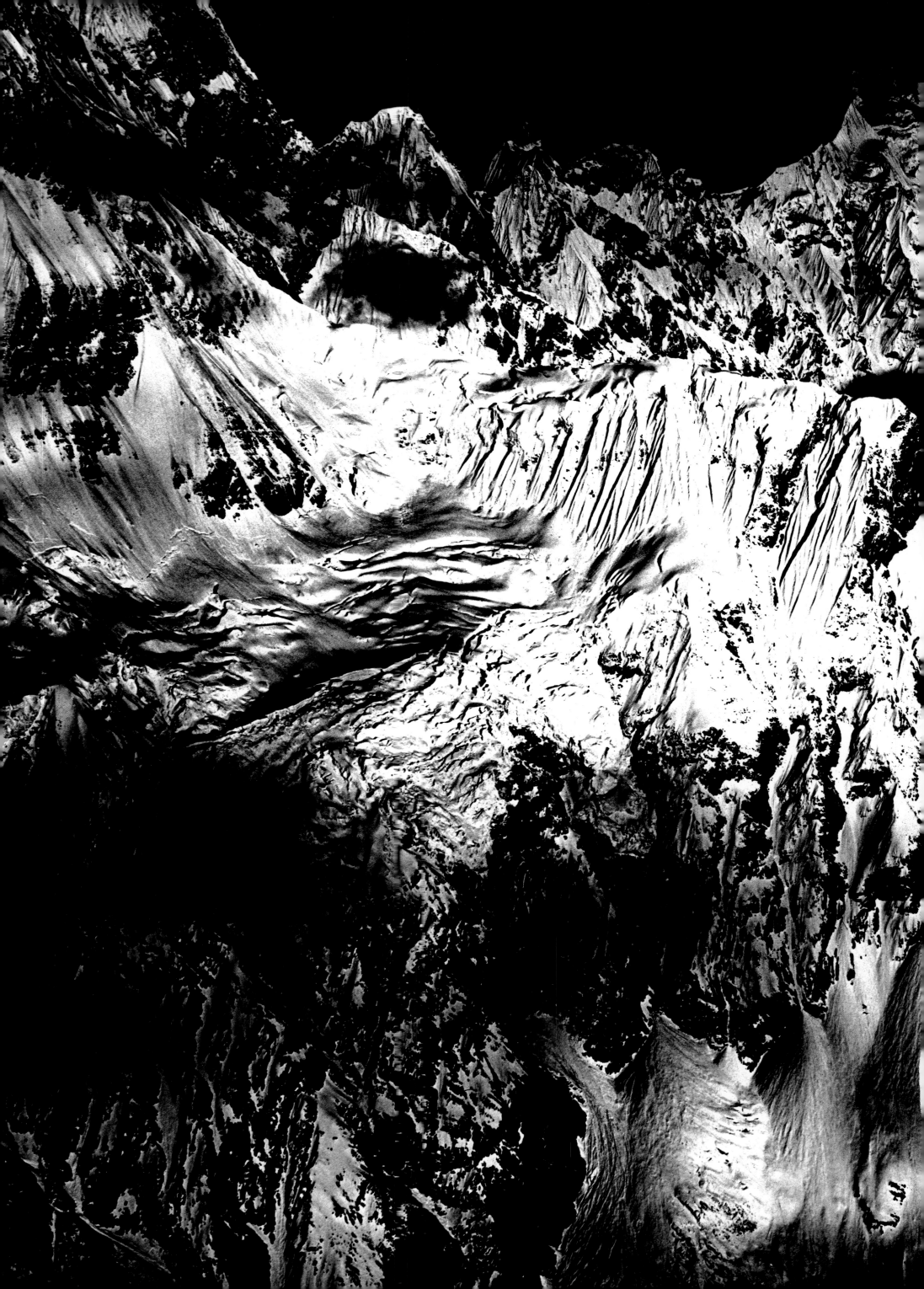

The Punjab Himalayas

Leaving its source in the highlands of Tibet, the Indus River cuts through the Kashmir Plateau and flows northwest. Before reaching Gilgit it curves, changes direction and flows southward through Pakistan. To the river's north lies the Karakorum; to its west, the Hindu Kush; and to its south, the Punjab Himalayas, also known as the Kashmir Himalayas. The range extends eastward as far as the Sutlej River. Within the Punjab Range, the treacherous Nanga Parbat (8,125 meters) and Nun Kun (7,000-plus meters) lord over all the other mountains. There are few notably high mountains in the range other than these two.

India and Pakistan are still disputing possession of this region. During the British occupation, Kashmir was one of 562 political units of India. When India and Pakistan gained independence on August 15, 1947, Kashmir also became independent. Because of strong intervention by the Nenru government, however, Kashmir affiliated herself with predominantly Hindu India. Since most people in Kashmir are Muslim, bitter disputes arose between India and Pakistan over disposition of the territory. While the dispute between those countries is less intense today, the basically religious struggle does not seem to be coming to an end.

It is hard to determine where the Kashmir border is. Since the *de facto* border is actually a cease-fire line, the political boundaries of the country are unstable. From my own observation it appeared that Nanga Parbat is under Pakistani rule and that Srinagar, 120 kilometers to the south, is controlled by India. The entire region was occupied by soldiers when I was there, and it was extremely difficult to get permission to enter the area to climb mountains, much less to take pictures.

THE INDIAN SIDE

During my travels to and from the Himalayan region I spent a great deal of time in India applying for permission to take photographs. After four years I had convinced myself that it was useless. I was not allowed to climb a single mountain, and should probably consider myself lucky to have entered the Indian protectorate of Sikkim. I photographed Darjeeling and vicinity because government permission was not needed, but the Garhwal Himalayas were entirely off limits. I persistently requested permission to enter the region to photograph Nanda Devi close up. The government refused despite all my efforts and the assistance of many other people.

After two years, the Indian government finally allowed me to travel to the mountains near Manali and Chamba in Himachal Pradesh and to return via Deo Tibba, Indrasan, Mulkila and Rhotang Pass. The permit was issued by the Indian Mountaineering Foundation of the Defense Ministry. It specified that: 1) photographing military installations was prohibited; 2) local commanders could attach any further restrictions they deemed necessary; and 3) all negatives would be submitted for censoring. I was overjoyed at finally receiving travel authorization. As it turned out, though, I placed too high a significance on its value.

I purchased the food, fuel and camping equipment I needed for the long journey and set off for Manali, where I met my first challenge. The commander of the area refused to allow me to enter, saying that my warrant should have been issued by the National Defense Ministry itself. There was no way to contact New Delhi—the telephone was available only for local calls. I had to drive all the way back to New Delhi to see Ministry officials and return to Manali with my permit properly authorized. That impressed on me how ineffective central government authority in India is. On my return to Manali, moreover, the commander refused me permission to photograph the area by applying the second of the permit's prohibitions. That, of course, made my permit worthless, and the commander issued me a new permit of his own. According to his permit I could walk as far as a village a few kilometers outside Manali toward the mountains. I thanked him for his generosity, although I knew that ordinary tourists could freely travel as far as Khoksar Pass, about twenty kilometers beyond the village he restricted me to. That was my reward for two years of trouble.

THE ROAD TO NANGA PARBAT

Obtaining permission from Pakistani authorities to explore Pakistani-controlled Kashmir was not easy. It seemed that all of Pakistan was under strict surveillance. One could not enter a government building anywhere unless accompanied by a staff member of his embassy. Every day for two months I travelled between Rawalpindi and Islamabad, between the Japanese Embassy and Pakistani government offices. I could write a book about those two months alone.

We entered the mountains in the Astor region, a most improbable area to gain entrance to. I suspected that Pakistani troops occupied the region. From here we took the path leading to the Lama area and finally to the Lake of Lama, the end of Sachen Glacier. The few days we spent camping on the shore of this beautiful lake were a relaxing break. Snow-covered mountains loomed in the distance over a thickly forested area.

We turned back to Gilgit and went up the Rakhiot Glacier. The region is south of and not far from the Indus but there is not a single tree or blade of grass to be seen. A deep valley carved by the Indus cuts through the desert. Murky water runs through the river basin, and it seemed that the spirit of the people strongly reflected the calamitous nature of the area.

It is normal to hire Hunza porters for expeditions, but since we could not enter the Hunza area I had to find porters in the Tato area. German expeditions to this region were constantly plagued by having to use Tato natives, and I suffered the same experience. The Tato porters made my journey to photograph Nanga Parbat the most trying part of my four-year exploration of the Himalayas.

There was no human habitation beyond Tato, and we could not readily turn back to Gilgit. The Tato porters took advantage of our situation and we had to meet various unreasonable demands they made in order to continue our journey. Daily strikes for more pay were a part of their work. Moreover they walked only three hours a day before setting their loads down—at camping sites they themselves chose. They worked as porters solely to pilfer, but we were afraid to admonish them because they were armed. The endless sabotage, strikes and stealing taxed us all greatly.

The scenery, however, was unbelievably beautiful. We camped at Märchen Wiese, the "Wonderland Pasture," a comfortable field on a hill above Rakhiot Glacier. The pasture resembled a well-manicured lawn. A stream rippled by, birds sang in the surrounding forests, and the north face of Nanga Parbat stood proudly against the deep blue sky. This was one of the very few cozy places in the Himalayas.

In Sanskrit, Nanga Parbat means "naked mountain." Germany alone sent seven expeditions here between 1932 and 1953, and more than thirty alpinists died before the mountain was successfully scaled. On top of the moraine along Rakhiot Glacier I found the grave of a German climber named Drexel. It seems he died of pneumonia during an expedition here in 1934, the year before I was born. The cross on the grave was in perfect condition and the gravestone well preserved. I set a bouquet of wild flowers on the grave.

PANORAMIC VIEW OF RAKHIOT GLACIER

One can see the whole of Rakhiot Glacier from the mountain behind Tato Village, a half-day climb. The mountain on the left is Middle Chongra Peak (6,455 meters); on the right is South Chongra Peak (6,448 meters). The milk-white meltwater from the glacier runs through Tato before pouring into the Upper Indus almost like a waterfall. Without exception, water from glaciers in the Himalayas is always muddy.

NANGA PARBAT

All the world's mountains above 8,000 meters are either in Nepal or the Karakorum Range, except for Nanga Parbat in the Punjab Range. Seven different tries were made and 31 alpinists died on Nanga Parbat before it fell to a German party in 1932. The mountain's treacherous nature is apparent in this photograph of its north face. The main peak, 8,125 meters, is visible on the right.

RAKHIOT GLACIER

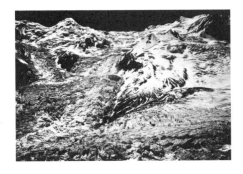

This photo was taken from a 300-meter-high plateau in the glacier at the foot of Nanga Parbat's north face. Most of the climbing routes up Nanga Parbat start from here, go up Rakhiot Peak (7,070 meters) (upper right), and continue across the ridge from there to the right. It was here that a snowslide killed 7 climbers and 9 sherpas in a German expedition in 1937.

GLACIER

Icefalls cover the Rakhiot Glacier at the bases of Chongra and Nanga Parbat, making the glacier's surface extremely rough. The glacier there is very dynamic. Where the glacier flows by Ganalo Peak in the west, however, the landscape turns smooth and the scene is calm and peaceful. This photograph shows a clean, white glacier, instead of the usual sight of strewn mud and rocks. Melted ice forms narrow streams flowing over the icy surface. Though the area is pleasant to the eye, I was hardly inspired to stroll there.

NANGA PARBAT RANGE

From the top of a mountain opposite the west end of Rakhiot Glacier I got a good panoramic view of the Nanga Parbat Range. On the far left is the 7,597-meter northwest peak of Silberzacken. Right of that is Nanga Parbat. The highest mountain in the foreground is North II Peak, 7,785 meters. The mountain to the right of North II that looks lower is actually the main peak, 8,125 meters. The highest mountain on the far right is Ganalo Peak, 6,606 meters. I took this photograph from a slope that was completely covered with grass and flowers—a sharp contrast with the sight before me.

SUNSET AT RAKHIOT GLACIER

From the middle of Rakhiot Glacier one gains a sweeping 180-degree view that takes in Ganalo Peak in the west, Nanga Parbat's north face and Chongra Peak in the east. The western sun shines directly on the jumbled mass of ice blocks in the glacier, and the scene turned from yellow to red, and gradually faded to faint purple before darkness set in. An evening glow remained on the glacier for about two hours after the sun had set behind Ganalo Peak.

DISTANT VIEW OF UNNAMED PEAK

A telephoto close-up of an unnamed peak along the ridge to Nanga Parbat. Or perhaps this is just a bump and not a separate peak. I was surprised to find so few prominent flutes around the Rakhiot Glacier area. The ridges here are all above 6,000 meters but the only flute worth photographing was this one. And even this one has none of the frightfulness of flutes in the Nepalese mountains.

SOURCE OF RAKHIOT GLACIER

Rakhiot Glacier begins moving near here, picks up a moraine on its western bank and heads toward the Rakhiot Valley. I took this photo from a hill in the middle of the glacier. A short distance from here there is a 100-meter drop, a precipice carved out of the rock by the glacier. The hill I was on was covered with flowers and was a perfect place for sunbathing. The thought of having to drink the vile glacier water if I lingered here, however, stopped me from staying very long.

SOUTH CHONGRA PEAK

South Chongra Peak (6,448 meters) viewed from a hill on the Ganalo Peak side. The ridge shadow on the glacier lengthened rapidly, and the yellow colors gradually turned to red. The snow's brightness waned quickly and I had to work fast to keep my exposure times adjusted correctly. Taking pictures in the early morning or the evening keeps a photographer extremely busy. Experience spells the difference in guessing cloud shifts. I risked my life to climb here, and this one photograph was all I got.

NANGA PARBAT RIDGE

From Märchen Wiese, the "Wonderland Pasture," it is a half-day walk to the river where the German expedition that climbed Nanga Parbat set up their base camp. At points higher than this river, only muddy water is available for drinking. This photo was taken at the end of the mountain path from the river, a two-hour climb. Rakhiot Glacier lies beyond this point, but it is like a dried-up river bed. It is another day's walk from here to the place where one can see ice in the glacier.

MIDDLE CHONGRA PEAK

This photo was taken in the evening as the landscape began to take on colors. The clouds kept the mountains hidden. I thought the contrast between the rock in this photo and the round shape of Chongra would be interesting. The light-dark contrast would be too emphatic in daytime, however, and I aimed for an evening shot. I watched the clouds for about two hours, waiting for a break, but this was the best shot I was able to take.

CHONGRA RANGE

The dark shadow is a hill in the middle of the glacier. The glacier flows from below the slopes of Ganlo Peak and turns to the left not far ahead of the place where I took this photo. There it joins with another glacier flowing directly from the front. The muddy surface seen here hardly fits the popular image of a glacier, but only fifty centimeters below the sand and mud is ice. I stood on an old moraine and flowers were blooming everywhere. The mountains here are, left to right, Chongra's main peak (6,830 meters), middle peak and south peak. The white mountain on the right is Rakhiot, 7,070 meters high.

MÄRCHEN WIESE

The "Wonderland Pasture" was named by the German expedition that climbed Nanga Parbat in 1932. The spot was certainly pleasant and the view spectacular, but the Two porters spoiled everything with their thievery and lazy, opportunistic behavior.

RAKHIOT PEAK AND RAKHIOT GLACIER

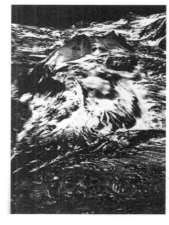

Glaciers in this area have shrunk considerably. The ice shelves are 30 to 100 meters below the moraine. Rocks are constantly falling down the steep banks and being swallowed up in crevices in the glacier. Alpinists generally pitch their fourth camp somewhere on this icefall when climbing Nanga Parbat.

UNNAMED PEAKS SOUTH OF NANGA PARBAT

I drove by jeep up Astor Valley past the town of Astor to Lama. We used yaks to carry our baggage from there to Lama Lake where we set up camp. The ceasefire line between India and Pakistan is between Nanga Parbat and Srinagar, a town about 120 kilometers to the south. There were many Pakistani soldiers in this area and they often stopped me to check my passport and climbing permit. This photograph was taken from a mountain ridge south of Lama Lake.

SOURCE OF CHONGRA GLACIER

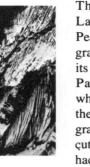

The mountain ridge south of Lama Lake connects to the main Chongra Peak (6,830 meters). Here I photographed a part of Chongra Glacier and its moraine wall. The view of Nanga Parbat was spectacular, especially when the red of the morning sun struck the mountain on its face. In this photograph, two-thirds of Nanga Parbat is cut off by the ridge of Rakhiot. If I had only been permitted to enter Rupar Valley. . . .

NANGA PARBAT FROM TALICHI

The finest view of Nanga Parbat on the road following the Indus River is from the area near Talichi Village. Only about twenty structures comprise the village, which was set up around an oasis in the grey-colored desert. In summer, fierce sandstorms strike every evening, and temperatures during the day rise to 105 degrees Fahrenheit and above. The turbid Indus flows a dark brown color here.

RIDGE OF NANGA PARBAT

This is the western ridge of Nanga Parbat taken from a ridge approached from Lama Lake. Below the ridge and mountain in the foreground is Sachen Glacier. People generally come only as far as Lama Lake, and only during the summer when they erect huts and bring animals to graze. This route is not fit for mountain climbing and no one would ordinarily come here unless for some specific purpose. We were probably the first party ever to have spent so much time wandering about in this area.

SIKKIM HIMALAYAS

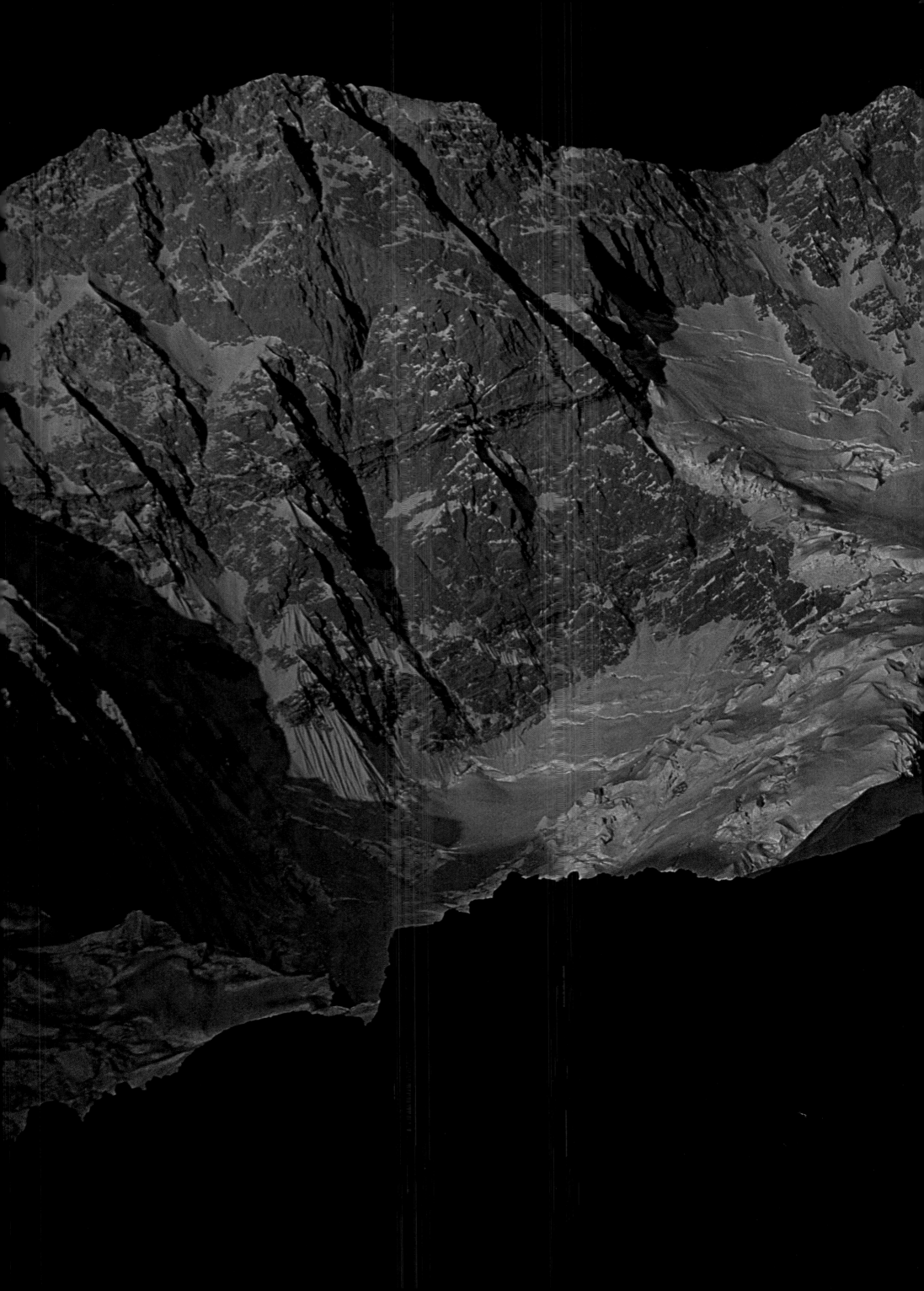

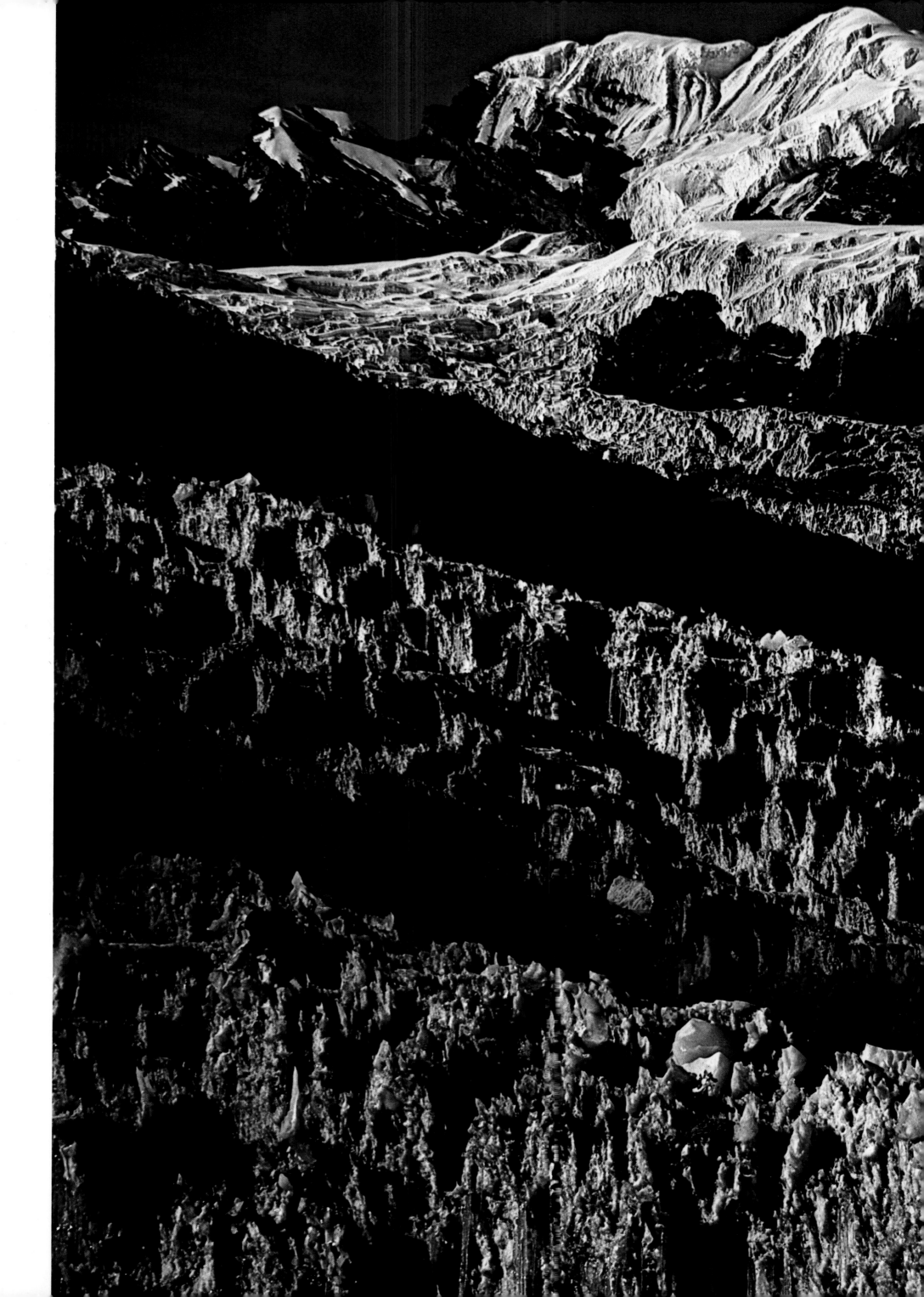

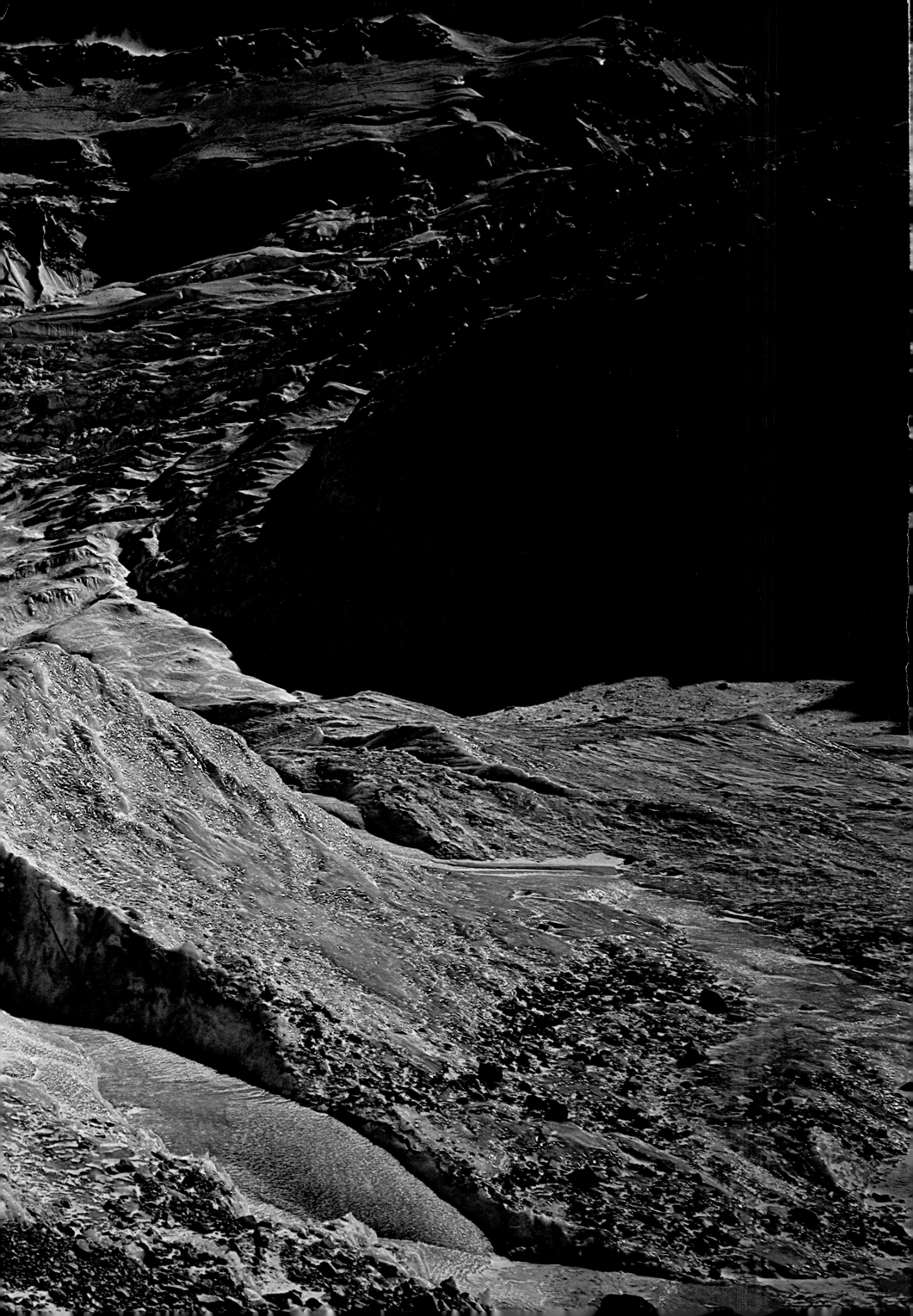

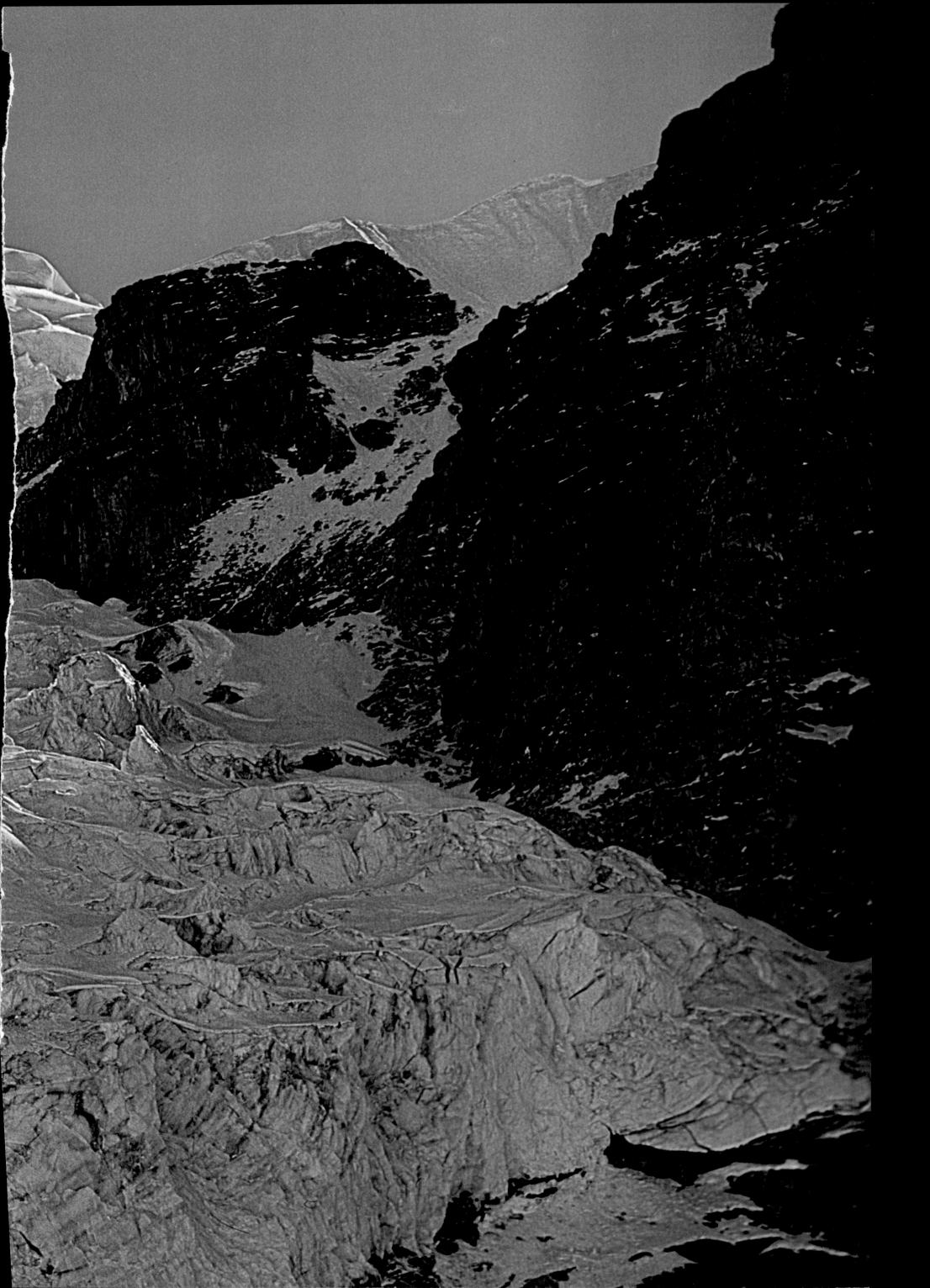

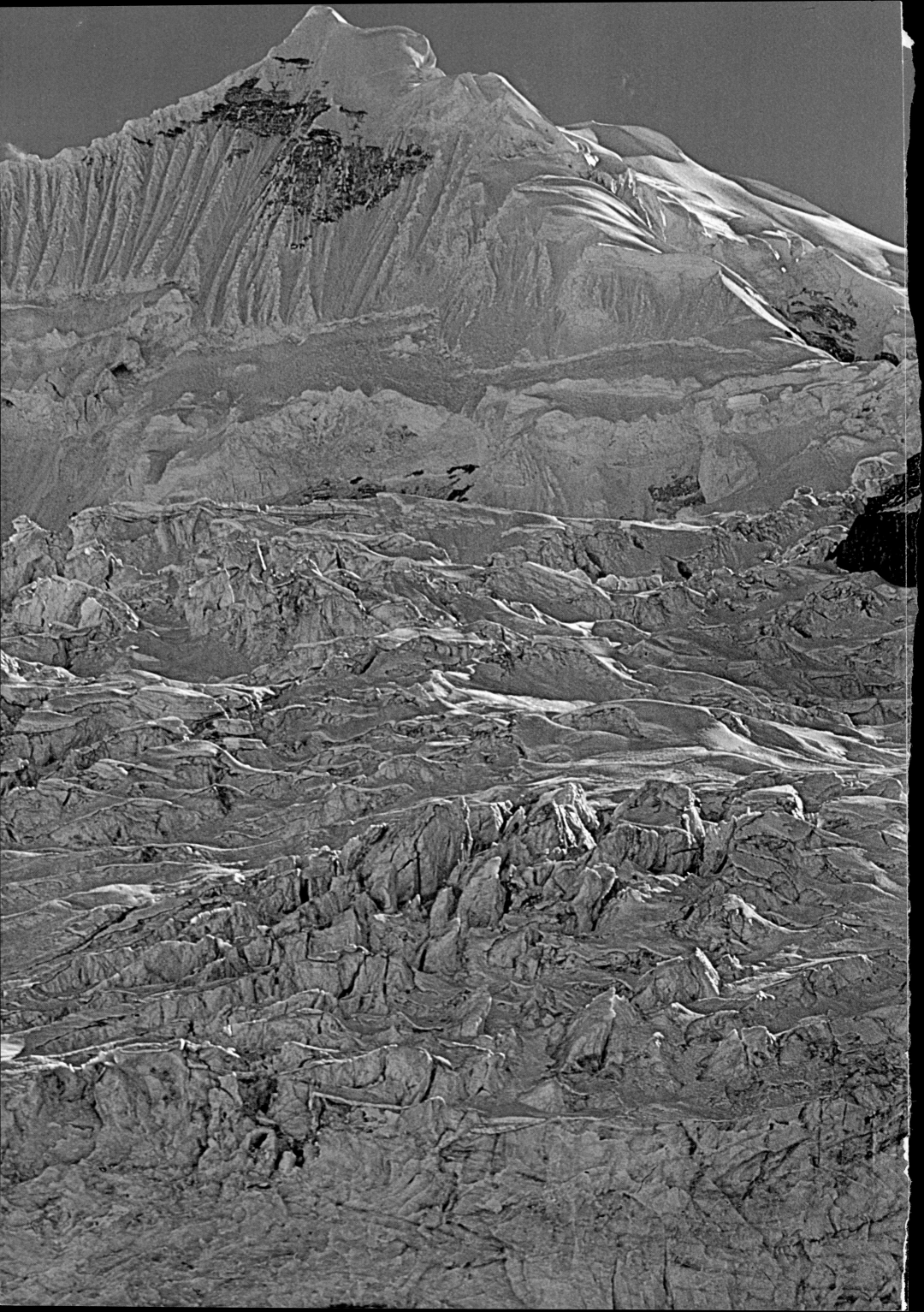

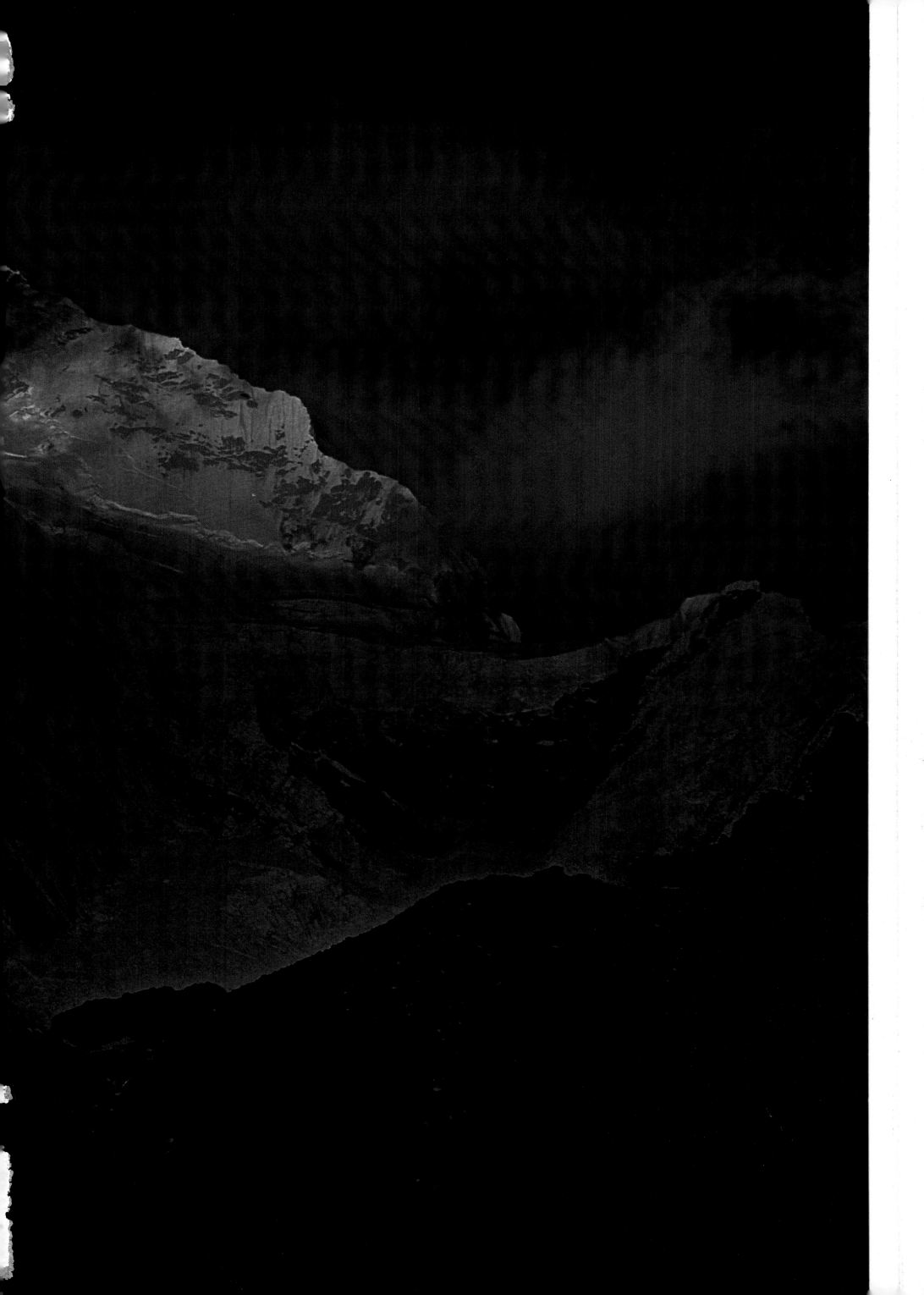

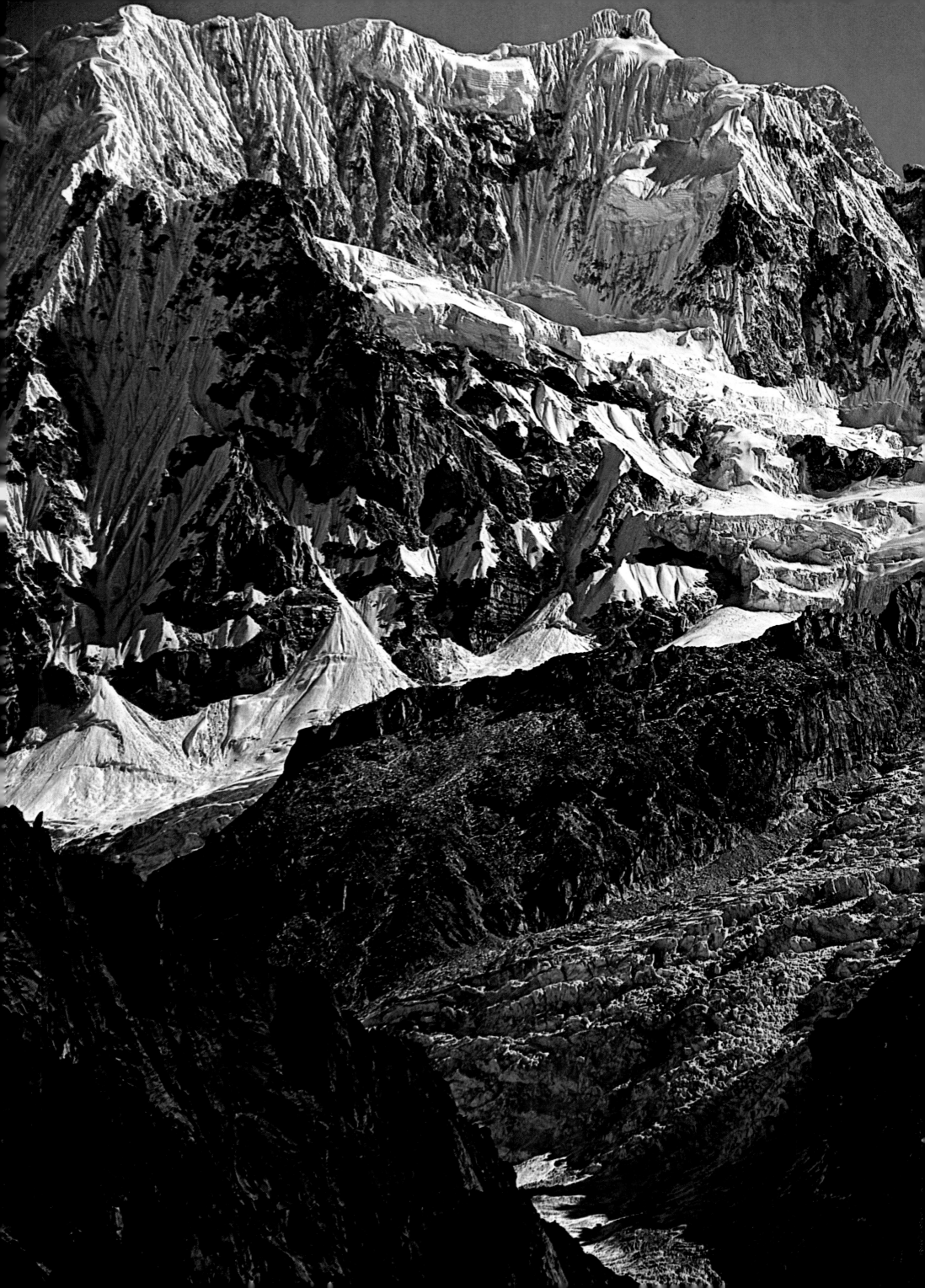

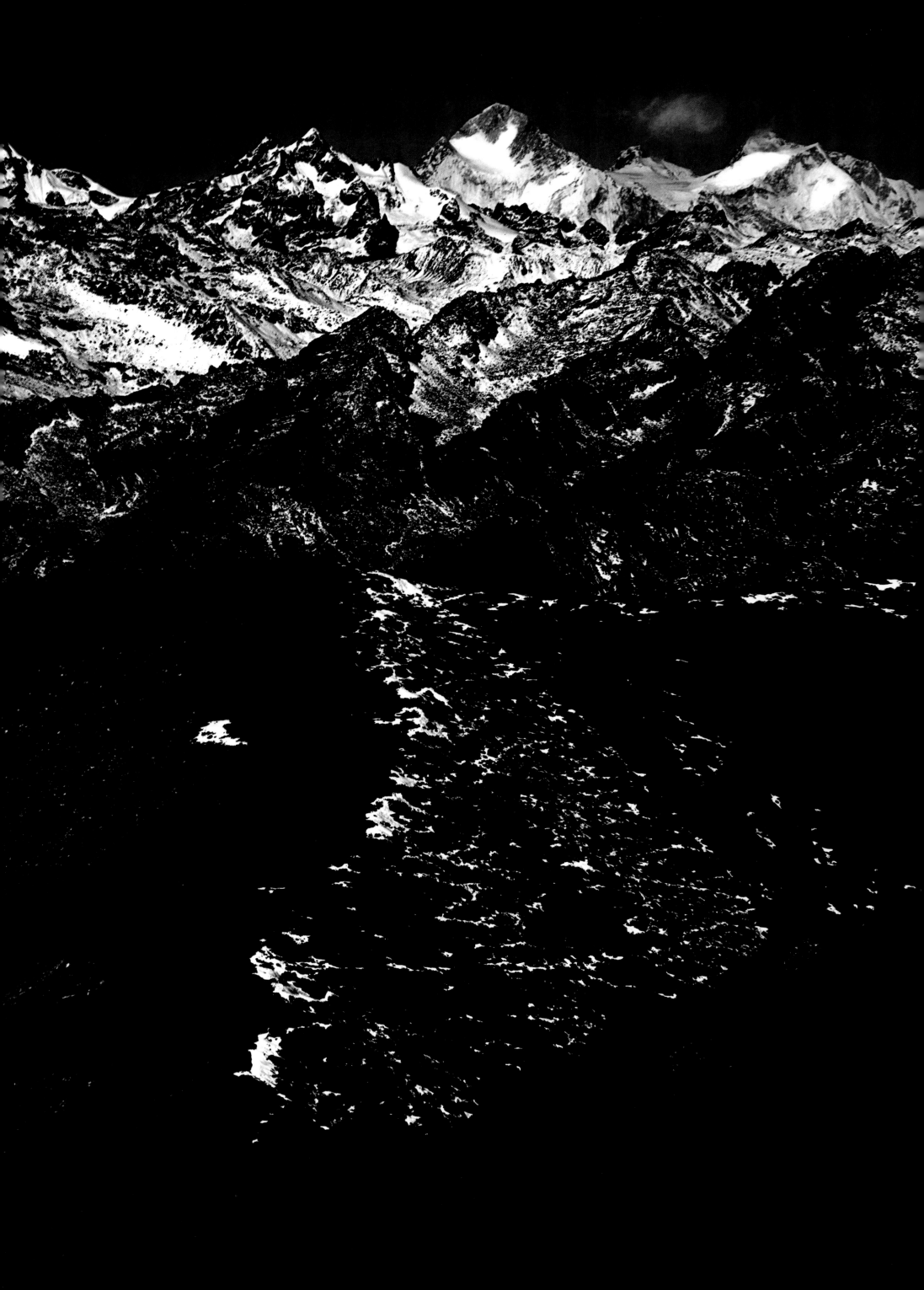

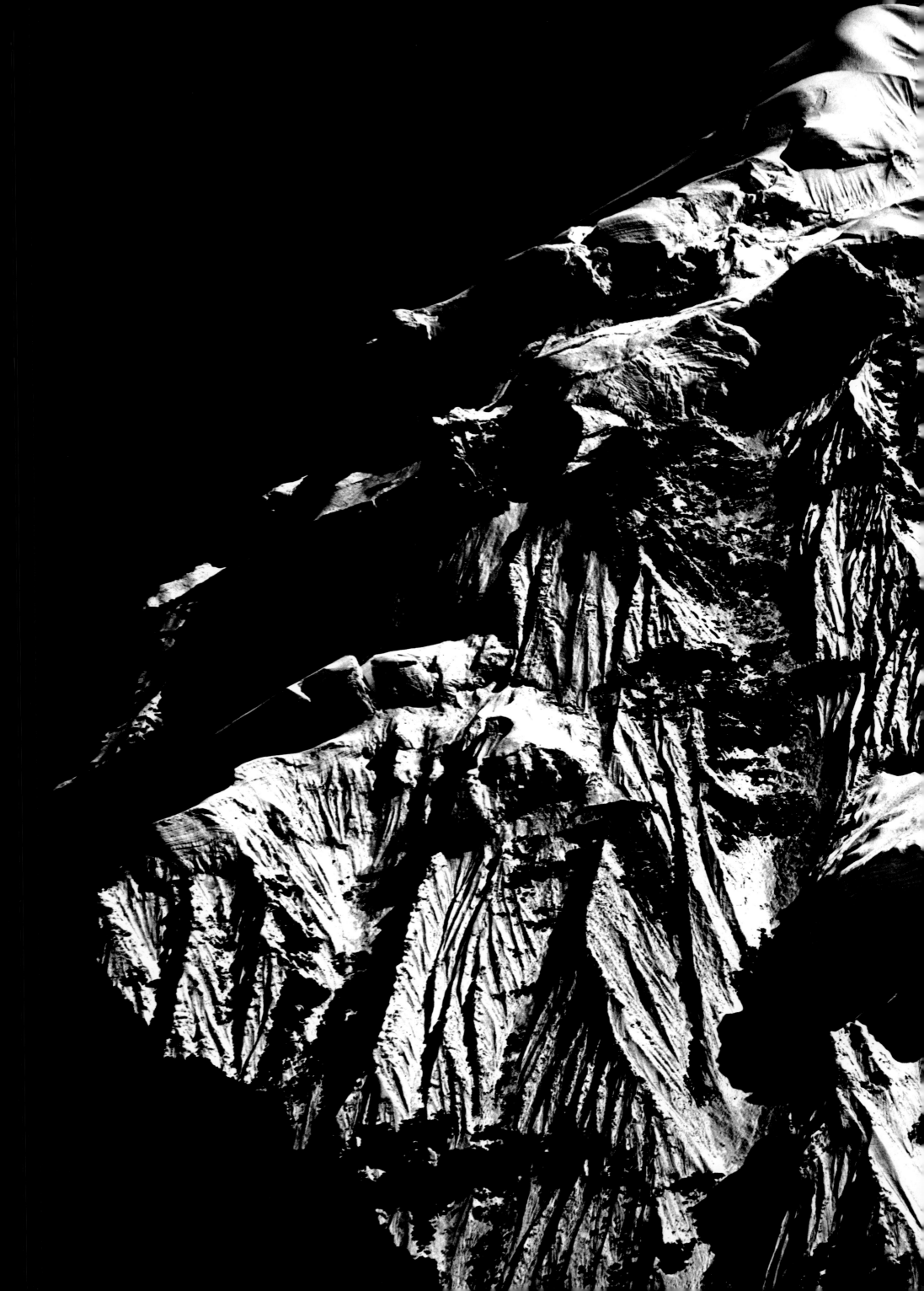

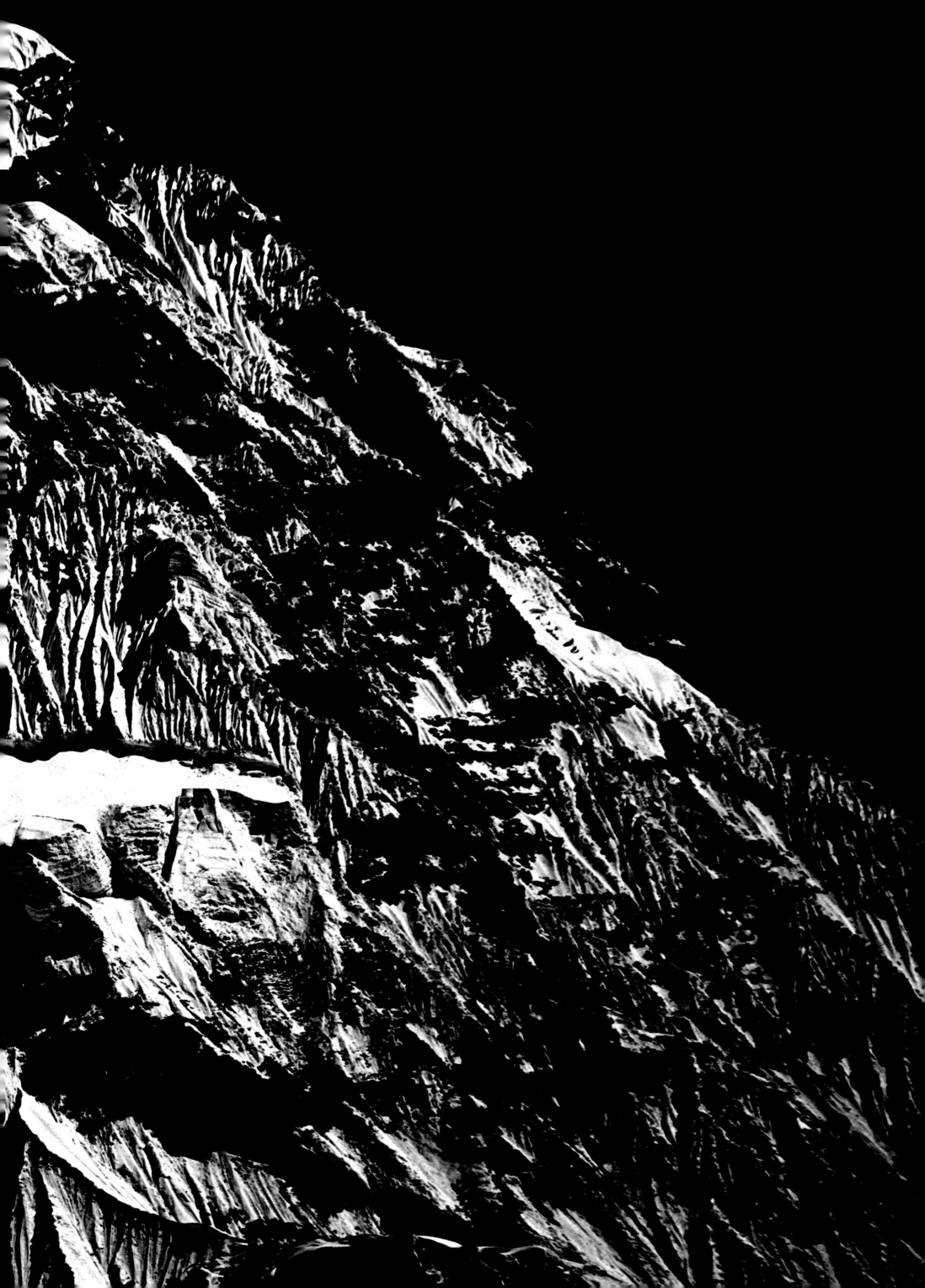

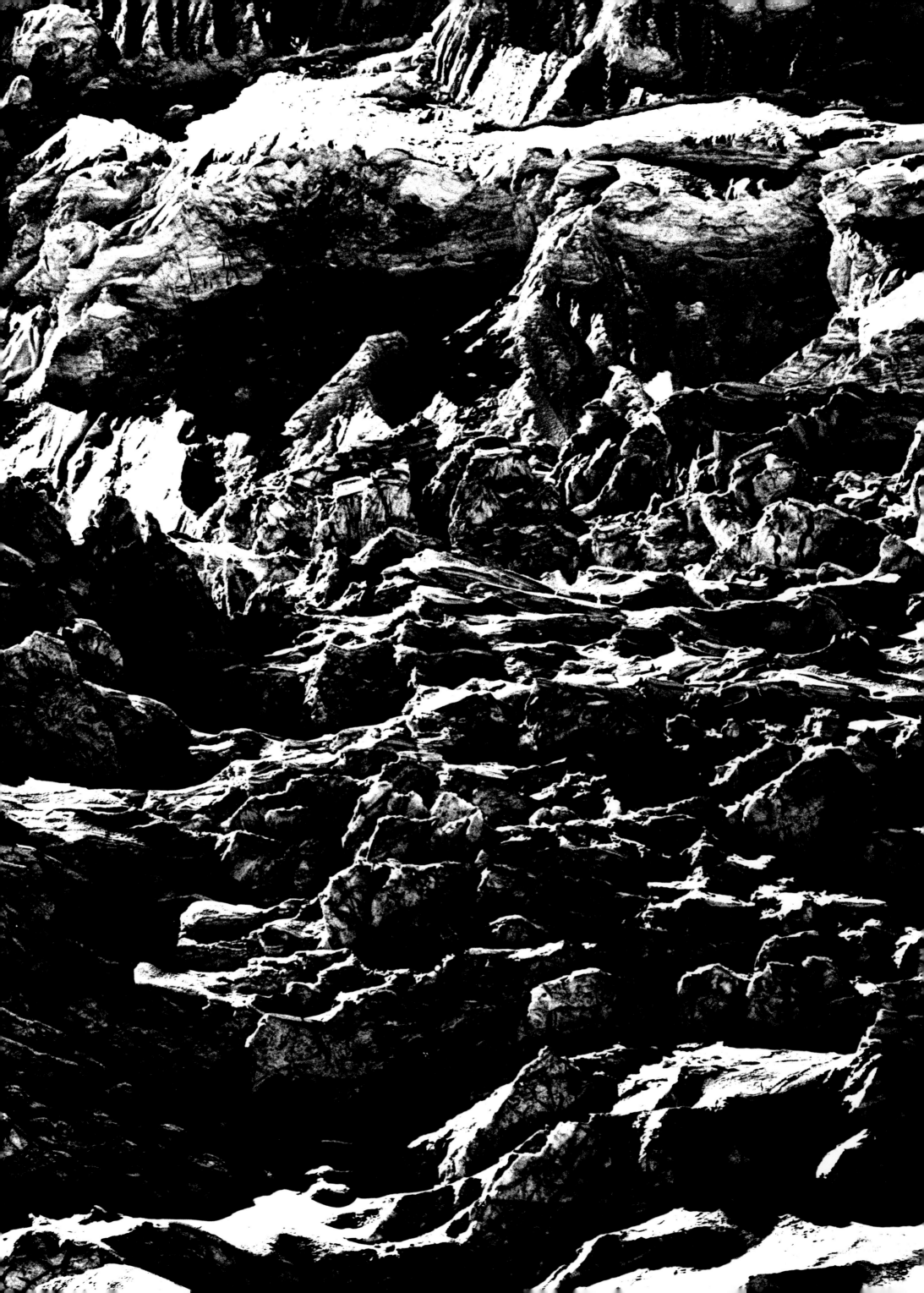

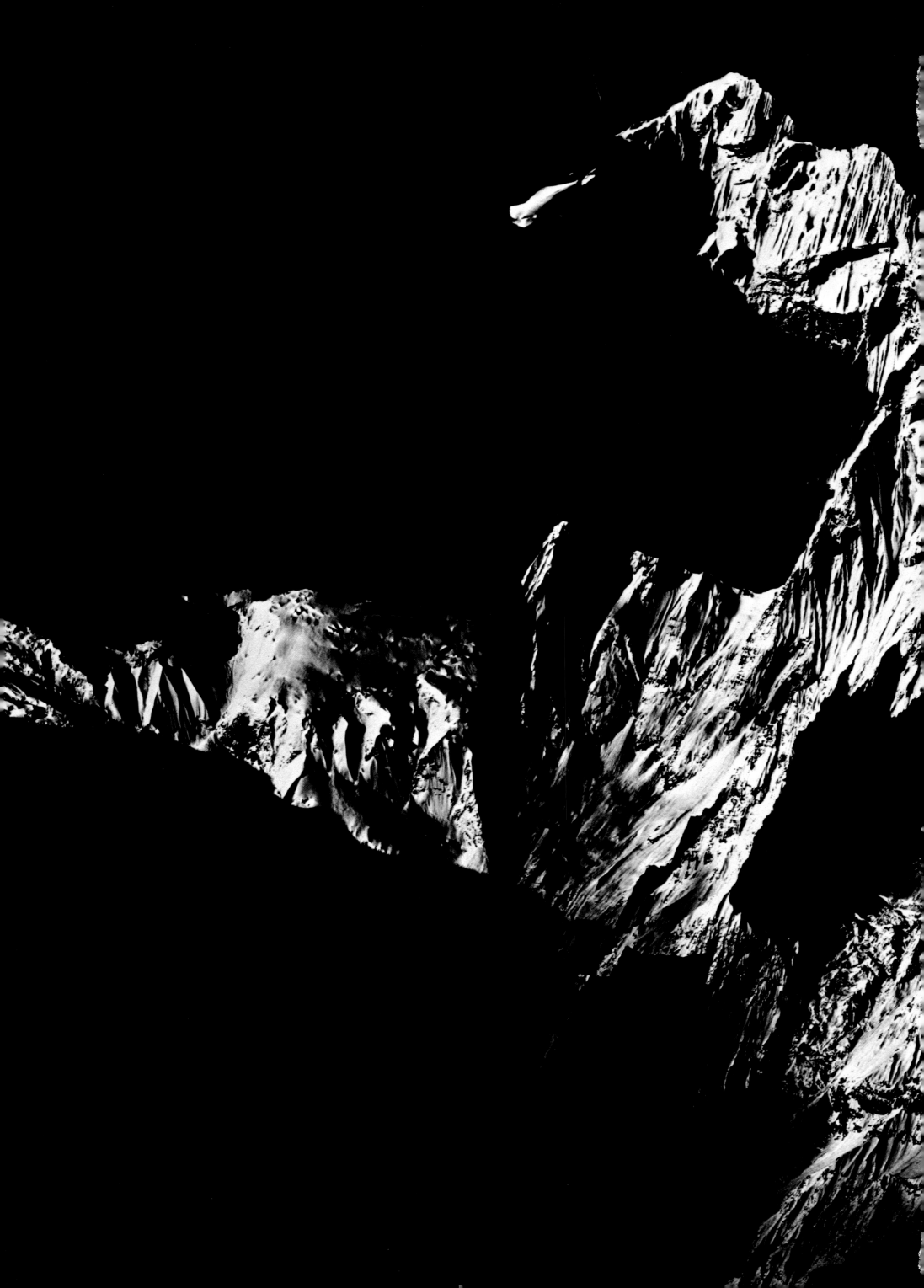

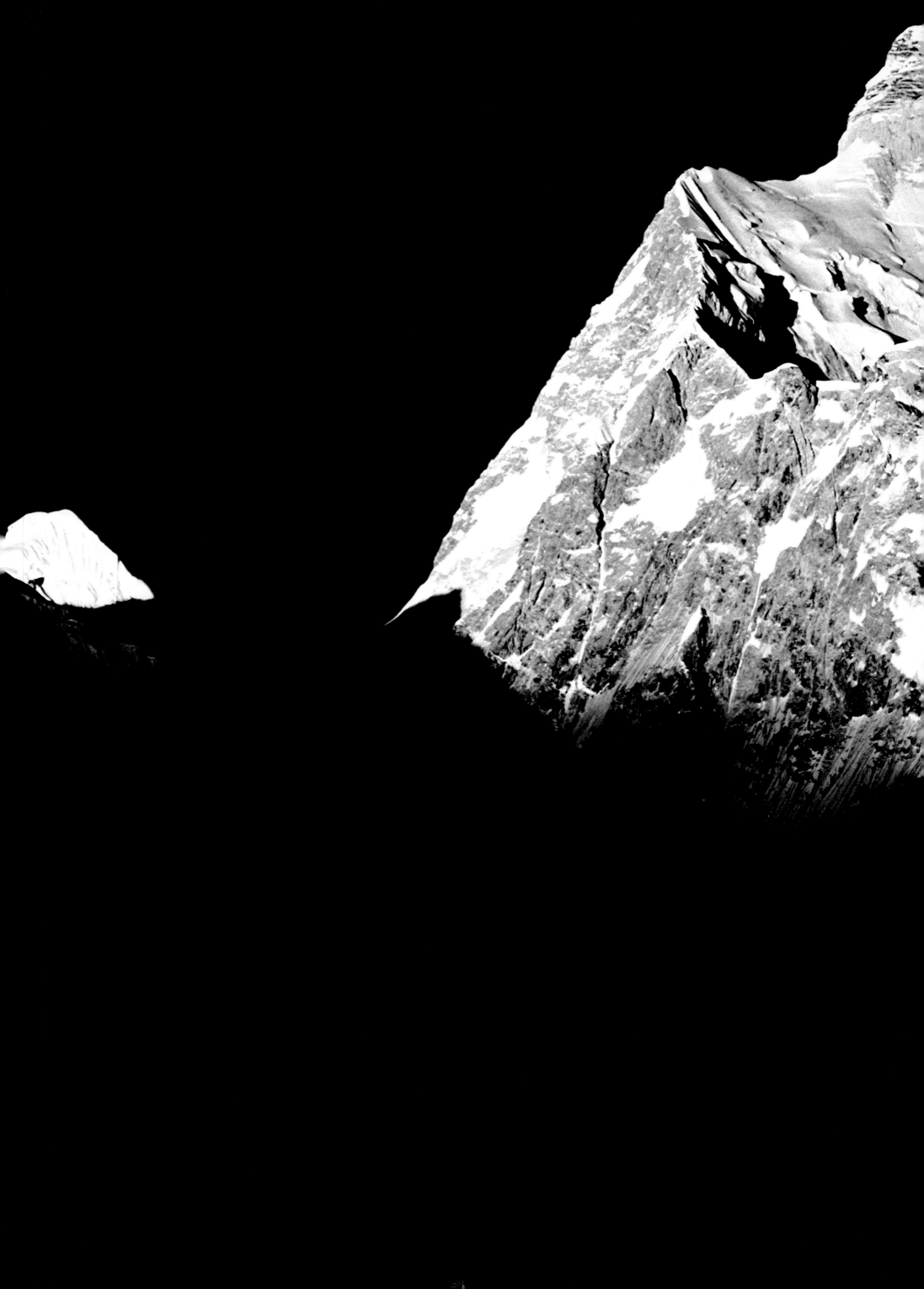

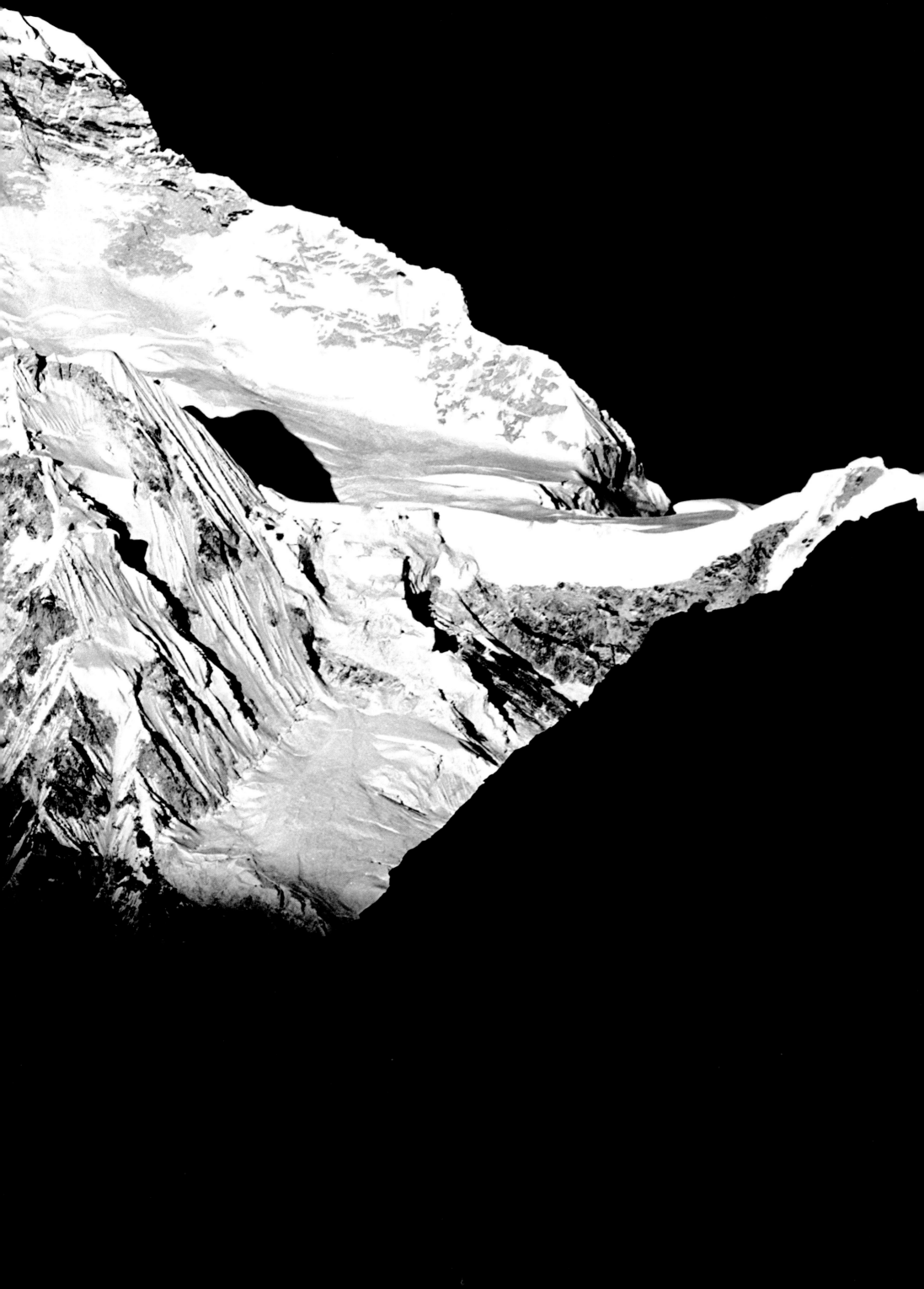

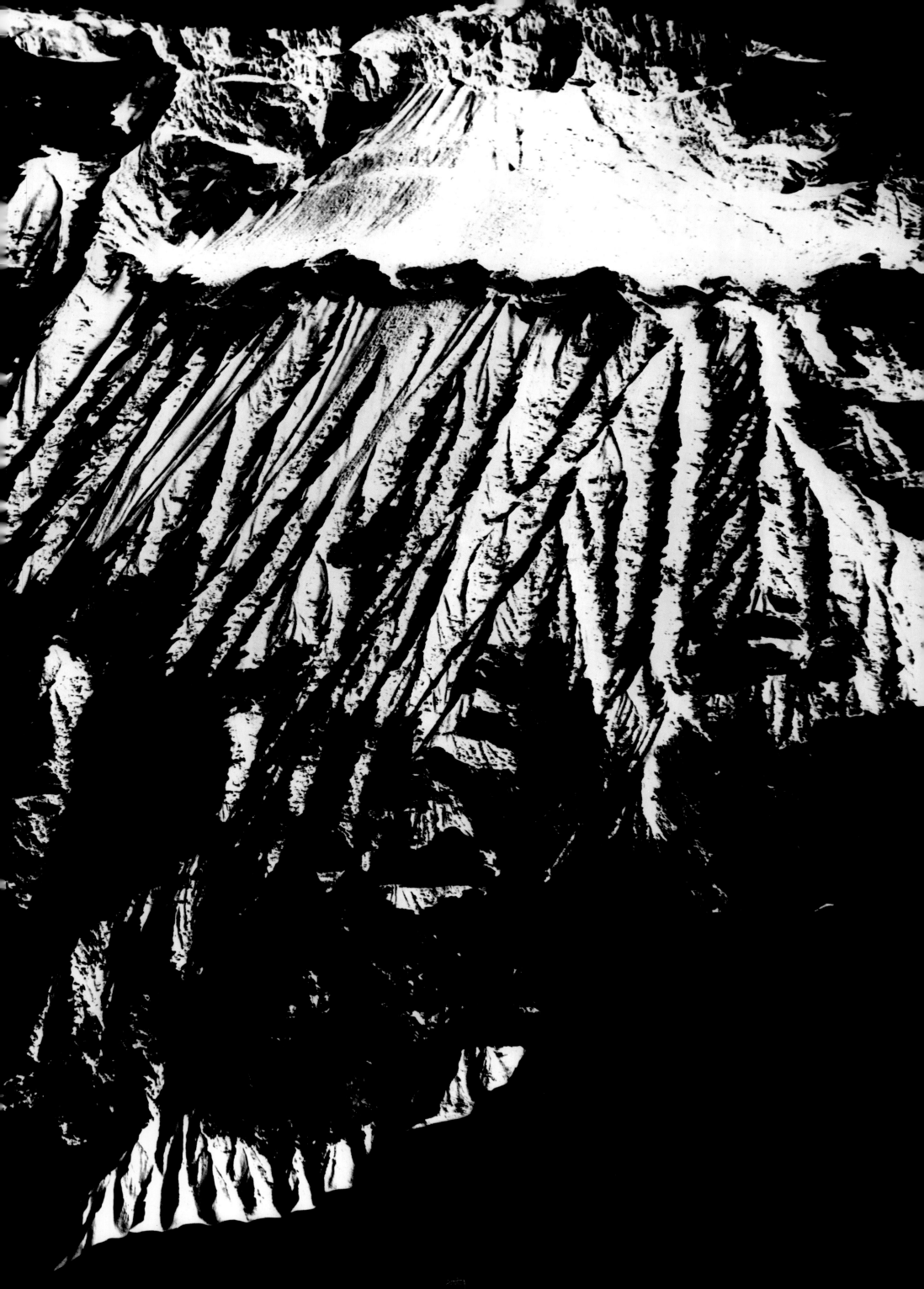

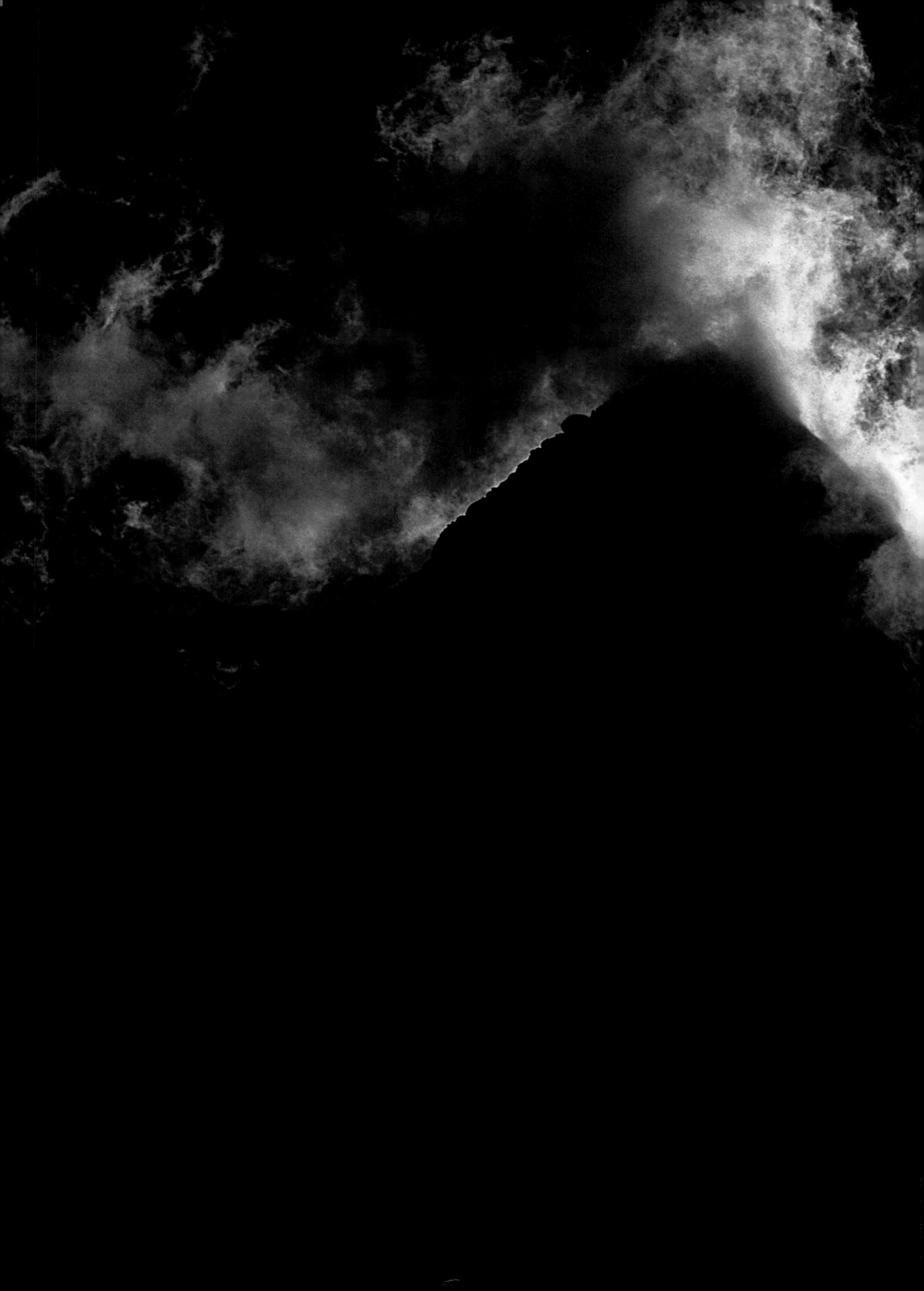

The Sikkim Himalayas

Because the Himalayas were formed from a north-south squeeze between the land masses of Central Asia and India, most of the ranges extend east to west. Only the Sikkim Himalayas on the Sikkim-Nepal border extend north to south. The earth's third highest peak, Kangchenjunga (8,598 meters), and thirteen mountains over 7,000 meters stand in this range. Particularly famous are Jannu in Nepal and Siniolchu in Sikkim.

Jannu has nicknames like "The Sleeping Lion," "The Sphinx" and others that hint at its reputation among alpinists. It is truly the most awesome of the high peaks in the 3,000-kilometer Himalaya chain. It competes with Kangchenjunga, the highest of the Sikkim Himalaya peaks, in its breathtaking appearance and its popularity among mountain climbers. Unfortunately, however, knowledge about Jannu is scant, since it lies in a country that has never readily let foreigners in.

Although Nepal relaxed its restrictions on foreign visitors in 1956, it reinstated its isolationist policy in 1963 and few foreigners are allowed to enter the country today. Those who do gain entry usually have their movements restricted. Ours was the only group ever allowed to travel throughout the Sikkim Himalayas.

Since the Sikkim Himalayas generally form the boundary between Nepal and Sikkim, one must explore the area at least once from the Sikkim side and once from Nepal to gain a complete view of the range. I began my expedition on the Sikkim side.

Mountains in this range were first scaled from Sikkim in the late 19th century. When India was a colony the British showed great interest in exploring the Himalayas, and sent many expeditions to the area. Darjeeling was the starting point for assaults on the mountains in the region. Darjeeling is only about seventy kilometers from the closest mountains, and from the city one can view the entire Sikkim Himalayas. The city sits 2,000 meters above sea level and once provided the British a cool retreat from the summer heat of India. After the area's population rapidly increased with an influx of Indians, Darjeeling became quite dirty and run down. Today, the squalor of the town contrasts sharply with the splendor of its surroundings.

To appreciate fully the grandeur of the Sikkim Himalayas one must stand on Tiger Hill, eleven kilometers southeast of Darjeeling. People around the world were introduced to the majesty of the Himalayas through photographs taken from that point, and most of the thousands of photographs taken of the Sikkim Himalayas show views from there. Naturally, our conception of the entire Himalayan complex can be influenced by scenes of the Sikkim Range.

ENTRY INTO SIKKIM

I never expected to receive permission to photograph the mountains of Sikkim and Bhutan. I heard about the possibility of entering those two countries just at a time when I was greatly disappointed because my requests to enter the Indian mountains had been denied. Mr. P.N. Mennon, General Director of the Northern Territorial Bureau of the Indian Ministry of Foreign Affairs, suggested the Sikkim alternative. I had requested admission to the Garhwal Himalayas and the Indian side of the Punjab Himalayas through the National Defense Ministry three years prior to that time. I had contacted the Ministry mostly through Mennon at that time, and got to know him very well. My disappointment at not being able to photograph the Garhwal and

Punjab Himalayas was so great that I could not get very excited about the alternate proposal. After talking with my assistants, however, I decided to apply for travel to Sikkim.

No complicated arrangements were necessary. I telephoned Mennon one day to tell him I would go to Sikkim if I could, and the next day I had the permit in my hand. He also suggested that I obtain permission to visit Bhutan. He could then issue an interline pass allowing me to enter the Bhutanese mountains directly from Sikkim. I soon obtained the assurance that I could go to Bhutan, but was told I would have to wait a few months before the government would issue the permit. Unfortunately, Mennon left his position two weeks before I was scheduled to receive permission, and the new director of the Northern Territory Bureau, Mr. Abraham, was unwilling to issue the interline pass. All of Mennon's efforts were wasted and I had to abandon the plan.

I could have asked the Japanese Ambassador to Bhutan, Sashichiro Matsui, who had close contact with the Imperial Family of Bhutan when he was the General Director of the Colombo Plan, to intercede in my behalf. However, I decided it was too big a favor to ask. Other help was offered, but I was reluctant to trouble so many people. Besides, I knew that travel to Bhutan was not worth such effort because photography was allowed only in the towns of Thimpu and Paro, neither of which seemed likely to offer interesting views.

On returning to Japan I discussed the situation with my publishers. Since the original plan covered all of the Himalaya Range, we felt it would be best to include at least some photographs taken in Bhutan. On the other hand, it would not be appropriate to represent Bhutan with snapshots of two small towns while shots of historic places and mountains represented the other countries in the region. Money was another factor in our decision. The trip to Bhutan for two snapshots would cost at least $5,500, including expenses for an assistant. If we spent $2,750 for each photograph in our book it would end up costing millions of dollars.

Although our plans to enter Bhutan collapsed, the trip to Sikkim went smoothly. First, we flew from New Delhi to Baghdogra. From there we drove to Darjeeling. We waited three days for the thick clouds hiding the mountains to clear, but had no luck. Since there was a time limit on our stay in Sikkim I had to leave Darjeeling and hope that I would get a clear view of the mountains on the way back.

Following the stipulations in our permit, we drove by jeep to Gangtok, the capital of Sikkim, via Kalimpong. Road constructions stopped us for two or three hours at a time. We also passed three checkpoints, which delayed us further. It was eight o'clock at night when we arrived in Gangtok.

I had heard that permission to stay in Sikkim was usually limited to one day, and three days at the longest. Hence, if one spends a whole day reaching Gangtok he has to drive back on the next. Such restrictions are quite an effective means of preventing visitors from seeing much of the country. But my friend Mennon obtained permission for us to remain in the country for eight days. He also arranged for us to travel about eighty kilometers north of Gangtok. We had not dared hope for permission to enter this more mountainous region.

Because of unexpected delays I had only five days left and had not yet reached the northern limit of my journey. We drove along the highway connecting India and Sikkim via Kalimpong. At night, a long line of Indian army trucks passed by and guns were hauled up the highway. Natu La, the pass where Indian and Chinese armies clash occasionally, is only eight kilometers northeast of Gangtok. Until we reached the road to the pass we were guided by an official from the Tourist Office. The road was not paved, but it was wide and well constructed. Kalimpong, Gangtok, Natu La, then around the foot of Mt. Chomolhari located in Bhutan, and on into Kangmar, Tibet: this was the main route through the mountains until the pass turned into a battlefield.

This closer view of the mountains did not produce any interesting photographic subjects. I had seen spectacular photographs of Kangchenjunga taken from Darjeeling, which is further from the mountain than Gangtok, and I had expected that a close-up of the mountains in the Kangchenjunga area would be even better. But the eastern side of the mountain was remarkably unimpressive and I could hardly believe that it was the same Kangchenjunga I had waited so eagerly to see. No part of this view of the mountain even hinted at its splendid fame. I soon took the road back to Darjeeling to spend the rest of my time photographing Kangchenjunga from there. The mountain is somewhat flat on top and appears more dramatic when partly hidden in clouds than on clear days.

NEPALESE SIDE OF THE SIKKIM HIMALAYAS

The trip to the Sikkim region was not satisfying as far as the quality of my photographs was concerned. I desperately wanted to take pictures of the Nepalese side; otherwise, only a view from the top of the mountains would provide satisfactory coverage of this mighty range. Although I held no hope of being permitted, I applied for entry into the Nepalese mountains. To me it was a miracle when I heard that my party would be admitted to the region. Since the country closed in 1963 I was the first foreigner allowed to tour the mountains. This was due solely to the endeavors of the Japanese embassy staff and the generosity of Brigadier General Sushil Shumsher J.B. Rana.

As soon as I obtained permission, I left Kathmandu Airport for Biratnagar. Arriving there I drove as far as Dharan Bazar, where we pitched our first camp in the Nepalese mountains. I was soon interrupted by Indian soldiers. Although the area was within Nepalese territory, India had set up a checkpoint and an official demanded that I present a permit from the Indian government. He ignored the guarantee from the Nepalese government. I had no doubts that we were in Nepal, but they claimed that the area was in India. I went to the checkpoint with the officer, explained who I was, and showed them all the credentials I had. I showed them the letter of introduction from the Japanese Ambassador to Nepal, Mr. Kira, and the letter to local police which the administrator of the National Police of Nepal, Mr. Thapa, had made me carry along. I also mentioned the names of Mr. Mennon of the Indian Ministry of Foreign Affairs and Mr. Sarhin, the Secretary General of the National Defense Ministry. They finally let me pass. A few months later when I went back to Kathmandu I mentioned the incident to the Nepalese Foreign Ministry, but the officers dismissed it with a laugh. Nevertheless, I often saw Indian officials in Nepalese territory acting like some kind of conquerors. I understand that Indian checkpoints in Nepal are gradually disappearing. It is only natural that they should.

So went my first night in the Nepalese mountains. Early the next day, January 6, 1970, we began our march. Our sherpas were named Happa Tenzing, Annu and Gartzen. We had also hired fifteen porters with the help of the police. Thus, our party numbered twenty-one men, including myself and my assistants Kihara and Tanioka.

We were told it would take about three weeks to walk to Ghunsa, where we could get a close-up view of the mountains. Since I expected no interesting subjects on the way I hastened our march by paying the porters extra to walk until dark every day. That let us complete the march from Dharan Bazar to Ghunsa in two weeks.

We then crossed Chunjerma Pass and passed the ruins of Tseram, an old village. Our maps showed four villages along our route, but all we saw were ruins. Nor did we come across the ruined monastery or the tombs of Lama monks mentioned in old descriptions of the area.

On our twentieth day out of Dharan Bazar I took my first photograph of the Nepalese-Sikkim Himalayas. It was a splendid view of Kangchenjunga towering over Yalung Glacier. The route of the British expedition which scaled the summit for the first time was clearly visible. The eastern face of Jannu was also in sight. Formed of unbelievably white snow and ice, the glacier sits a few thousand meters high at the top and slides down to meet the Eastern Jannu Glacier. The view was far more spectacular than I had imagined.

In the fall of 1899, the Italian alpine photographer Vittorio Sella and the English climber Freshfield, who later became the head of the British Alpine Society, journeyed around Kangchen-junga. That, in fact, was one of the most important events in the history of photography. Their party crossed Johnsan Pass on the borders of Sikkim, Tibet and Nepal to enter Nepal. As the country was closed to foreigners, however, they were chased out. The chase began when they were found by a Nepalese soldier at Kangbacheng Village. On the way back to Sikkim, Sella and Freshfield crossed Chunjerma Pass, and the now famous view of Jannu was photographed. It made the Italian photographer so famous that his name is still heard in photography circles. I stood on the same spot where Sella stood over seventy years ago. Facing the same mountain, I reflected on what his emotions might have been.

It took us two days to walk from Ghunsa to Tseram. We marched through snowstorms and were battered by violent winds continuously. My ears were frostbitten. The second day was worse than the first because two of our porters deserted us. Their loads had to be carried by a sherpa and my assistants.

Our maps were not reliable. Since the area has never been fully surveyed it is difficult to obtain accurate charts. Besides the map I carried with me from Japan, I had purchased another in India. Before arriving at Tserma we went through five passes, only three of which were marked on one map and four on the other. Chunjerma Pass had to be one of them. Although the number of passes differed, on both maps the pass closest to Tseram was called Chunjerma. Both maps turned out to be wrong, but I believed them and consequently had to waste time later finding the real Chunjerma Pass. This waste of time brought unexpected danger to the entire party.

The fifth pass, the one closest to Tseram, was far from where the historical photograph was taken, so we headed back to the third pass. When I arrived there, Tanioka, who had gone on ahead, told me he had seen Jannu. But when I arrived all of the mountains were shrouded in thick clouds. Half doubting Tanioka and half hoping he was right, I decided to camp there and wait for the clouds to clear.

The weather was worsening and it seemed most unlikely that Jannu would show itself clearly. I would hardly have believed we were in the right spot even if I had seen Jannu myself, but decided to spend the night there anyway. We pitched our tents in the snow-and-ice-covered pass. It was difficult to set up camp at 5,000 meters because of the strong winds. The thermometer we had could register no lower than –20°C, but I judged that the temperature was below –30°C.

While we were eating, a sherpa burst into our tent to tell us that Jannu was right above our heads. Everybody in the tent dashed out to see. The red glow of the evening sky dotted with constantly moving clouds was the backdrop for the mountain I had long been dreaming of. The majestic appearance and overwhelming massiveness of the mountain were right in front of me. I felt I was being consumed by it.

The mountains in a Japanese poem that came to my mind must have been Japanese mountains. However, I felt I was sharing the emotion of the poet as I faced Jannu, the Himalayan mountain I had yearned most to see. I spent three days in this icy, frozen, stormy pass and photographed the ever-changing Jannu every minute I could.

We returned to Ghunsa to rest and replenish our supplies. Then we started out again by following the Ghunsa River to the north until we arrived at Pang Pema. We stayed there three days. On the way back to Kangbacheng, I detoured to the top of Ramtang Glacier and also stopped by Jannu Glacier. Although this was the middle of the dry season, it started to snow. In the three years I had spent exploring the Himalayas I had never encountered such unusual weather. We were not at all prepared for snow, and became completely bogged down for seven days.

Since our original plan was to return to Ghunsa Village in two days, food suddenly became a serious problem. We exhausted our food supplies after four days, except for emergency rations, and on the eighth day decided to try and make it to Ghunsa.

We split into three groups, leaving the tent area at thirty-minute intervals. That way at least one group might survive if a snowslide struck. Right below Kangbacheng we had to negotiate a steep expanse two or three kilometers long. It was the most dangerous part of our escape plan, and even as we watched we saw snow roar down across the area we must traverse. It seemed suicidal to attempt, but we could not stay where we were.

I was in the third group and watched the first two groups far ahead running, slipping and stumbling through the snow. With all the sliding and falling, they advanced very slowly. And since the first group had to break through new snow, the distance between them and the second group soon shortened. The groups met, in fact, in the middle of the steep expanse. The scars of massive snowslides were visible above and below them. Only luck would prevent another from crashing down at the very moment we were watching. I had to look away.

I had met and survived danger countless times in Japan and in other countries, and I think I must lead a charmed life. I am not personally afraid of danger or death, but in my Himalaya travels I never considered merely my own safety. I might take chances myself, but took every precaution not to jeopardize the lives of the sherpas and my assistants. It could not be mere luck that all the members of our party survived this calamity without serious injuries. In fact, in my three years of exploring the Himalayas I was fortunate that no one was killed in any of the parties I led, despite the constant dangers. My experiences in the Himalayas made me believe in the existence of an awesome power that is difficult to describe.

CHAMLANG AND MAKALU

Chunjerma Pass is fifteen kilometers west into Nepal from the Sikkim border. Taken from that pass this photo shows Chamlang (7,319 meters) on the left and Makalu (8,475 meters) on the right. The red-colored mountain barely visible on the right edge of this photograph is Everest, and the bluish mountains in the foreground are the Lumba Sumba Himal. In the valley under the clouds are Phole and Ghunsa villages. Also in that valley is the Ghunsa River, which originates in the Kangchenjunga Glacier. I took this photo around 5:00 a.m.

KANGCHENJUNGA

After taking a long detour to the left on the second day of the trip from Tseram along Yalung Glacier, I set up my camera to photograph the world's second highest mountain. Kangchenjunga's main peak (8,598 meters) is in the center. To the left is the west peak (8,420 meters) and on the right is the south peak (8,474 meters). At 8,000 meters the mountain's wall seemed to spew forth red-colored clouds. It was a strange dreamlike scene.

NUPCHU

The route from Kangbachen winds through a valley and up to a wide field called Mindhu. The natives probably bring animals to graze here in summer but in winter there is neither man nor animal in the whole area. Further along this same route are Nupchu Glacier and Nupchu icefall. From here it is fairly easy to approach the mountain. An expedition from Japan's Osaka Prefectural University first climbed this 7,028-meter mountain in 1962.

SHARPHU

Sharphu was discovered by a joint party of alpinists from Tokyo Metropolitan University and Osaka Prefectural University when they climbed Nupchu in 1962. This area is equivalent to being blank on maps because it has never been surveyed. Sharphu is listed on maps as 7,200 meters, probably an estimate. This photograph was taken from a village in Kangbachen after the tail winds of a blizzard had cleared the skies.

UNNAMED PEAK NEAR YALUNG GLACIER

This unnamed peak on the left bank of the Yalung Glacier was photographed from the moraine at the upper part of the glacier. The rocks in the foreground are larger than they appear to be, and we made our way up the glacier by jumping from one rock to the next. The surface snow was coated with a thin sheet of ice that did not hold our weight and we sank two feet with every step. The Yalung Glacier is quite old and has shrunk considerably. There was a 100-meter drop from the moraine to the glacier's surface.

TELEPHOTO VIEW OF MAKALU

This is a telephoto close-up of the earth's fifth highest peak, Makalu (8,475 meters), viewed from Chunjerma Pass. At the left, Chamlang (7,319 meters) is partially visible. Everest is on the right. I caught the moment when the red from the rising sun turned its brightest yellow. The yellow slowly turns whiter until by 10 a.m. it is blue. Clouds start to form after the sun is up. Before I fully realized it, huge cauliflower-shaped clouds had formed and were moving straight toward my position.

SOURCE OF RAMTANG GLACIER

This photograph shows the start of Ramtang Glacier, and was taken from our camp. The mountain in the center is Kangbachen (7,902 meters). The mountain to the right of the snowblown ridge is a 7,532-meter unnamed peak. It is unusual and surprising that a mountain above 7,000 meters is not named, but there are many such high unnamed peaks in the Himalayas. The ice of the glaciers in this area shines a golden color, as if gold dust were mixed with the ice.

JANNU GLACIER

Jannu Glacier viewed from a mountain near Kangbachen Village. The Ghunsa River, which originates from the Kangchenjunga Glacier, flows from left to right of the cairn in the foreground. The river's flow is halted by Jannu Glacier cutting into it from due east. The glaciers here have spent themselves and are in their dying stages.

WHITE WAVE

To reach the source of the Ramtang Glacier one must traverse Kangchenjunga Glacier, which flows north to south from Ramtang. I pitched camp on the glacier's blue ice and spent three days photographing the area. This photo shows White Wave (6,960 meters), located on the right side of the glacier. The mountain's shape is not particularly pleasing but I was overwhelmed by the ice and the icefall the mountain has given birth to. It extended almost further than I could see.

JANNU'S EAST WALL

Taken from the top of the Yalung Glacier moraine, this photo shows Jannu's east wall and ridge extending northeastward. Further along the ridge is a 7,532-meter unnamed peak. The same ridge eventually runs into Kangbachen Peak, 7,902 meters. Jannu (7,710 meters), one of the most difficult mountains to scale, fell to a French expedition in 1962. The 4,000-meter vertical drops of the mountain's eastern and northern ice walls appear invincible.

JANNU FROM CHUNJERMA PASS

Seventy-four years ago the Italian alpine photographer Vittorio Sella captured this same view of Jannu. He came here in September; I took this photograph in February. We pitched camp in the pass, and I am certain my sherpas will never forget me for exposing them to the ice and fierce winds. The photograph shows the southwest side of Jannu in late afternoon. The 1962 French expedition climbed along the ridge seen on the right.

MOUNTAINS AROUND YAMATARI GLACIER

Our next camp site after leaving Chunjerma Pass was in a field through which flowed the Mudhimbuk River—actually, a stream. It was a famed camping site but was covered with snow when we arrived and was not particularly pleasant. A half-day climb up from here is a ridge that affords a panoramic view of Yamatari Glacier. Jannu is further left than this photograph shows. What I thought was a mountain in this photograph may be only a high spot along a ridge.

SUB-MOUNTAIN OF WEDGE PEAK

I took this photograph from a large field at Lhonak. In summer the area becomes a pasture for animals the Ghunsa bring. The enclosure in the foreground is a simple animal shelter. Looking across from here one can see the Kangchenjunga Glacier flowing from left to right. Every evening dense fog rose from the down-stream part of the glacier. In this photo, the sub-mountains of Wedge Peak reflect the sun's evening glow. Tibet is only fifteen kilometers north of here.

TELEPHOTO OF NEPAL HIMALAYAS

Between Tamo and Chunjerma Passes I walked the 5,932-meter ridge of Boktoh. Looking back I took this telephoto close-up of the Nepal mountains. In the center stands 8,475-meter Makalu, and on the far right is Chomo Lönzo, 7,790 meters high. Beyond that is Everest. Lumba Sumba Himal mountains are on the left, not so very far from where I stood. The Three Sisters are to the immediate left of Makalu.

UNNAMED PEAK ABOVE JANNU GLACIER

Climbing up Jannu Glacier I got a view of this mountain on the left bank of the glacier. At first I thought it was White Wave, but after studying its features and measuring distances I realized I was wrong. An unnamed peak marked on my map also did not seem to fit. Although I showed this photograph to numerous Himalayan specialists no one could help me identify it. This is probably a mountain that does not show up on any maps. It had a certain boldness about it.

ICEFALL ALONG WHITE WAVE

This photograph shows part of the icefall and blocks of ice that White Wave has given birth to. As I emphasized the contrast of black and white the scene changed from one of mountains and snow to something that looked like the entrails of a giant beast. This type of landscape shows the wondrous creativity of nature. I feel strangely moved when I view scenes like this.

JANNU AND YAMATARI GLACIER

This glacier is in its final stages of deterioration. Most of the ice is gone, and—as seen in the left foreground —water flows along the bed of the moraine. Similar shrinkage is occurring at Yalung and Jannu Glaciers as well. Glaciers with deep, solidly frozen bases such as Ngojumba seem to be diminishing in number. The mountain in the center is Jannu. The glacier behind the ridge on the right is Yalung. Boktoh (5,932 meters) stands further right and to the front of the ridge, but I left it out to keep the photograph balanced.

UNNAMED PEAK IN MINDHU

Going up the valley northwest of Kangbachen one comes to the foot of Nupchu (7,028 meters). To the left of Nupchu is Sharphu, while on its right is an unnamed peak of undetermined height. Even large mountains like Sharphu did not appear on maps of this area until 1962. It is probably not even known whether this unnamed peak stands by itself or is one of a group. In the foreground the remnants of a glacier can be seen.

WEDGE PEAK

This shot is also from the large grassfield at Lhonak. Seen from this angle Wedge Peak (6,750 meters) does not seem its usual self. The stone walls in the foreground form a simple animal pen. The flags in the center of the photograph are believed by Tibetans to drive away evil spirits. The inscriptions on these red and white bits of cloth are simple prayers.

WALL ON RIGHT BANK OF RAMTANG GLACIER

To reach the source of Ramtang Glacier one must first walk up the moraine, then cut out onto the glacier and continue climbing up. The climb is quite dangerous. On the left, rocks fly down from the steep moraine wall. The right side is formed by the frozen north wall of White Wave (6,960 meters). I took this picture of part of the wall early in the morning. The ice blocks on the glacier looked like so many little monsters waking up and ready to perform a dance of welcome for us.

MOONLIGHT ON JANNU

Light problems make it difficult to take a clear photo of Jannu's entire north wall in the daytime. I decided moonlight would give me a better photograph. But the lunar phase at the time was not ideal, and I could get only this rather flat view of Jannu's face. The snow-covered landscape looked blue to the naked eye. Stars appear as curved white lines in the sky because of the earth's rotation. It was suggested that the bright streak in the photo might be an orbiting satellite.

JANNU

Jannu is called variously the "Treacherous Mountain," the "Sphinx," and the "Sleeping Lion." The names probably can be traced to photographs by the famous Italian photographer Vittorio Sella. I stood at the same place in Chunjerma Pass he did 71 years ago. The short lapse of time undoubtedly witnessed no change in the shape of the mountain or in the sky above it. I was greatly moved as I closed my shutter.

WEDGE PEAK AT SUNSET

Wedge Peak (6,750 meters) viewed from Pang Pema at sundown. In the evening, the wind blowing across Kangchenjunga Glacier reverberates against this rocky wall and causes a low, rumbling noise. The Kangchenjunga mountains viewed from Pang Pema are incomparable. We were not authorized to go further than Pang Pema. Ten kilometers away is Johnsan Pass, the gateway to Tibet.

UNNAMED PEAK NEAR RAMTANG GLACIER

The mountain rising on the left at the source of the Ramtang Glacier is unnamed. I thought it was Ramtang Peak at first, but the position is wrong. Many mountains in this area are positioned differently from what maps show, and altitude figures are mostly guesses. Maps simply do not help in identifying some peaks. I took this photograph about nine in the morning when the sun rose over Kangbachen. The unnamed peak is small but quite photogenic.

SIKKIM HIMALAYAS FROM DARJEELING

The mountains of the Himalayas closest to human habitation are the Sikkim Himalayas. Darjeeling is only 70 kilometers from the mountains. Tiger Hill outside Darjeeling is one of the five best spots for photographing the Himalayas. It equals the views from Damang Pass and Nagarkot in Nepal. From left to right are Jannu, 7,710 meters; Ratang, 6,678 meters; Kabru, 7,338 meters; and Talung, 7,349 meters. Kangchenjunga, 8,598 meters, is in the clouds. On the far right is Pandim, 6,691 meters.

WHITE WAVE AND SERACS

A glacier's lower part is normally covered with rocks and mud or slush, and the ice itself is usually not exposed. To reach the ice-covered frozen shelf it is necessary to follow the glacier up as far as its source. Seracs of clear ice like the one in the forefront are seen here and there on a glacier. They are certainly miraculous wonders of nature. I climbed part way up one and chopped a place in the ice to set up my tripod.

OLD MAN

On the twelfth day after leaving Dharam Bazar we made camp at Amcheresa. Although the place has a name there are no houses or people there. The old man pictured was travelling with his son and camped at the same place. They camped in the open. We marched together after that for three days to Ghunsa. Although there was nothing special about those three days I have retained a vivid impression of the old man and his son.

JANNU'S NORTH WALL

This photograph of Jannu's north wall was taken from the top of a mountain behind Kangbachen. Jannu is regarded as a fearful mountain, and it actually can appear shaped like some monstrous bird with wings spread. I studied the north face from various angles and am convinced there are few other rock walls in the Great Himalayas as awesome as Jannu's north wall. I examined the summit area with my 500mm telescopic lens and believe climbing the wall would be a hopeless task.

OLD WOMAN IN PHOLE

Ghunsa is the largest village in this area, but in winter it is deserted. The villagers move to Phole, a town further down the mountain. Phole is only three hours walking distance from Ghunsa but it is perceptibly warmer there. Phole also has a police station, the only one in the area. I saw more policemen than villagers, and the machineguns they carried made them seem more like soldiers. This cheerful old woman helped the sherpas when we camped outside Phole, not far from the Tibetan border.

KANGBACHEN

On the left in this photograph is Kangbachen, a settlement of about twenty houses. From the moss on their foundations and the trees around the houses we estimated these dwellings to be from one hundred to two hundred years old. No one lives here in winter. Mountains in the photograph are Jannu on the left and an unnamed 6,699-meter peak next to it. What appears to be a peak on the far right is merely a swell on a ridge. The moraine from Jannu Glacier in the center of the photograph is about 50 meters high.

WOMAN AT GANGTOK MARKET

Gangtok is the capital of Sikkim. A group of Indian photographers in the area to produce a documentary film recommended that I visit the downtown marketplace. But the market disappointed me. I had spent several months visiting colorful marketplaces in cities along the southern and western coasts of Africa and to me nothing in Gangtok looked particularly unique. This girl, however, was the most beautiful girl I saw in Sikkim. The child next to her is probably her sister.

HINDU KUSH

HINDU KUSH

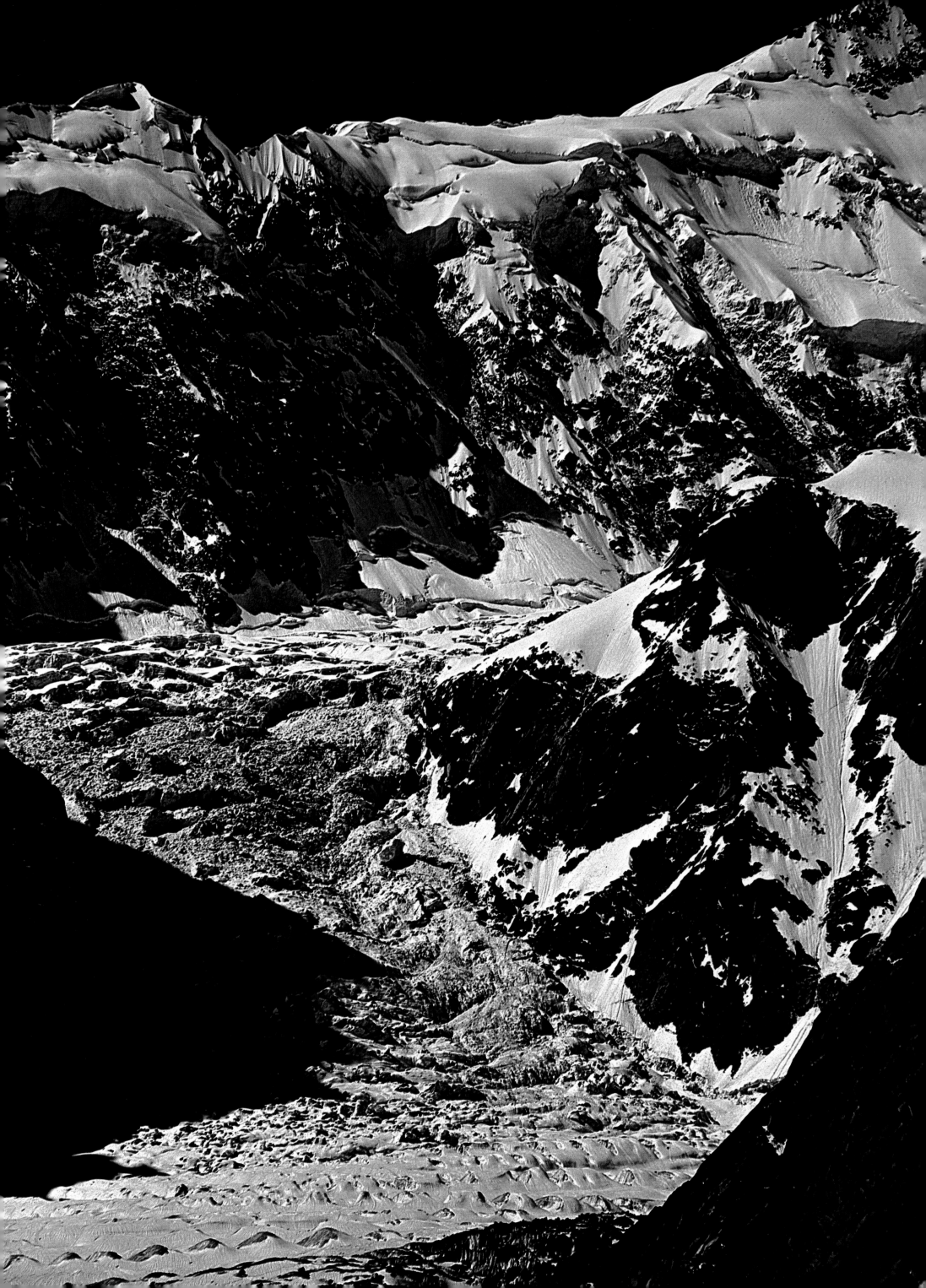

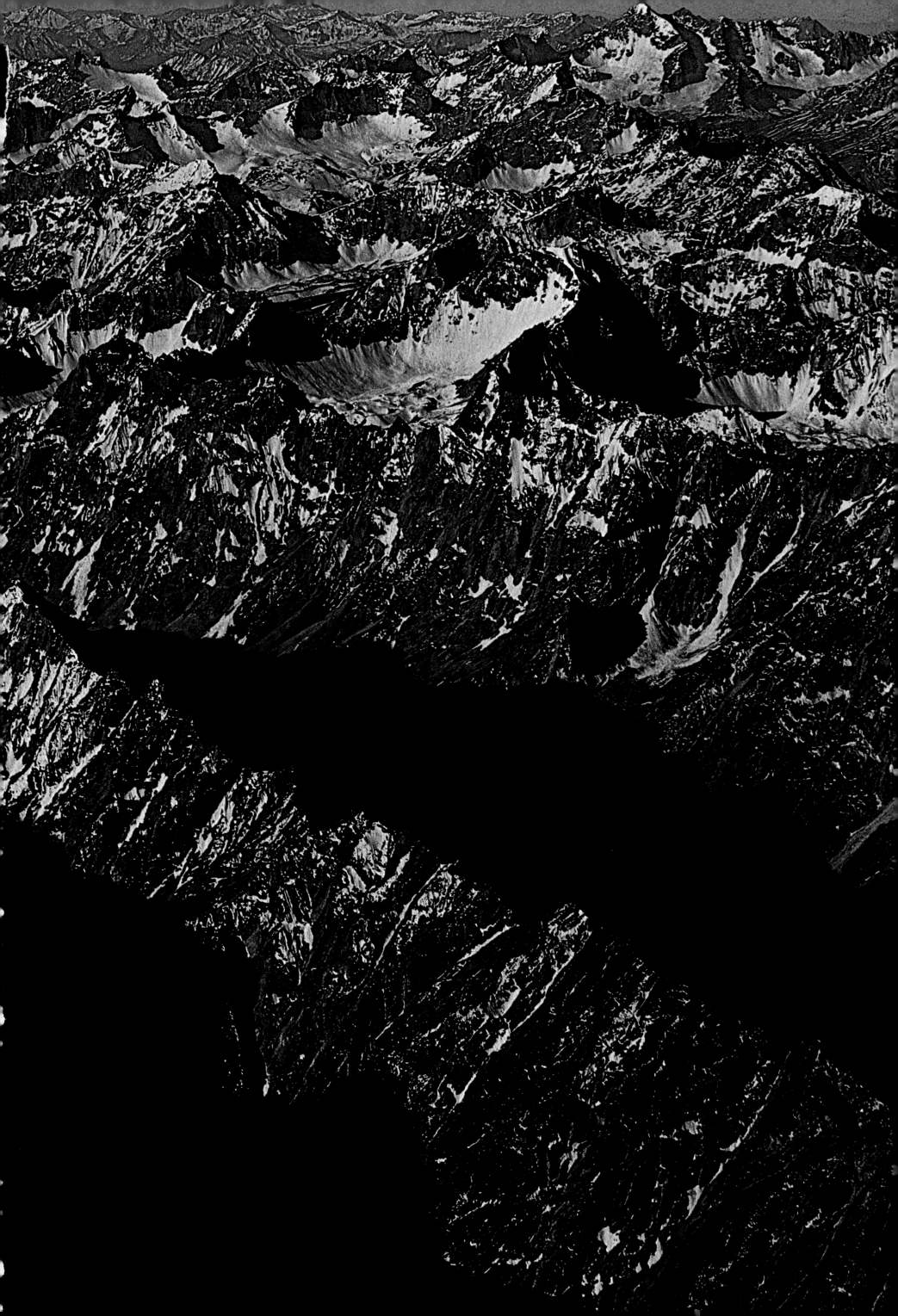

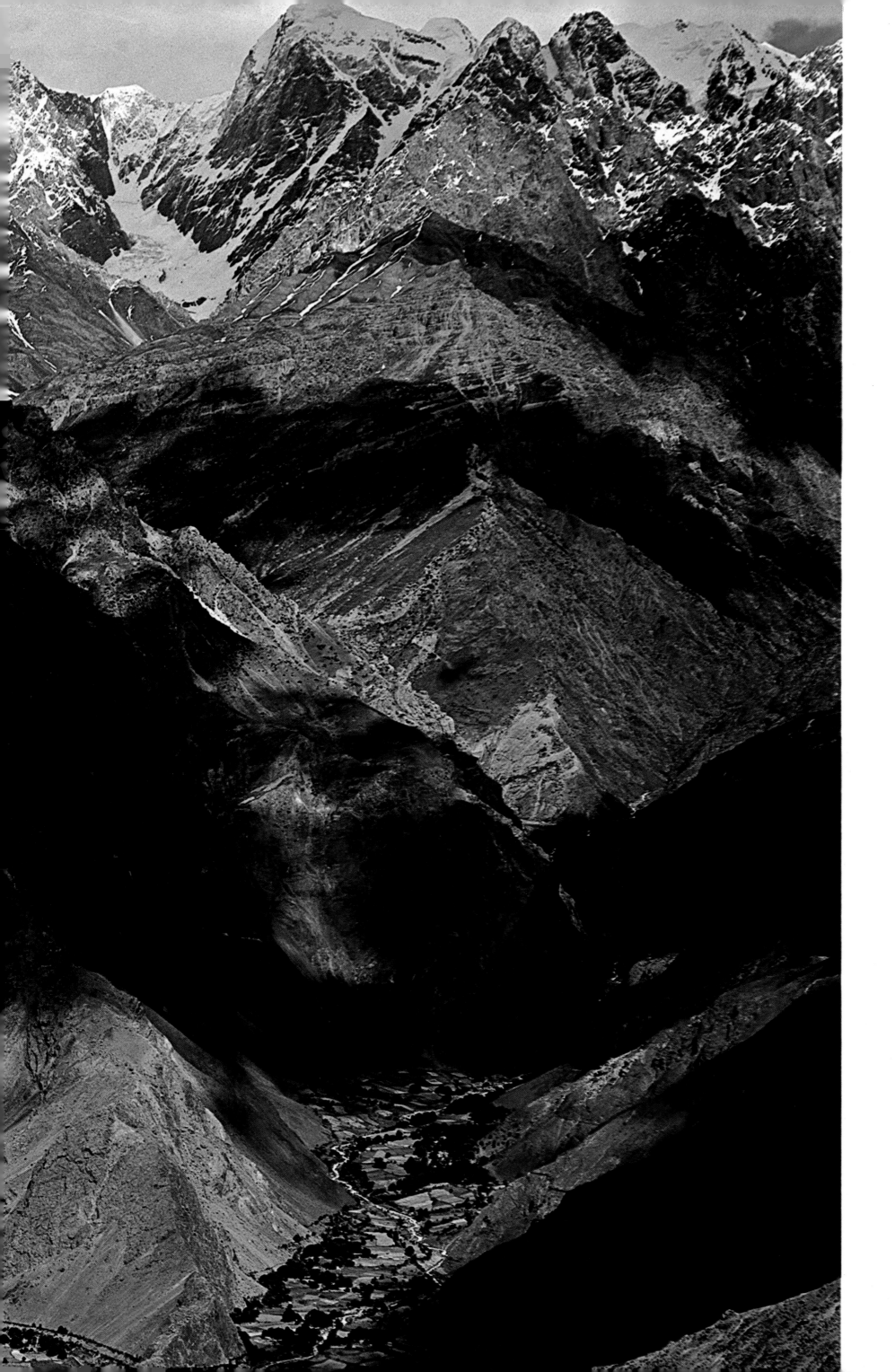

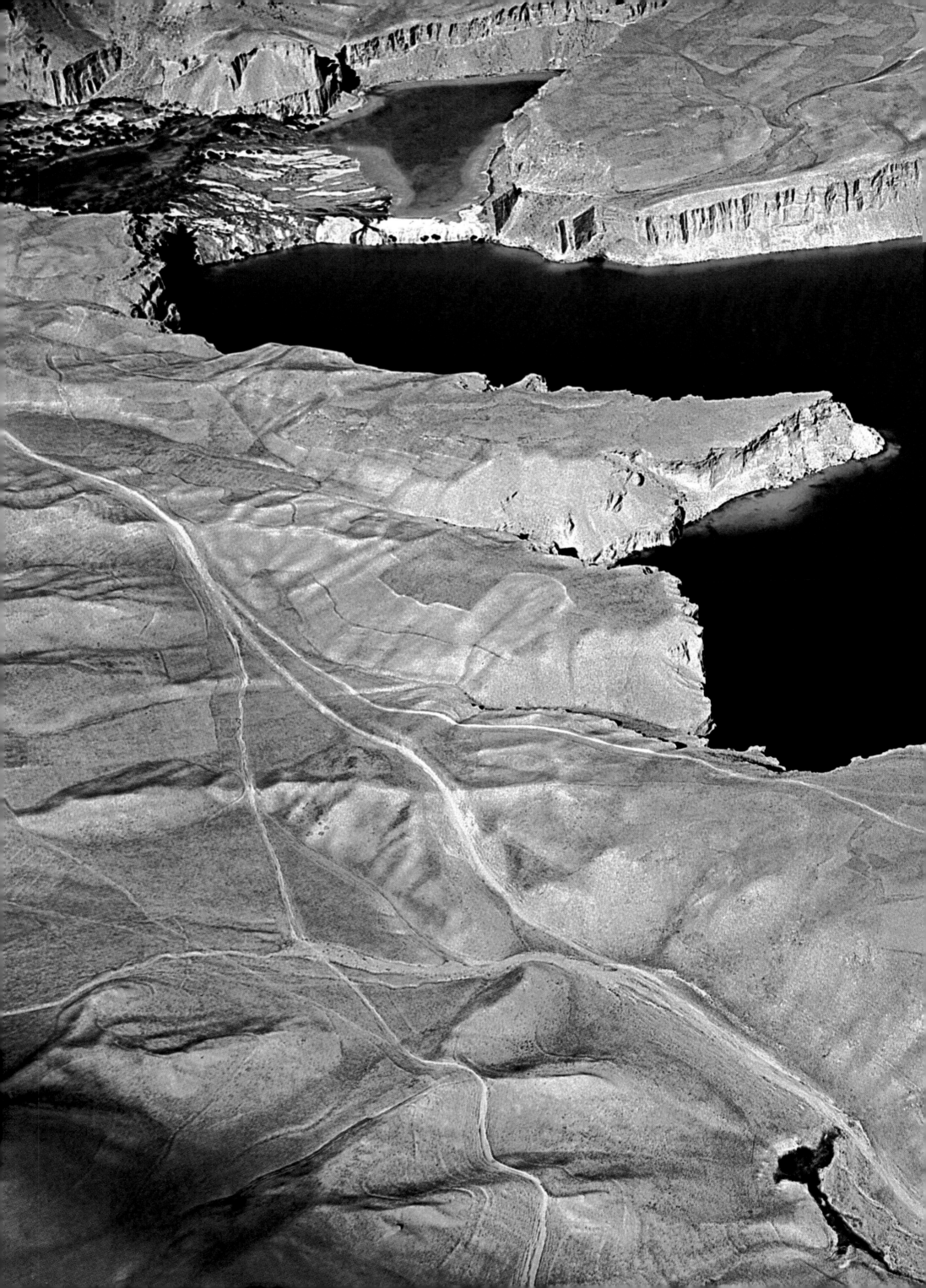

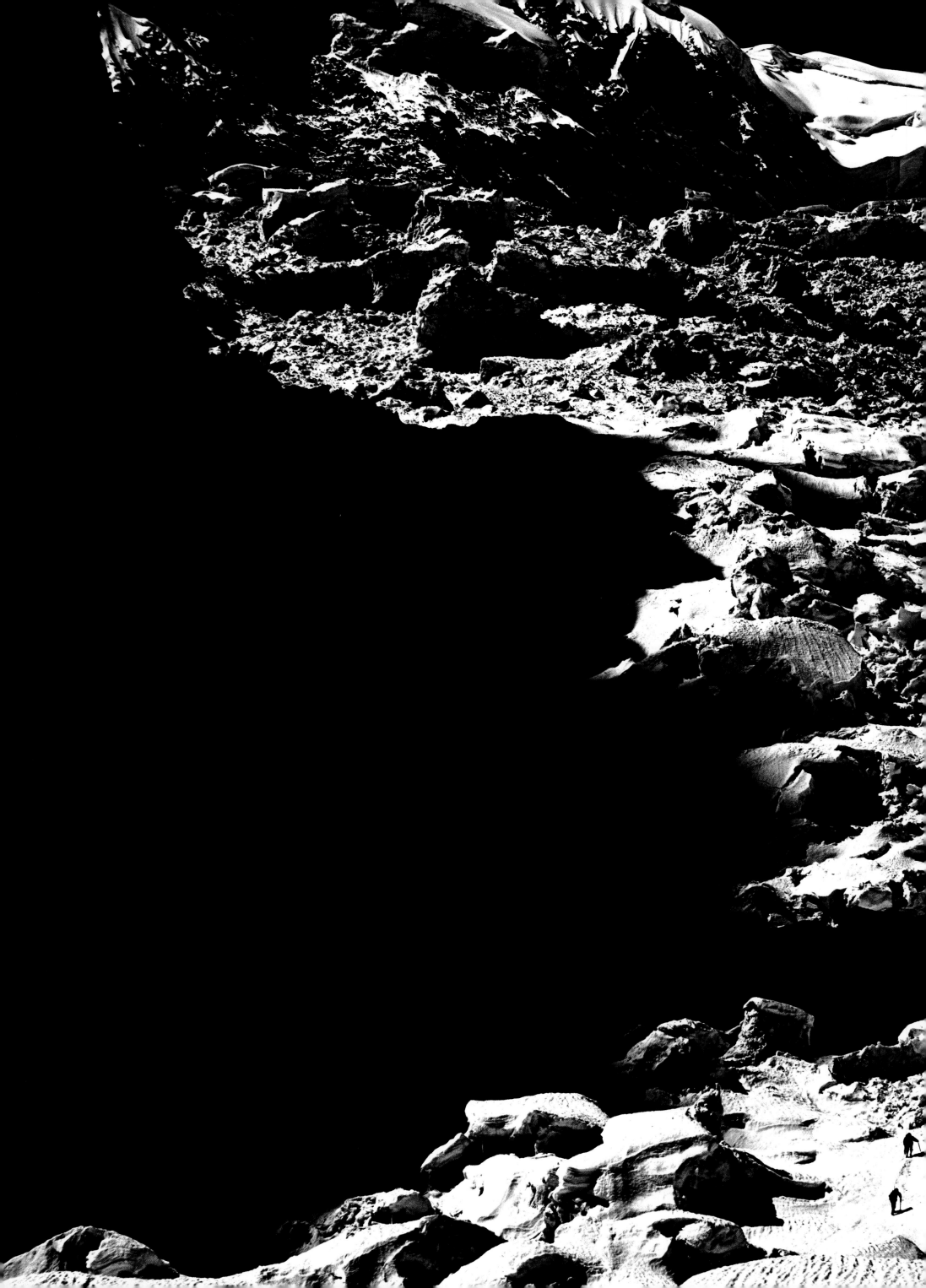

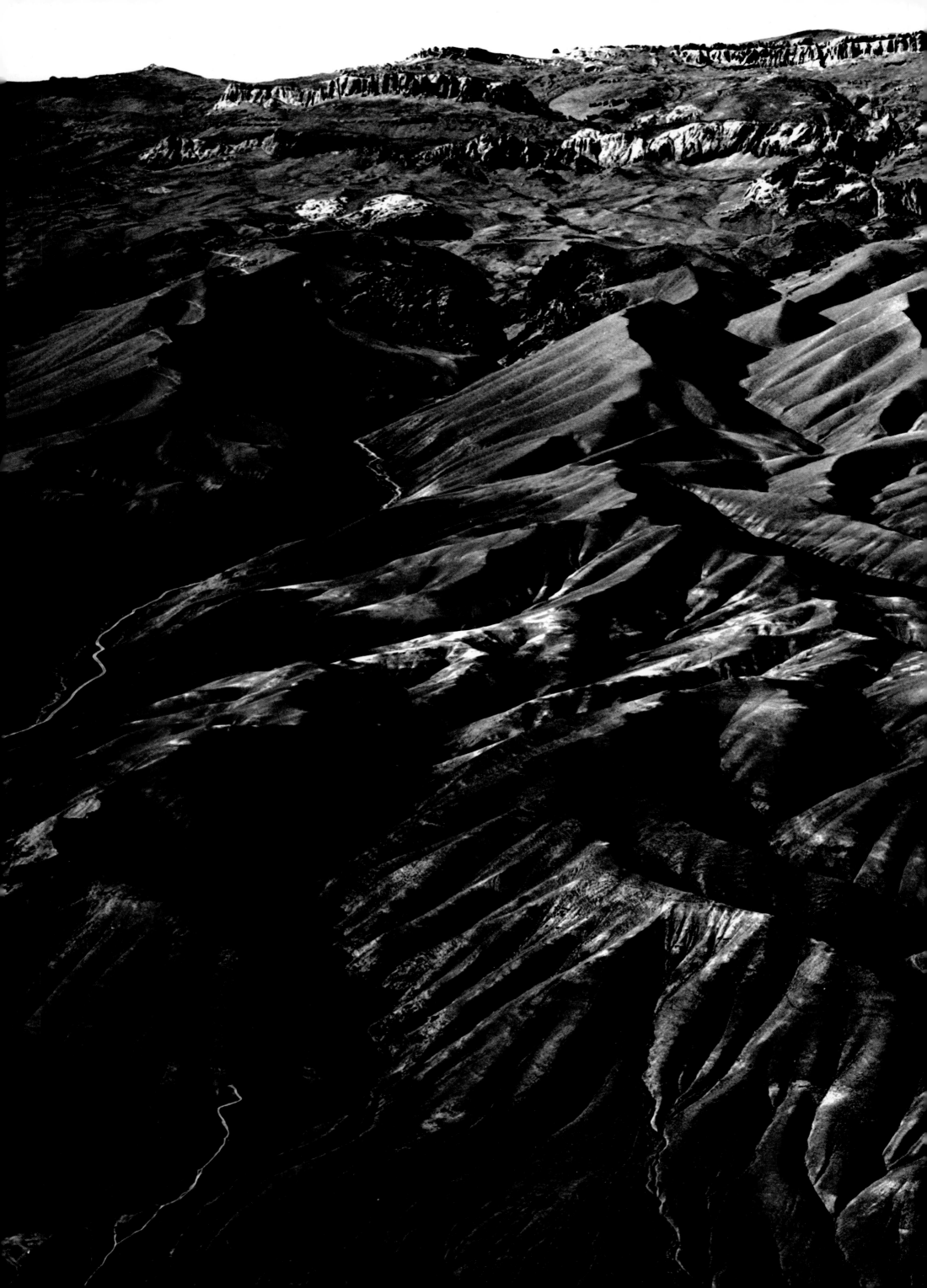

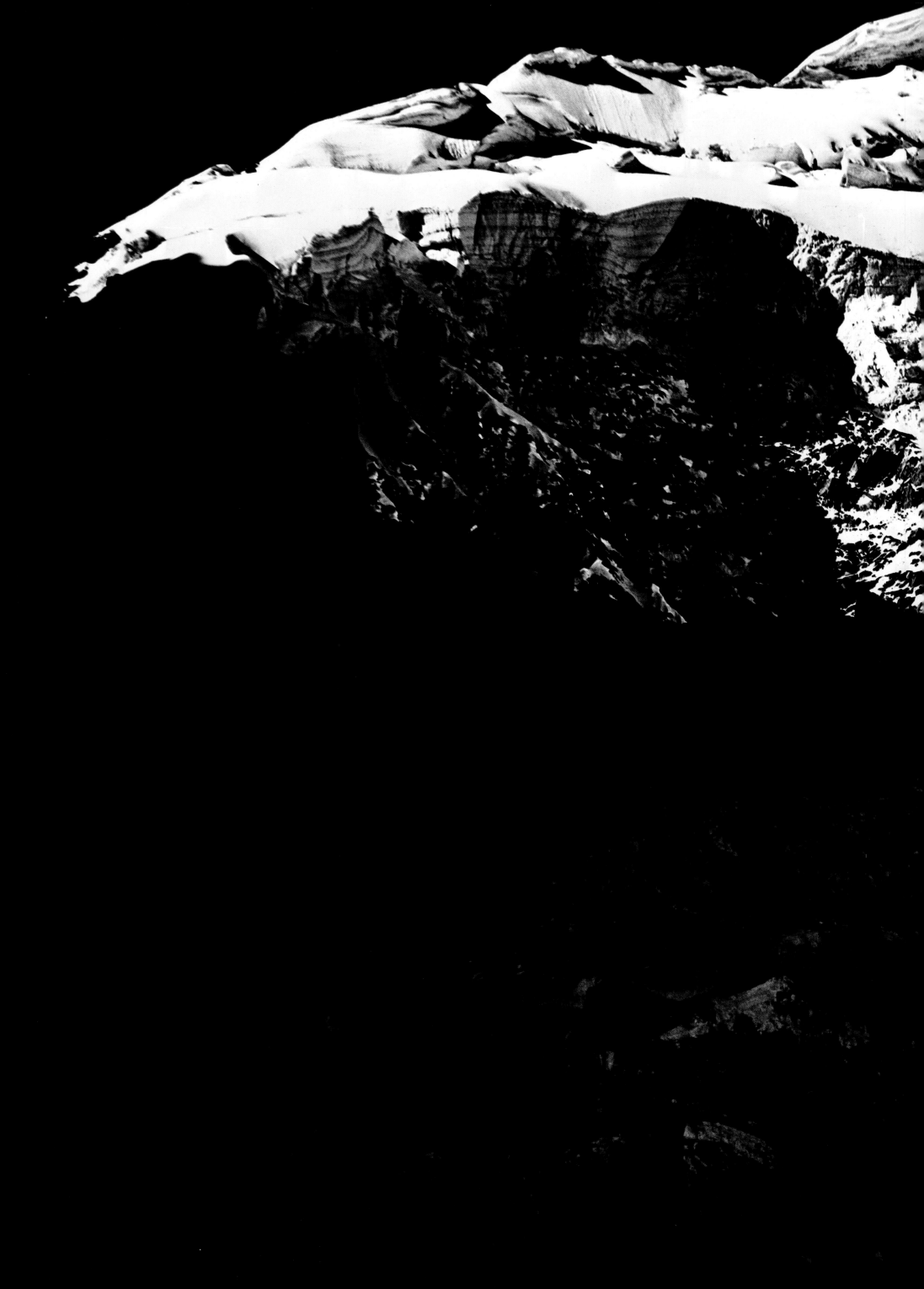

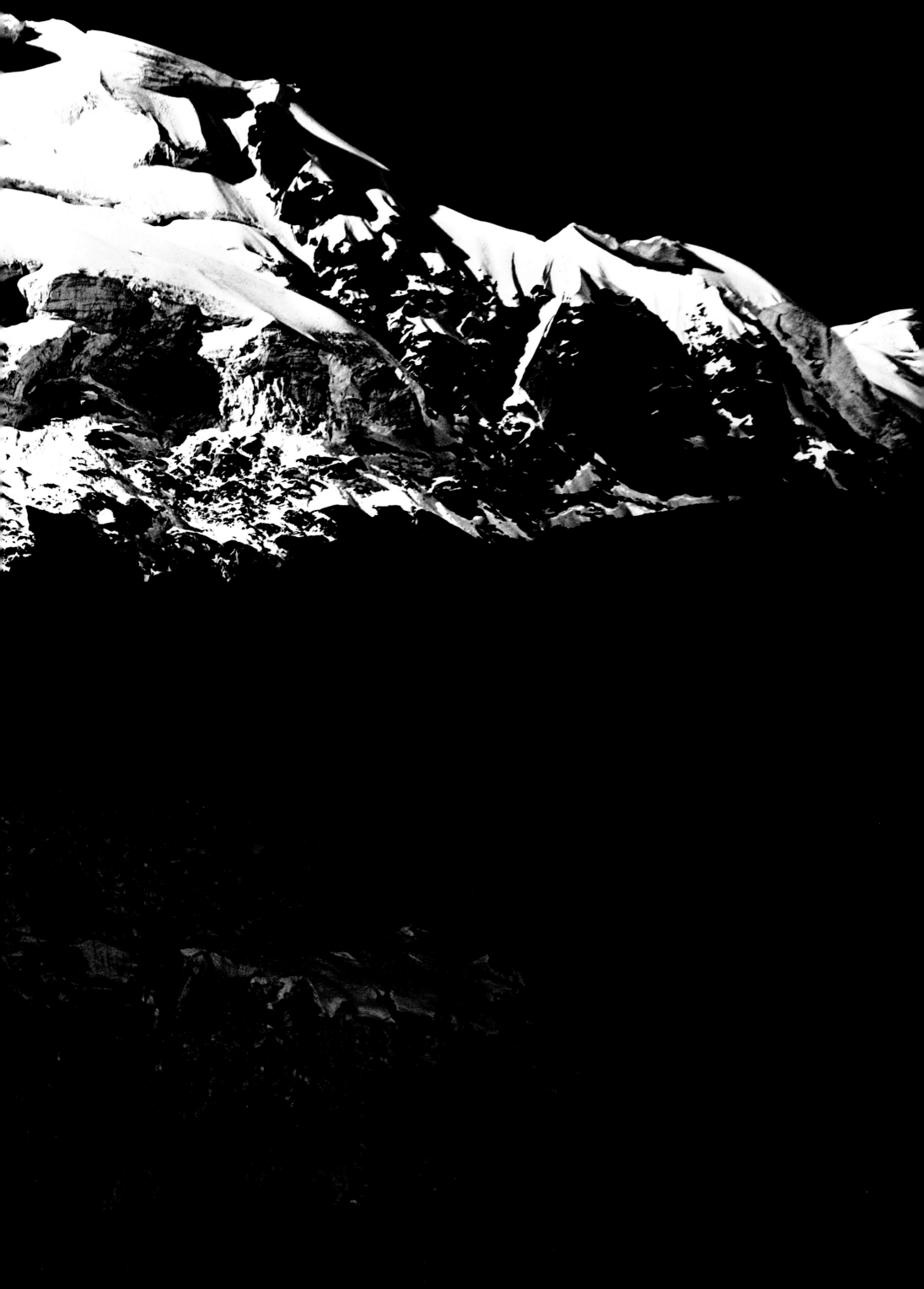

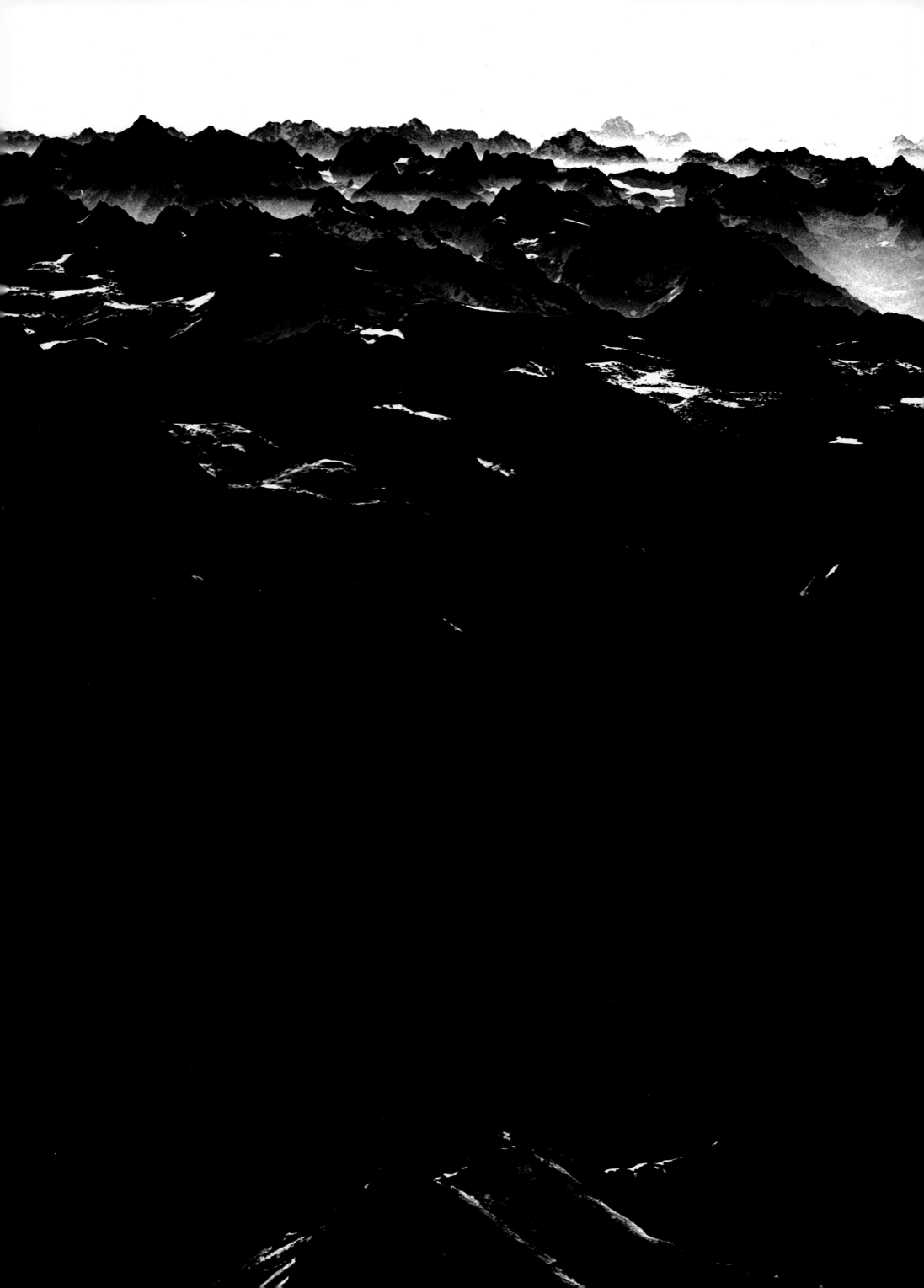

The Hindu Kush Range

The Hindu Kush mountain range extends southwest from the southern extreme of the Pamir Plateau. The range's easternmost point is 68° east longitude. Most of the high peaks in the range are along the West Pakistan/Afghanistan border and its surrounding area. The Hindu Kush mountains mentioned in this book are the mountains in that area. We must be specific, for some geographers discuss the Hindu Kush range as extending for 1,200 kilometers. Those authorities include the mountains of Koh-i-Baba and Safed Koh in the Hindu Kush, which extends it to Iran's border. If one includes those mountains, however, the Himalayas themselves acquire a total length of 4,000 kilometers.

The mountains in the Himalayas vary considerably in height. Those located west of 68° east longitude are only 2000 to 4000 meters high, and scarcely compare with the other mountains in the range. Because most of the Himalaya mountains are 6,000 to 7,000 meters high it seems unnecessary to include such low ''mountains'' in the range as well. Accordingly, the Himalayan Range in this book is 3,000 kilometers long, extending from the eastern edge of the Assam Himalayas at 96° east longitude to the western edge of the Hindu Kush at 68° east longitude.

West Pakistan's Tirich Mir, 7,706 meters above sea level, is the highest peak of the Hindu Kush. Along the Afghanistan border lie beautiful mountains such as Istor-o-Nal (7,403 meters) and Noshaq (7,492 meters). Several passes formerly of great aid to travellers heading from Kabul towards the Indus Plain are also located along this border; among these, the Khyber Pass (1,029 meters above sea level) is still in use today. Khawak Pass is where the invading armies of Timurlane and Alexander the Great crossed the Himalayas.

PAKISTANI SIDE

In recalling my trip to Pakistan, the name ''Hindu Kush'' first brings to mind my arduous travel across torturously hot deserts. Except for a few refreshing hours each morning and evening, the desert heat was unbearably intense. Desert travel, in fact, was more trying than later travel through icy –40°C weather in the mountains. The temperature at mid-day rose so high that breathing grew difficult. Whenever we came across a stream of water, we would immerse our heads completely to cool off and then leisurely soak our feet. But the heat finally overwhelmed us. After four or five days, it became impossible to continue walking. The soles of our feet blistered from the heat, and when the blisters broke we had to charter donkeys and horses. All my life, I shall never forget that trip across the fiery sands.

I flew to Chitral to visit Shahsadar Burhranudin Khan, whom I had met several times in Rawalpindi. He has a strong attachment to Japan and the Japanese, and was of invaluable assistance to me personally on many occasions. ''Shahsadar'' is, I learned, a title similar in meaning to ''Lord.'' Chitral was once an independent country and Shahsadar was its king. During World War II, he was commanding officer of the Indian national army organized under Chandra Bose which fought for Indian independence with the assistance of the Japanese army. Shahsadar played an important role in the Impar operation against the British; his affection for the Japanese, he explained, stems from those days. His kindness far surpassed ordinary goodwill, and he literally spared no effort in meeting my every need. When our caravan, including ten porters and one guide, left Chitral, my assistant and I rode out on horses that were gifts from Shahsadar.

On the first day of the trip, we went through Siogot. On the second day, we came to narrow mountain paths and were forced to descend from our horses and proceed on foot. We passed Susm and crossed Owir An (4,338 meters) on the third day, crawling our way up the steep, snowy slope. The sun's bright reflection from the snow added to our difficulties. From time to time I scooped up handfuls of snow to stuff in my cap. As it melted and ran down my face, the cold water provided a refreshing relief from the heat.

Our destination was Tirich Glacier. The difficult Owir An is not included in the normal course; I selected that route for the fine panoramic view it offers, well suited for taking pictures. At Kosht we returned to the regular route, crossed Zani An Pass and finally entered the glacier site. I spent one week there taking pictures.

On the way back, we passed by Bandok and descended to Kosht after crossing the Kosht An. As far as I know, ours was the first Japanese party ever to take this course. The road had disappeared in the snow, and without a guide my assistant and I were hard pressed to find the way by ourselves. Our guide had left us earlier for reasons which deserve some explanation.

Trouble with him occurred before we came to Kosht. We had set up camp, and it was time for the guide and my assistant to begin fixing supper. At that juncture, the guide left for the toilet. The word "toilet" is a euphemism, of course, for during our trek we merely retired to any convenient grassy area to answer nature's call. To speak bluntly, the natives of this area did not usually bother with niceties such as toilet paper, and afterwards were generally satisfied to rinse their hands off perfunctorily in cold water, sometimes rubbing them lightly with a stone. On this occasion, when our guide returned and began slicing vegetables for dinner, the assistant standing next to him grew upset and insisted that he wash his hands with soap. Insulted, the guide protested that he had washed in the river. A brief argument ensued, which the guide terminated by announcing his resignation. With no further ado, he took his only possession, a pistol, down from the tree where it hung and fastened it at his waist. Then, thrusting his salary in his pocket, he strode off for home.

Had he been a sherpa from Nepal, such an incident would probably never have taken place. In the Punjab region, human relationships were extremely difficult to manage. Porters from the area have a strong sense of community; if one of them quits his job, all do. Furthermore, they frown upon the idea of hiring porters from different villages.

From Kosht we took the regular route, which leads to Maroi by way of Reshun. From Maroi on, the path is just wide enough for a jeep to pass; upon our arrival in Maroi, we found a jeep waiting which Shahsadar had thoughtfully sent ahead for us—a welcome sight, indeed.

AFGHANISTAN REGION

In July 1969, I obtained permission to take aerial photographs of the Afghanistani region of the Hindu Kush Range. I wanted good weather for the pictures, and hoped to catch the mountains covered in new snow. With these goals in mind, I went to Kabul again at the end of October, accompanied by two assistants. Unfortunately, the weather was quite bad. We waited for twenty days in vain, and were finally forced to postpone the work until June of the following year. In late June 1970, I returned to Kabul for the third time, arriving on the Bakhtar Afghan Airlines, owned and operated by the Afghanistan government. Obtaining permission to photograph the Band-i-Amir area had been a simple procedure, but approaching the Russo-Pakistani border by plane was to prove much more difficult.

Our pilot refused to make the trip unless the company obtained positive guarantees from both the Russian and Pakistani governments that they would not shoot at us when we drew near the border. The Afghanistan government immediately wired the air force headquarters of both countries, located in Tashkent (USSR) and Rawalpindi (Pakistan), respectively. After twenty-four hours there were still no answers, so the government wired them again. Both Russia and Pakistan were on friendly terms with Afghanistan, and the government was optimistic that they would comply with our request. Accordingly, we decided to fly to Kunduz and wait for final confirmation there. My plan was to photograph the mountains from the plane just after sunrise the next day. At dinner time that evening, our pilot brought in the word that both countries had agreed to the plan, and the news was toasted exuberantly by all.

According to the pilot, flying unauthorized near the border can be quite a harrowing experience. He himself was once chased by a Russian MIG fighter plane. After taking off from an airport on the Iranian border on his way home to Kabul, he veered somewhat to the north upon encountering a desert windspout ahead. No sooner had he done so than the MIG came in hot pursuit, ordering him to land in Russian territory. He managed to escape safely, after explaining about the windspout and protesting that the Russians themselves were violating the Afghanistan sky. He added that the Russian MIG's all had missiles, and that one little touch of their release button would mean the end.

Before sunrise the next morning, we all assembled at the airport. The radio operator there was busily tapping out a reply to a wireless call. Last night's permission, it seemed, had been abruptly revoked. Whether it was Russia or Pakistan was unclear, but one of the countries had announced that it was accepted international custom to shoot at aircraft that invaded a national border. No one, the pilot included, could account for the sudden about-face in attitude.

It seemed as though we flew for perhaps ten minutes before Noshaq and other high peaks on the border first picked up the morning sun's light. Forty kilometers from the border, the pilot said he could go no further, and began circling south. On our way back to Kabul I photographed the mountains in the central area of the Hindu Kush.

Paying for our chartered flight proved no easy matter either. The sum we had settled on beforehand was totally ignored, and I was charged sixty per cent more than originally agreed on. They told me I could not board my plane for New Delhi until I met their demand, and to prove their point began telephoning various government authorities in my presence. Ten or more men actually gathered in a circle around me threateningly, until I conceded to pay the additional amount.

The Himalayas are indeed beautiful. I know of no other place on earth which can match their splendid scenery. Unfortunately, the attitudes of the people living in some areas there often contrast all too unhappily with the dazzling beauty of the surroundings. I deeply regret that memories of unpleasant experiences I had during my travels there remain to spoil my recollections of an otherwise enjoyable stay.

ISTOR-O-NAL

Istor-o-Nal (7,403 meters) is the second highest peak in the Hindu Kush Range. Because of its shape the main peak was named "Hoof of a Horse" (Istor-o-Nal) in 1928 by D. M. Bahn, an Indian officer of the land survey department. Lower Tirich Glacier is at the foot of the mountain. The southeast peak at 7,365 meters is most prominent in this photo. Second to the right of it is its east peak, 7,276 meters.

LOWER TIRICH GLACIER

Lower Tirich Glacier is in the center of this photo and flows to the left. In the near foreground is Upper Tirich Glacier flowing to the right. The latter makes a large curve to the south and finally meets the north wall of Tirich Mir (7,706 meters). The glaciers in this area form a complex maze. The mountain shown here is Peak 33, approximately 6,200 meters high. The high peak on the right is unnamed.

KUNOTAK ZOM

Kunotak Zom (5,878 meters) is the first high mountain one sees upon entering the Tirich Glacier from Shekhniyak. One hardly believes that it is under 6,000 meters high. This mountain is clearly visible even from the beginning of the Istor-o-Nal ascent route at the source of Lower Tirich Glacier. Of the two categories of mountains—those beautiful to look at and those that inspire climbers—Kunotak Zom fits in the latter category.

TIRICH MIR EAST FACE

From the middle of Lower Tirich Glacier I caught the moon lingering above the east face of the mountain right after sunrise. The east peak, 7,691 meters high, obscures the slightly higher main peak. I worked hard selecting the best position for my camera. Closer to the mountains the peaks looked deceptively low. By moving to the left I could include part of the east peak, but Peak 33 would then be hidden behind other mountains. This was the ideal vantage point.

MID HINDU KUSH

One almost doubts that the earth's surface can look like this, but this is the central part of the Afghanistan side of the Hindu Kush mountains. The left foreground is framed by the Koh-i-Yezmi peaks, 5,252 meters above sea level. The peak in the shadows above them to the left is 5,315 meters high, and the white mountain in the upper left is 5,457 meters. In the upper part of the photo the mountains of Koh-i-Sarband-Sagau and a 5,556-meter unnamed peak are visible. At the upper right is Koh-i-Kosokar-Gantiwa and its sub-mountains. Below the shadows in the right foreground lies the Pawloghar River.

GHUL LASHT ZOM

From the right bank of Tirich Glacier I caught an interesting view of Ghul Lasht Zom. The white mountain is Ghul Lasht Zom (6,611 meters) and the black one is Peak III (6,361 meters). The white summit on the left is Dertna Peak, 6,100 meters high.

BUNI ZOM AND ITS SUB-MOUNTAINS

The village in the foreground is Reshun. The mountains are, from left to right, Shah Dok, 5,538 meters, the north peak of Buni Zom, 6,338 meters; the main peak, 6,551 meters; and the south peak, 6,220 meters (right back ground). Looming high in the center of the photograph is Khorabohrt Zom, 5,850 meters. The white, larger mountain on the right is Chakhori Zom II, 5,957 meters. To its right and further back is the main peak at 6,000 meters. All are dry, brown mountains, typical of the Hindu Kush range.

BAND-I-AMIR

My climbing friends and I do not think of a mountain not covered with snow as a "real" mountain, and I balk at calling the desert area northwest of Kabul part of the Hindu Kush. But books by cultural geographers call Bamiyan and Band-i-Amir a basin in the Hindu Kush. I followed those precedents, therefore, and included the area in this album. This photo is simply a lake in the desert, but I found the color of the deep water very beautiful.

MOUNTAINS ALONG LOWER TIRICH GLACIER

Because the mountains around it are so large, this glacier looks much smaller than it actually is. What appear to be small hollows on the glacier are really ten meters or more in diameter. Also, the brown rock-and-sand covered area is an ice table a hundred feet thick. The mountains seem to have grown from a frozen ocean. The mountains are Kunotak Zom, left (5,878 meters); a 6,214-meter unnamed peak, center; and Peak 33, about 6,200 meters high, right.

MARCH ALONG LOWER TIRICH GLACIER

Here icefalls can be seen in the middle of the glacier. The top of the glacier extends beyond the icefall to the north wall of Tirich Mir. The Upper Tirich Glacier swings in a great curve to the right foreground and flows to Tirich Mir's north wall. The glacier is stopped by the north wall's ridge, however, and does not actually meet the wall. The icefalls in the area are extremely dangerous, and no one has yet climbed through them to the sources of the glaciers. My assistants are out on a reconnaissance climb.

VILLAGE IN DESERT

This was taken while flying back to Kabul after completing the expedition into the frozen mountains of the Hindu Kush. The village was located between Anjuman Pass and Kabul to the west of the Hindu Kush. There is no vegetation in this area, only desert and barren rocky mountains. Small clumps of green are occasionally seen around small springs or where the water from melted snow flows. Some people live in those areas, barely staying alive. This photo expresses some of the difficult struggle for survival these people experience.

BARREN MOUNTAINS

This area, where steppe and desert meet, is eighty kilometers north of Kabul. It does not rain here in summer, and melted snow is the only source of water. I had observed the struggle for survival in the cold of 4,000-meter-high Namche Bazar in Nepal. Living in this desert is no less difficult. Small mud cottages are visible here.

WOMAN FROM KABUL

Muslim women rarely show their faces, and having their pictures taken is out of the question. In 1959, it became legal for women to wear western clothing, yet they still cling to many old customs. Recently, a photographer was clubbed to death by local residents for trying to photograph a Muslim woman. Even if this woman had agreed to pose, the other residents would have protested. For taking this picture we were rewarded with rocks and spittle.

UNNAMED PEAK FROM LOWER TIRICH GLACIER

View of an unnamed peak from the basin of Lower Tirich Glacier icefall. The path of the icefall is steeper than it appears in the photograph, and the massive blocks seemed ready to topple down on me. One block is perhaps twenty meters in diameter. It was frightening to imagine what would happen if they started sliding down. Snowslides constantly roared down the right half of the icefall.

BAND-I-AMIR AND DESERT

From overhead all the lakes here appear to be at the same altitude. Actually, they are on a terraced slope. There are also a few waterfalls. From here I could see the snow-covered mountains of the Hindu Kush in the east (not in this photo). Pilots flying international flights at 8,000 meters are guided by these lakes.

MOUNTAIN RANGE IN MID HINDU KUSH

In few places can one find so many mountains in one small area. In Nepal, I had seen countless mountains over 6,000 meters high. Those mountains can probably be sorted into small ranges. But here in the Hindu Kush there are no particularly prominent peaks and all of the mountains are tightly grouped. The one slightly visible in the upper right corner is Koh-i-Mondi, 6,248 meters above sea level.

THE GREAT HIMALAYAS
by Kyuya Fukada

The Great Himalayas *Kyuya Fukada*

I

In the beginning, there were no Himalayas. Formerly there lay between present-day Tibet and India only a vast stretch of shallow sea. The reasons are still not known why the land masses on either side moved toward each other and forced the underwater land area upward, but the rising land gradually formed into the great range of mountains seen today. Fossils of marine life, while deformed and difficult to recognize, are found at heights above 8,000 meters in this area. They bear out the theory that the Himalayas were once submerged.

I have a small piece of limestone displayed on a shelf in my study. The stone, so soft that one can scratch it with his fingernail, is from Mt. Everest's summit. It was given to me by Mr. Naomi Uemura, who climbed to the top of the mountain on May 11, 1970. The layers of limestone that cover all of Mt. Everest above 8,000 meters were once under water but now lie on a foundation of hard, uplifted rock.

Actually, the Himalayas are still rising because of continuing pressure from the hard earth crust north and south of them. Scientists report that since the end of the last glacial epoch, that is, over the past 20,000 years, the Himalayas have grown 1,500 to 2,000 meters higher. The annual growth rate is 7.5 to 10 centimeters. That means one meter every ten years, and ten meters every 100 years. Mountaineers and other mountain enthusiasts take pleasure in knowing that the Himalayas are growing taller even though the present age is one in which most of the earth is gradually being eroded by weathering and corrosion

Until fairly recently, Mt. Everest's official height was accepted to be 8,840 meters above sea level. The measurement dated from the mid-nineteenth century. Recent surveys have updated the mountain's height to 8,848 meters, an increase of eight meters in approximately 100 years. Other peaks in the 8,000-meter class, such as Dhaulagiri and Annapurna, all of which were measured from the Ganges Plain at about the same time in the nineteenth century, have grown as well. Perhaps getting excited over the increased height of a mountain may seem strange to some people. For the lover of high mountains, however, an increase of even one meter is a thrilling thought.

There is further evidence that the Himalayas rose from lowlands. Several rivers having their sources in Tibet, for instance, flow between the soaring walls of the Himalayas into the great plains of India. This is a characteristic peculiar to Himalayan geography. I know that in the Japan Alps there are no rivers flowing through the main range that runs from Mt. Shirouma in the north to Mt. Norikura in the south. But deep valleys cut through the Himalayas in many places, rivers that have been flowing from Tibet since long before the Himalayas were formed. As the Himalayas gradually rose, these rivers cut their way across the range from north to south.

All the famous rivers of Nepal, i.e., the Arun in the east, the Trisuli and the Kali in the central and the Karnali in the west cut across the main range of the Himalayas, and have formed deep valleys. The banks of these rivers are extremely steep, and it is not unusual to see some of them rising 4,000–5,000 meters straight up from the bottoms of the channels. The Kali River, flowing between Annapurna and Dhaulagiri, is about 1,500 meters above sea level. Only 6½ kilometers away the majestic Dhaulagiri towers 8,172 meters.

To help readers visualize the steep rise of the mountains allow me to give a few more statistics. About four kilometers from the bed of the Hunza River, which is approximately 1,800 meters high, is Mt. Rakaposhi at 7,788 meters. Twenty-two kilometers from the Indus River, 1,200 meters high, is Nanga Parbat with an elevation of 8,125 meters. Only thirteen kilometers from the bed of the Trisuli River, at about 1,800 meters, stands Langtang Lirung at 7,245 meters.

The valleys here have long served as trade routes between Tibet and India. Accounts written by Himalayan travellers frequently tell of Tibetan traders leading donkeys and sheep laden with salt down these deep valley routes and of Nepalese merchants going northward along the same paths with loads of rice to trade on the other side of the mountains. Culture and religion have been exchanged and numerous people have migrated to other lands over these routes through the Himalayas.

Between the two areas separated by the range there are great climatic differences, of course, and therefore differences in vegetation. The south side of the Himalayas is quite humid, making its flora luxuriant, while most areas on the north side are dry and the land is barren.

Most books about climbing the Himalayas begin with accounts of the sweltering heat in India. Next the damp zone with its abundant exotic plants is discussed. That zone is usually marched through, but in this book we fly over it by plane. After the damp zone come grassy highlands and some of the world's freshest air. Here the real climbing begins. After walking for some time through the foot of the mountains, the piedmont, we reach an altitude of 4,000–5,000 meters. No life exists here, and a world of snow and ice surrounds us. We have thus passed through two different types of climate, the tropical and the subtropical, and have finally entered an arctic-like region.

II

"Himalaya" comes from an old Sanskrit word meaning "house of snow." Actually, it combines two words, *him* and *alaya,* the first meaning "snow" and the second meaning "dwelling place." In Buddhist scriptures compiled in Chinese the word appears as either *hsü*eh-ts'ang, "storehouse of snow," or *hsü*eh-chu, "repository of snow," rather faithful renderings of the Sanskrit original. One readily imagines the ancients standing on the plains of India, looking toward the snow-covered peaks shining magnificently in the north and choosing a name to describe them.

The Himalayas are the world's mightiest mountains. No other chain has mountains higher than 7,000 meters above sea level, whereas the Himalayan range boasts of fourteen peaks over 8,000 meters and hundreds over 7,000 meters. Eight of the fourteen tallest are in Nepal and one (Gosainthan, or Shisha Pangma) is in Tibet, not far from that country's border with Nepal.

1.	Everest	8,848 meters
2.	Kangchenjunga	8,585 meters
3.	Lhotse	8,501 meters
4.	Makalu	8,470 meters
5.	Dhaulagiri	8,167 meters
6.	Cho Oyu	8,153 meters
7.	Manaslu	8,125 meters
8.	Annapurna	8,091 meters
9.	Gosainthan	8,013 meters

These peaks constitute what we generally call the Himalaya Range, forming a great, 2,700-kilometer-long arc between the Indus River in the west and the Brahmaputra River in the east. At the western end of the arc is another great range called the Karakorum. There have been disputes as to the validity of considering these mountains part of the Himalayas, and one scholar regards the two as entirely different chains, distinct because they are separated by the upper reaches of the Indus River (more precisely, the Shyok River, a tributary of the Indus). But another scholar asserts that there is no important reason to regard them as independent since neither geographic nor structural differences between them can be discerned.

Whether they are the same or not from an academic standpoint, it is, in my opinion, only common sense to include the Karakorum when we talk of the Himalayas. In fact, it was very common in the nineteenth century to talk about the Karakorum Himalayas. With Karakorum excluded, the stature of the other Himalayas would diminish considerably for the simple reason that the Karakorum includes four of the highest peaks in the world, each over 8,000 meters. The second highest mountain in the world, K2, stands in the Karakorum Range. The four major peaks there are: K2, 8,611 meters; Hidden Peak, 8,068 meters; Broad Peak, 8,047 meters; and Gasherbrum II, 8,035 meters.

To the west of the Karakorum lies another great range of mountains called the Hindu Kush, which has only recently attracted the attention of mountaineers. Several peaks in the range soar above 7,000 meters. It is possible to consider this range a part of the Himalayas in the broad sense. The Hindu Kush stands between the Oxus and Indus Rivers, and once served as the political boundary between Central Asia and the Indian subcontinent. Today it lies along the border between Afghanistan and West Pakistan.

I am inclined to go even further in extending the scope of the Himalayas to include all the high mountains in Central Asia. Given the idea of a "storehouse of snow" and considering the similarities in religions, customs and ways of life shared by the Asiatic peoples in this vast region, calling all the mountains the Himalayas would by no means be farfetched. One of the standard reference books on the Himalayas, *Sketch of the Geography and Geology of the Himalayan Mountains and Tibet*, by Burrard, includes the entire mountainous areas of Sinkiang in China, the Hindu Kush in Afghanistan and the Pamir Plateau in Tadzhikistan, U.S.S.R.

In the whole region there are fourteen peaks over 8,000 meters and hundreds more over 7,000 meters, including some 200 which are notable. And although they are considered rare on other continents the mountains over 5,000 meters in Central Asia are so numerous that no one has ever bothered to count them. Moreover, many of the greatest rivers in the world, i.e., the Yellow (Huang Ho), the Yangtze, the Mekong, the Irrawaddy, the Brahmaputra, the Ganges, the Indus and the Oxus (Amu-Dar'ya) have their headwaters in the Himalayas.

In this discussion I consider the Himalaya Range as extending through eight countries: the U.S.S.R., the People's Republic of China, India, Bhutan, Sikkim, Nepal, Pakistan and Afghanistan. This area is called the "roof of the world." Since there are still many spots here unspoiled by human curiosity, the Himalayas can be considered the greatest storehouse of secrets in the world. Range upon range of magnificent mountains, snow-clad, ancient, with peaks abundant in mystery and sublime beauty, the great Himalayas will never cease to fascinate the peoples of the world.

III

I have a large map hanging on my study wall. On a scale of one to fifteen thousand, the map is entitled *The Himalaya Mountains and Surrounding Regions* and is published by the Land Survey Council of India. It covers the area between 68 and 102 degrees east longitude and between 26 and 44 degrees north latitude, the region that contains every mountain in the world over 7,000 meters high. Only here did the earth's crust make such a stupendous skyward thrust.

At the western end of the map I have is the Hindu Kush range, which can be divided into western, central and eastern sections. As the range extends toward the east, the mountains increase in height. In the Pakistan/Afghanistan border region, the eastern section, we count more than ten peaks over 7,000 meters high. The four greatest of these are Tirich Mir, Noshaq, Istor-o-Nal and Saraghrar. It is interesting that no mountains in the Hindu Kush were climbed prior to 1945. In fact, most of the peaks fell in the 1960's. A staggering number of expeditional parties have come to these mountains in the last several years. In 1969, 25 parties, of which nine were Japanese, attacked peaks in the Hindu Kush. The interest in climbing mountains here was due partly to the fact that the authorities of other countries in the Himalayan area had begun refusing entry to foreign climbers, particularly to the Nepal Himalayas and the Karakorum. What is more, climbing these mountains requires comparatively light equipment, and the weather in the region is generally less exacting than weather in other parts of the Himalayas.

Ten years ago we could count on the fingers of one hand the peaks conquered in the Hindu Kush. Since about 1961, however, almost all the virgin summits of the range were climbed one by one. But some are still untouched. Even those ignored previously as unimpressive mounds of rocks on the upper ridges of higher mountains have gradually begun to attract attention and to become "important" targets for conquest. Until quite recently, it was everybody's understanding that the highest peak in the Hindu Kush was Tirich Mir, a mountain already climbed. But the top of the mountain has since been elaborately subdivided into a main peak, an east peak, west peak I and west peak IV. Therefore, each successful climb of these sub-peaks has its own value and is carefully recorded.

When defined in this fashion, we have nearly 200 peaks over 6,000 meters in the Hindu Kush. Of those, 145 have been climbed, with authenticated photographs and records backing the climbs. Indeed, no peaks in all of Central Asia are more frequented today by climbers than those in the Hindu Kush. Yet it is difficult to say that the Hindu Kush mountains have been thoroughly charted. Take for example the following incident.

Istor-o-Nal (7,403 meters), one of the four highest peaks in the Hindu Kush, was believed to have been the first peak in the range that was conquered. It supposedly fell to an American party in 1955. No one doubted that party's success. Thirteen years later, a party of four Japanese women reported reaching the same summit. After returning to Japan the group published an account of their explorations, *7,403 Meters in the Himalayas*.

A great number of people all over the world are obsessed with high mountains and read all new books on the subject. Their knowledge of mountains they have never been to themselves is considerable and they can recognize at a glance every curve and corner of ridges on famous peaks. When one such mountain buff in Japan saw the frontispiece photo of the book on Istor-o-Nal, his suspicions were aroused. Was the peak the female party climbed really the highest part of Istor-o-Nal? He immediately set out to investigate. He gathered as many photographs and written accounts of Istor-o-Nal as he could, and then consulted with experts and buffs throughout the world. He was finally convinced that the peak the party reached was not the real summit but one of the peaks west of the top. And he further established that the earlier American party had made a similar mistake and that the peak they had stood on was a lesser peak on the western ridge. Thus it was proven that the true summit of Istor-o-Nal was still unclimbed. A Spanish party climbed it, however, in 1969, the same year as the disclosure.

The western section of the Hindu Kush and another range which runs parallel to the western section are together called the Hindu Raj sub-range. That sub-range has lately begun to attract alpinists. Between the two sections runs the Yarkhun River. It successively becomes the Mastuj River, the Chitral, the Kunar and, after meeting the Kabul, pours into the Indus River. The Hindu Kush and the Karakorum meet at the source of the Yarkhun River.

IV

I will now turn to the Pamir region. It was to this area, a vast stretch of high ground called the Pamir Plateau, that geographers first gave the name "the roof of the world." After running northward along the West Pakistan/Afghanistan border, the Hindu Kush turns to the east and continues on a bit further together with the Oxus River. The famous Wakhan Valley is located there. Hsüan-tsang, the distinguished Chinese Buddhist monk who travelled to India, and Marco Polo, the Italian adventurer, are believed to have journeyed to this area, gone up the Oxus River and entered the mountains in Pamir.

In about the middle of the Wakhan Valley we find another large river flowing from the north, the Pamir River, which had long been mistaken for the Oxus. Until the beginning of the twentieth century there were no exact political boundaries in this region. Since there was danger of a military clash between Russia and Great Britain—ruler at the time of India and present-day Pakistan—the concerned parties chose the Wakhan Valley as a buffer zone. The valley was in Afghanistan territory and the Pamir River, then thought to be the Oxus, served as the boundary.

On their journeys upstream, Hsüan-tsang and Marco Polo discovered a large and beautiful lake near the source of the Pamir River. Hsüan-tsang called it the "Lake of the Great Dragon," and described it as the most splendid spot in the world. The Italian traveller apparently was not in a christening mood but observed that the highlands around the lake abounded in excellent grasses for livestock. He remarked that a thin cow that grazed in the area for ten days would become a fat cow. Actually, we see many wild, crooked-horned sheep in the area today. They are known to explorers as the Ovis Poli, Polo's sheep.

After Hsüan-tsang and Marco Polo, no man saw the lake until 1838 when Captain John Wood, an English explorer, rediscovered it and named it Lake Victoria. Later, the great explorer Sir Mark Aurel Stein also stood by the lake and, as reported, was deeply impressed by its placidity and great beauty.

The vast mountainous region between the Pamir and Oxus Rivers is the Wakhan Range, which boasts of several peaks over 6,000 meters and a number of lesser peaks. As far as I know, no one has ever climbed these mountains. Up along the Oxus is Wakhjir Pass, where the Pamir and the Karakorum ranges meet. It usually was across this pass that people entered the Pamir region. Or they could go northward from Gilgit through either the Mintaka Pass or the Kilik Pass to the Pamir Road.

Hsüan-tsang calls Pamir "Pomiro." Marco Polo calls it "Pamiel." At any rate, Pamir is a very old place name, and there are numerous theories concerning its etymology, none of which fully satisfies anybody. In Japan it is usually called the Pamir Highlands, but it is a mistake to regard it as a highlands, for this vast mountainous region is too complex to describe by any such name. The region, in fact, can be divided into eight zones. The geographical distinctions are too detailed for discussion here.

Apart from the two celebrated travellers of many centuries ago, Silk Road traders and caravans went into Pamir through the Tash Kurghan Pass and reached Kashgar in Sinkiang-Uighul in China. Kashgar, located at the western edge of the Taklamakan Desert, has been an important town for traders ever since ancient times. The town overlooks two lofty peaks, Kungur and Mustagh Ata, both above 7,500 meters.

Kungur has two prominent peaks. Kungur II is the higher. The summit of Kungur I was reached in 1956 by a joint party of climbers from the U.S.S.R. and the People's Republic of China. Five years later, a Chinese party of women reached the same summit again. The two leaders, native Tibetans, set the altitude record for female alpinists. Kungur II is still unclimbed. There are undoubtedly many mountaineers outside China anxious to climb this peak, but as long as the Chinese government continues to exclude foreigners they can only wait and hope.

The range between Kungur and Mustagh Ata is sometimes called the Kashgar Range. In the hinterlands of China are numerous unclimbed mountains which are extremely enticing to climbers. Perhaps for this reason there are many Japanese alpinists anxious for their government to resume diplomatic ties with the Chinese.

Most of the Pamir region belongs to Russia. Between this long mountain range and the great Trans Alai mountains runs the Kyzylsu River. The original Silk Road begins here at Kashgar, runs westward through the Torugart Pass on the borders of present-day China and Russia, down to the Kyzylsu, and finally reaches the Oxus River.

The highest mountains in the U.S.S.R. are in Pamir and in the Tien Shan district. The Russians have a reputation for being sports lovers, and Russian climbers have scaled the highest peaks in their country many times. They have climbed Pik Communism, the highest mountain in Russia, over variations of the most dangerous routes, and hundreds of climbers have reached the top of Pik Lenin, the third highest mountain in the country. I am sure no other mountain in the world over 7,000 meters has received as many visitors. The U.S.S.R. is indeed a people's country.

V

Many people confuse Pamir and Tien Shan. This is often true even of those who greatly admire and closely study the mountains of Central Asia. The Tien Shan is a great, long range extending to the north of the Pamir, the two being roughly divided by a west to east line connecting the Fergana Basin and Kashgar.

The Tien Shan, moreover, makes complicated turns. Its main range, after moving away from the Pamir in the south, changes its course to run west to east along the border between the Republic of Kirghiz in the U.S.S.R. and the northern edge of the Sinkiang-Uighul region of China. The mountains take a sharp turn northward from there and then shift almost due east. Away from the border, the range gradually flattens until it disappears into the sands of the Gobi Desert.

Tien Shan is an old name given by the Chinese during the Han Dynasty. The Tien Shan of ancient times, however, included only the easternmost part of the present-day range, and it was not a high range. The Tien Shan North Route and Tien Shan South Route, famous as old silk routes, run through the north and south piedmonts of the Tien Shan Range. The most prominent peak among the eastern mountains of the range is Bogdo Ula, which is 5,470 meters high—although the figure is disputed. But since Urumchi, a nearby town, is only 900 meters above sea level, one can easily imagine how magnificent Bogdo Ula must look from the town. It is small wonder that the mountain is treated in old Chinese writings as one of China's most celebrated peaks.

In 1908, German explorer Meltzbach climbed Bogdo Ula and later published a detailed account of his expedition. Near the summit, he says, there is nothing but steep glaciation, and viewed from there the peak seems to defy human approach. In 1949, Shipton and Tilman, noted Himalayan experts, attempted the summit but failed.

The highest peaks in the Tien Shan Range are all in the central region. Pyotor Petrovich Semyonov, a Russian explorer, first entered this area in 1856, via Alma Ata, capital of the Republic of Kazakh, U.S.S.R. He was also the first to approach Khan Tengri, the most celebrated mountain in the Tien Shan. Semyonov so loved the Tien Shan Range that he took on another name for himself, Tienshansky.

Khan of Khan Tengri means "king," and *tengri* means "spirits." Taken together, therefore, the name means something like "King of the Spirits." The name is very suitable indeed, for from olden times the mountain has been an object of worship by people living on the south side of the range. For a long time, people never thought of climbing the mountain. The peak looked too lofty to approach, and it was not until 1931 that the mountain fell to a Russian party. The Russians, after overcoming tremendous difficulties, reached the summit from the Kazakh side.

Khan Tengri had long been believed to be the highest mountain in the Tien Shan Range. In 1937, however, a higher peak was discovered and named Pik Pobejda (Peak of Victory). This is the second highest mountain in the Soviet Union after Pik Communism.

Since the Tien Shan is one of the world's most expansive mountain ranges, it has been given different names according to the particular section. The western and central sections, running northward along the border between Russia and China, are called the Meridian Range. There are, in turn, several sub-ranges which extend like parallel tree branches well into the U.S.S.R. in the west. As these sub-ranges move west, their altitudes rapidly diminish until the mountains lose themselves entirely in the desert of Kyzyl-Kum.

Between these parallel lines of mountains is the famous Lake Issyk-Kul. Hsüan-tsang reportedly passed this lake after he crossed the Tien Shan from Sinkiang-Uighul. He called it the Great Clear Lake. The Tien Shan Valley roads have been trodden by many, serving as silk routes connecting the East and the West. The army led by Timur (Tamerlane), who once made Samarkand his capital, also used these routes.

Legend has it that there was once an island in Issyk-Kul on which was built a palace where Timur occasionally came to rest. The palace, legend tells us, is now submerged. The story could very well be more than mere legend, for an investigation of the bottom of the lake begun in 1958 by Russian archeologists unearthed remnants of what might have been brick walls and what might pass for water pipes. Moreover, the archeologists retrieved such remains of civilization as cooking pots, stone mortars, broken pieces of glass, coins, copperware and other artefacts, proving that there was once a thriving city on the shore of the lake.

The Tien Shan mountains are now closed to foreign mountaineers. Immediately after you take off from the airport of Tashkent, the most important city in west Turkistan, you will see the white crests of mountains soaring in the east. That is the Tien Shan Range. I have flown over them twice, and both times they left me almost breathless. The magnificent view of these mountains is quite moving.

VI

The Tien Shan cuts the northern edge of the Taklamakan Desert while the Kunlun Shan borders it in the south. The name Kunlun has nostalgic overtones for Orientals as a holy mountain that was higher than anyone could possibly imagine.

Like the name Tien Shan, the name Kunlun is also ancient. It appears in China's oldest books, although in those days it referred generally to the great mountains in China's west. Ferdinand von Richthofen, a nineteenth-century geographer, threw the first light on the topography of the Kunlun. He was the best geographer on the subject of Asia, was the teacher of Sven Hedin and was the inventor of the term ''Silk Road.'' Richthofen divided the Kunlun Range into three regions, the western, central and eastern, and considered it over-all as the greatest and oldest mountain range in the world. Oddly enough, not a single peak in it has ever been climbed, making the lure of the mountains all the stronger.

According to Richthofen's classification, the west Kunlun extends between 76 and 89 degrees east longitude, covering the areas from the eastern edge of Pamir to the south-central border of the Taklamakan Desert. The water that pours from these mountains winds its way down to wet the northern foothills and form lovely oases here and there. The Taklamakan South Road connects these oases. Undoubtedly, both Hsüan-tsang and Marco Polo walked it. The most prosperous of these oasis cities is Khotan, a city with a long history. The Yurung Kash (White Jade) and the Kara Kash (Black Jade) rivers, fed by melted snow and ice from the Kunlun Range, meet to form the Khotan River. That river winds its way northward over desert sands until they completely dry it up. The beautiful Khotan jade that has been cherished from ancient times was originally quarried in the valleys of the Yurung Kash and the Kara Kash.

The best-known mountains among the Kunlun are those from which these two rivers start to flow. This district has several peaks above 7,000 meters that have never been climbed. Although W. H. Johnson claimed to have attained the summit of an unknown peak of 7,000 meters here in 1866-1867, records of the achievement have proved to be false. His attempt, however, may have been the only attempt to climb any peak in the entire Kunlun Shan. There have been several explorers who have crossed the range and travelled through the valleys of the mountains, but nobody has ever reached a summit. It is difficult to visualize the vastness of the broad and multi-branched Kunlun. In the Arka Tagh, a minor sub-range, maps show a 7,724-meter-high peak called Ulug Mustag. This is very likely a kind of phantom peak, for no photograph of the mountain exists. In one of Sven Hedin's accounts of his explorations in Central Asia is a sketch of a mountain which is supposed to be Ulug Mustag. The mountain's existence, however, is still unproven.

The central part of the Kunlun lies between 89 degrees and 104 degrees east latitude. The width of the range increases considerably and to the north of the main range many sub-ranges branch out in parallel lines. It strides over Tibet, Tsinghai, Shensi, Kansu, and Sinkiang and has several peaks over 7,000 meters. From this vast expanse of mountains the great rivers of Asia start to flow: the Hwang Ho, the Yangtze, the Mekong and the Salween.

Actually, the Kunlun Range has been denuded by erosion and its body largely destroyed It has no jagged peaks today, only round, smooth ridges. Judging from its present form, we might suppose that it was once much higher and steeper than the Himalayas. Old age has taken its toll. At any rate, the stately Kunlun Range stands like a huge monument, the oldest of the great ranges.

According to Richthofen, the central Kunlun contains the Bayan Kara and Hsi-ch'ing ranges. There are two prominent peaks in these ranges: Minyag Gongkar (7,587 meters), which was conquered by an American party in 1932; and Amne Machin, which had long been a mysterious mountain and was once believed to be higher than Mt. Everest. The mystery was solved in 1960, when a party of Chinese scientists reached the top and established that it measured 7,160 meters.

The eastern Kunlun stands between 104 and 113 degrees longitude, at the eastern end of the entire complex. This is the tail end of the Kunlun, which is made up of a few branch ranges. A succession of low mountains runs to the east from there, ending at 118 degrees. It is also possible to include them in the Kunlun Range.

VII

The term ''The Roof of the World'' was originally applied to the Pamir Plateau, once believed to be the highest land area in the world. In fact, many of the great mountain ranges in Asia originate here: the Hindu Kush to the west, the Tien Shan to the northeast, the Kunlun to the east, and the Karakorum to the south.

The Karakorum is exceeded only by the Nepal Himalayas in number of great peaks and height of its highest peaks. The Karakorum, which all mountaineers dream of visiting, has nineteen peaks over 7,600 meters, of which four are over 8,000 meters. In addition, there are five great glaciers in the Karakorum. They are, from west to east, the Batura Glacier (58 kilometers), the Hispar Glacier (61 kilometers), the Biafo Glacier (59 kilometers), the Baltoro Glacier (58 kilometers) and the Siachen Glacier (72 kilometers). These giant glaciers move like great silver snakes down the slopes of the Karakorum mountains. They are flanked by sharp icy ridges.

The highest of the peaks in the range is K2, the second highest mountain in the world. It was only natural that K2 was the first peak to draw the attention of mountain climbers in this area. Montogomerie measured this mountain for the first time from a high point near Kashmir in 1857. He was convinced of its extraordinary height and called it K2 (Karakorum 2), which was the mountain's survey number. In 1858, when he calculated the results of his measurements, he proved that it was the second highest mountain in the world.

In 1861, Godwin Austen became the first man to step onto these virgin glaciers. He closely approached K2's peak. Although some people later wanted to name it Godwin Austen Peak, many felt that it was wrong to name it after an individual, and Montogomerie's survey number, K2, became the mountain's official name. On reflection, could anyone have made a better choice for this mountain's name?

It took fifty years of explorations and attempts before K2's summit was reached in 1954. Six different parties repeatedly assaulted the mountain, and a number of lives were lost. The route chosen was always the steep Abruzzi Ridge on the south, named after Duke Abruzzi, cousin to Emmanuel III of Italy and the first climber to attempt this icy ridge. Several American parties before and after World War II attempted to conquer K2 but each time were forced to retreat just below the summit. Victory finally came to an Italian party, heirs to the tradition of Luigi Amedeo, Duke Abruzzi.

All four peaks over 8,000 meters in the Karakorum stand on the north side of the Baltoro Glacier, making this particular glacier the most frequently trodden. After several days of climbing the glacier one reaches a great open space called Concordia, where many glaciers flow together to form the Baltoro. At the far end of Concordia soars a wide-shouldered mountain called Broad Peak (8,047 m.). The glacier divides here, and at the end of the left fork one can see the impossibly high summit pyramid of K2. If you follow the right fork, you will come to the other two magnificent peaks in the Karakorum over 8,000 meters, Gasherbrum II and Hidden Peak.

On the south shore of the Baltoro Glacier stands another group of great peaks: Chogolisa and Baltoro Kangri, which fell to Japanese parties, and Masherbrum and Sia Kangri. All these peaks over 7,000 meters are the subjects of many climbing stories.

Other Karakorum glaciers have many high, ice-covered peaks which rise up around them. The north edge of Hispar Glacier is flanked by Khiangyag Kish and the south edge by Diran Peak. To the right of Siachen Glacier is Saltoro Kangri and at the south edge of Batura Glacier is Batura Peak, on which a Japanese party once met defeat.

As in other mountain regions in Central Asia, the distinguished peaks in the Karakorum range were first climbed in post-1945 years. Mountaineers from all over the world, anxious to explore unknown regions, headed toward the Karakorum. If the Pakistani government had not recently prohibited climbers from entering the Karakorum, perhaps all the peaks would have been scaled by now.

The Karakorum differs from Nepal in many respects. First, there is little greenery in Karakorum, which is almost unaffected by the monsoon rains and stays quite dry. Since climbers have a long journey along the glaciers, and since sherpas are not available, one must hire either Baltic or Hunzan porters. The inhabitants of this region closely resemble Caucasians physically, whereas the Nepalese look Oriental. The natives, moreover, are Muslims, not Lamaists like the Nepalese.

The term Karakorum is of Turkish origin, meaning "black pebbles." The name is hardly fitting to describe brilliantly shining peaks clad in white. However, there are black rocks at Karakorum Pass east of the main range, once an important pass for traders entering Central Asia. What was originally the name for the pass became the name for the range.

VIII

At the southeastern extreme of the Karakorum is another great range extending over 2,200 kilometers. These are the true Himalayas. For convenience, we can subdivide them as follows:

(From west to east)
1. Punjab Himalayas
2. Garhwal Himalayas
3. Nepal Himalayas
4. Sikkim Himalayas
5. Bhutan and Assam Himalayas

The highest peak in the Punjab Himalayas is Nanga Parbat. No other mountain in the Himalayas has a climbing history more dramatic than this one. It has already claimed over thirty lives. Once it was called the "Devil's Mountain," and even the bravest sherpa used to shrink from any attempt to climb it. Over 8,000 meters high, it rises from the highlands near the Indus and has always attracted mountaineers.

As early as 1895 a party of climbers visited Nanga Parbat. It was led by Alfred F. Mummery, a courageous man who had established his climbing reputation in the Alps. The Alps, however, bore no comparison to the Himalayas. Mummery discovered this a little too late, for he could not find any route up the mountain, guarded as it was by gigantic walls of hard ice. Mummery finally decided to attempt the Diamir Wall on the western slope. Neither he nor the two Gurkhas who accompanied him ever came down. From the outset, Nanga Parbat's demonic nature was apparent.

The real heyday of Himalaya climbing began after World War I, and Nanga Parbat was one of the targets of mountaineers in that period. In 1932, a German party led by Willy Merkl focused on the Rakhiot Glacier on the northern slope. Fighting their way through deep snow carried by the wet monsoon, they somehow managed to reach the ridge above the glacier. But from there they could not go an inch higher.

In the following year, Merkl led an even more powerful and well-equipped party to the same glacier. Advancing on the icy ridge, Merkl and his men passed Silberzacken, and then reached a snow-covered plateau. The summit was right above them. Success, the leader thought, was in his grasp. But the Devil's Mountain was not to give in easily. It defended itself with deep snow and a violent storm. Merkl and his men had to retreat, and on the way down the slope nine of the party, including the leader, lost their lives.

The next German expedition, in 1937, suffered an even greater loss. But the tragedy happened in an instant. The party's leader, seven other climbers and nine sherpas—the party's whole force at Camp IV—were buried under a terrific avalanche which struck at midnight. No one got out alive.

But the day had to come when this seemingly impregnable mountain would succumb to human persistence. In 1953, a joint party of Germans and Austrians moved to avenge the previous deaths. The leader, Karl Herrigkoffer, was Merkl's brother-in-law. The man who reached the summit was Hermann Buhl. He started alone at 2:30 a.m. on July 3rd from Camp V, which was on the ridge above the Rakhiot Glacier. He passed Silberzacken, passed the snow plateau and approached the summit. At seven p.m. he reached the top. But it was dark when Buhl started down, and he carried neither tent nor sleeping bag. Miraculously, Buhl spent the night leaning against a steep, icy cliff. It was late afternoon the next day when he returned, completely exhausted, to his companions at Camp V. He had eaten almost nothing since his departure the day before. Buhl had demonstrated superhuman willpower.

Nanga Parbat had been conquered. But the attraction of this mountain remained powerful, ever inviting climbers to its ice-covered rock walls. The next party, also German, attempted the Diamir Wall, the one Mummery once tried without success. Its members made two trial climbs before three men reached the summit in 1962 after unbelievable difficulties. But only two of the three made it safely back to camp. The third slipped coming down and fell to his death.

The next try was made on the Rupar Wall on the south slope. Three reconnaissance expeditions were necessary before this difficult route was climbed in 1970. But as if to pay for this third success, one of the climbers fell to his death on the way down. Nanga Parbat is the only peak over 8,000 meters in all the Himalayas that has been climbed by three different routes.

Nun Kun Peak is another famous mountain in the Punjab Himalayas. Though it is only slightly over 7,000 meters high, it early attracted the attention of mountaineers from all over the world. Since 1898 it has been visited by climbers from Britain, the Netherlands, and the U.S.A. Nun's summit was finally reached in 1958 by a Swiss missionary and a French woman climber. A very cosmopolitan peak indeed.

IX

The Garhwal Himalayas are separated from the Punjab Himalayas by the Sutlej River, a tributary of the Indus. Into these mountains flow many tributaries of the upper Ganges, parting from the Ganges like the prongs of a rake. Since this area was once a British colony, the Garhwal was the first part of the Himalayas to be explored and surveyed. Though there is no peak over 8,000 meters in this area, there are many which are tempting to mountaineers who want to climb with comparatively light equipment. The first Japanese Himalayan expedition was made in 1938 to Nanda Kot in this area. That party was from Rikkyo University in Tokyo.

The Garhwal's main attraction is not solemn dignity but rather a charm that permits climbers to work their way slowly to the top of the ice-covered peaks and then experience the exhilaration of descending into beautiful flower-decked valleys. No strain—nothing but pleasure. It is the consensus of all those who have climbed in the Garhwal Himalayas that only there can one enjoy the beauty of nature as well as a rigorous but not impossible climb up a high mountain.

That is not to suggest that climbing in the Garhwal is a picnic. Numerous peaks are over 7,000 meters high. Kamet Peak, the second highest in the Garhwal, was tried ten times before it fell. The eleventh and victorious climb was headed by F.S. Smythe of Britain. One of his companions to the top, R.L. Holdsworth, wore skis up to the Col, 7,025 meters high. This was the highest altitude at which men had ever skied until 1970, when Yuichiro Miura of Japan skied down the upper slopes of Mt. Everest.

R.L. Holdsworth also set a rather odd record on the top of Kamet Peak. He smoked. Holdsworth smoked heavily but nobody expected him to try to smoke on the summit of a Himalayan mountain. Although he must have been dead tired, he sat down on the snow and lighted his pipe. Nobody could refrain from admiring him. With all the attention paid today to the harms of smoking, some people might wonder what special effects smoking has on man at a height of 7,756 meters. That is not our concern here, however. His was a record, albeit a very strange one.

The highest of the Garhwal peaks is Nanda Devi, 7,817 meters high. It is considered the pearl of the Himalayas because of its loveliness. The graceful symmetry of its double peaks, the main and the east, thrusting themselves up to the sky, is indeed a visual treat—a rare example of perfect twin peaks. Even T.G. Longstaff, who knows almost everything about these mountains, praised Nanda Devi. He believes there is no mountain in the world more beautiful than Nanda Devi.

It would perhaps be strange if a mountain of such beauty were not an object of worship. In fact, since ancient times inhabitants of the region have revered this mountain as a dwelling place of the gods. The many routes leading to Tibet through the Garhwal Himalayas once carried heavy traffic, and it is no wonder that numerous religions are connected with these mountains. It is well-known that many Hindus and Buddhists go on pilgrimage to various sacred spots along the upper streams of the Alaknanda River. The names for mountains and passes in the area often have religious meanings. Nanda Devi means "Blessed Goddess."

It was natural that foreign mountaineers charted this mountain at an early date. But like Kamet, Nanda Devi refused for years to yield to the many climbers that tried to overcome her. It is extremely difficult even to approach her foothills, the entrance to which is guarded by long, deep gorges. After several failures, one party finally succeeded in crossing these gorges and in 1934 entered the south foothills of the mountain. Two years later the summit was reached by two men, H.W. Tilman and N.E. Odell. Tilman then remarked, says one book, that Nanda Devi had finally succumbed, that man had at last made the goddess bow her proud head. But after making that remark in the exhilaration of victory, he said he became indescribably sad.

Fifteen years later, in 1951, a French party led by Roger Duplat attacked Nanda Devi. Their plan was to attain the main summit and then traverse the four-kilometer summit range to the East Peak. This was a plan unheard of in the 1950's, when the idea of trying variation routes was only beginning to be adopted in climbing the Himalayas.

The result of this brave undertaking was sad. Duplat and a companion started for the summit from Camp IV and were last seen climbing up into a dense curtain of mist. "If some day I die in the mountains . . . " is a line from a song Duplat wrote. The words are particularly poignant because of Duplat's death.

The Garhwal Himalayas are considered the loveliest of all the mountains in Central Asia. It is a loveliness unsurpassed by the primitive splendor of the Karakorum, the Caucasian grace of the Hindu Kush, or the icy ruggedness of the Nepal Himalayas. The mountains and valleys, forests and grassfields, butterflies and flowers—everything exists in perfect harmony, to produce a supreme sensual pleasure. And few places in the world can boast of being so rich in legend and tradition. How unfortunate it is that politics have closed the Garhwal Himalayas to visitors since 1945.

X

The Garhwal ends at the Kali River. The range from there eastward is the Nepal Himalayas. Nepal had long closed her doors to all foreigners and enjoyed domestic tranquility. Eventually, however, even Nepal could not resist progress and opened her doors in 1949. Those most delighted with the move were probably foreign mountaineers, for the world's highest mountains stand row upon row in Nepal. There are eight peaks soaring above 8,000 meters and twenty exceed 7,500 meters. A part of the Nepal range can be seen from the Tibetan side but most of it was still uncharted in 1949. No wonder mountaineers became excited.

Soon after Nepal opened her doors a French expedition received permission to climb Annapurna. The French party reached the top in its first attempt, thereby making Annapurna the first of the giants in Nepal to fall. The French success, moreover, stirred mountaineers the world over. Up to that time, no Himalayan mountain had fallen in an initial attempt. Usually, a mountain was scouted in one year and climbed perhaps in the next. Even with such precautions there had been many failures in the past. The French expedition to Annapurna, however, scouted and attacked at the same time. Annapurna's great height made the feat all the more spectacular.

Although the French success was a milestone in Himalayan climbing, the group's leader said they had merely applied techniques they learned in the European Alps. But their equipment was new: nylon tents and ropes, boots with synthetic rubber soles, and tools and utensils of lightweight metal alloys. Today, it is commonplace to use such gear, but the French Annapurna expedition was highly innovative. The secret of the French party's success undoubtedly lay in its quick Alpine-style attack with light equipment.

The party paid a dear price for victory, however. Two of the members who reached the summit were severely frost-bitten and blinded by snow. Although they were rescued from death their fingers and toes had to be cut off as they were carried down on stretchers. While in the hospital, one of the two, M. Herzog—the leader of the party—wrote an exciting book about the conquest of Annapurna which became very popular among all mountain lovers.

This was actually the beginning of climbs on mountains higher than 8,000 meters. Men from all countries began competing to conquer the super-peaks, which led to coinage of the expression "the Himalayan Olympics." It was natural for the British to aim for Everest. Before the war they had attempted Everest seven times, and had been defeated seven times. Approach from Nepal was forbidden, of course, and climbs in those days had to be attempted up the north slope from Tibet. In 1949, the situation was completely reversed. Nepal could be entered but Tibet could not.

A scouting party sent to find a potential route up the south slope chose one above Khumbu Glacier. Climbers in the Himalayas frequently "stand on their predecessors' shoulders," as the expression goes. A Swiss party almost made the summit following the route the British discovered. A later British party finally reached the summit by benefitting from the Swiss experiences. The successful climb was made in 1953. The names of (now Sir) Edmund Hillary and Tenzing Norkay instantly spread throughout the world.

The decade following the French success on Annapurna in 1950 can be called the Golden Age of Himalaya mountaineering. Fourteen peaks over 8,000 meters in the Himalayas, including the Karakorum, fell one after the other to parties from Austria, England, France, Germany, Italy, Japan, Switzerland, and the U.S.A. Japanese climbers reached Manaslu's top on May 9, 1956. The party scouted the mountain and made three test climbs before planting the Rising Sun on the peak. That success excited in Japan not only a Himalaya fever but also an increased general enthusiasm in mountaineering.

There were some stubborn mountains in Nepal. Dhaulagiri resisted challenges by parties of seven different countries, including France, Switzerland, Argentina, Germany and Austria, before falling to the Swiss, in 1960. The only unconquered peak over 8,000 was Gosainthan. Since that mountain stood inside Tibetan territory, however, even though not far from the border with Nepal, western mountaineers could do nothing but look up and admire it. Only climbers from the People's Republic of China could attempt it.

The Chinese sent a scouting party to Gosainthan in 1963 and in 1964 organized an enormous 195-member expeditionary party. The number of members may surprise westerners, for the Chinese do not distinguish between regular members and porters. The plan was to reach the top of Shisha Pangma (Tibetan name) on May Day 1964. They came very close, missing by just one day. Ten people reached the summit, and fifty-three stood on the slope above 7,500 meters.

XI

Today, all the Himalayan peaks over 8,000 meters and almost all over 7,000 meters have been conquered. There are only a few high mountains in the Nepal Himalayas which have been ignored. Knowledge of and experience in Himalaya climbing is now so plentiful that there is no such thing as an impregnable peak.

In the Alps, where there are no unclimbed peaks, there was a period of climbing variation routes before rock-climbing—the hardest way to climb a mountain—came into vogue. Climbing in the Nepal Himalayas seems to be following that example. In the Himalayas, in fact, nobody ever tried traversing a mountain, that is, going up one route and coming down another. In 1963, traversing was undertaken for the first time, and it was done on Mt. Everest. Himalaya climbers in the past were only interested in unclimbed mountains. But Mt. Everest is an exception. As the highest mountain in the world it is hard to resist. Since the British success in 1953, Everest's top has been reached six times by various parties, including the Japanese in 1970.

Each party has contributed something new to the techniques of climbing Everest. The Swiss, the second successful party, succeeded in reaching the summits of Mt. Everest and Lhotse almost simultaneously. The third successful party was said to have been Chinese. They are believed to have climbed on the Tibetan route which the British had unsuccessfully attempted earlier. The Americans, the fourth successful party, did something nobody had ever done before on Everest—traversing.

Two of the Americans reached the top of Everest along the classic route from the southeastern ridge. Two more of the party attained the summit via the steep western ridge and then crossed the summit ridge to the opposite slope. When they reached the summit, however, it was dusk. Their plan was to rendezvous on the summit with the two members who climbed from the southeast. But because of the late hour, the first two men to reach the top started down, believing the attempt on the western ridge had failed. Although it was completely dark, the western ridge team headed quickly down the southeast ridge. They actually caught up with their companions, and all four men were overjoyed at the unexpected rendezvous. Ahead of them, however, was the dangerous business of climbing down the steep, narrow ridge in pitch darkness. Their oxygen was spent and the only flashlight they carried was running down. There was nothing the four could do except sit huddled together on a bare platform of icy rocks. They spent the night at 8,500 meters without a tent, sleeping bags, oxygen, or light. When they finally rejoined their other companions, three were suffering from severe frost-bite.

The next successful party, a group of Indians, attained the summit in 1965. They were determined to succeed, having failed twice previously. They had no ambition to set any records. All they wanted was to reach the top via the proven route. To ensure success, however, they organized four teams to aim for the summit simultaneously—and inadvertently set a record. Never before had nine members of one party stood on Everest's summit.

In 1970, a Japanese party planned to climb to the top via the classic route with one team, and to climb the south wall with another—an ambitious plan indeed. To climb up the gigantic, perpendicular wall of ice-covered rocks on the southwestern slope of Mt. Everest! The wall in question dropped 2,150 meters straight down from the top to Western Kum, where the base camp was set up. The section above 8,000 meters was completely vertical, with many frightening overhangs. The plan was ambitious, but it was not reckless. The Japanese had sent out scouting parties before and after the monsoon season in 1969 and were convinced that an attack on the south wall would not be impossible above 8,000 meters.

The Japanese party was enormous. It consisted of two groups, the one that was to take the classic route—the southeastern ridge—and the group that was to scale the south wall. There were 39 regular members, 7 sherpas, 79 additional members to work above the base camp and 1,000 porters. Equipment and food weighed thirty tons. Expenditures ran about $290,000, the largest amount ever spent on a single Himalayan expedition. The group succeeded in reaching the summit via the southeastern ridge, but the ambitious attempt from the south wall failed. They reached 8,000 meters, but because rocks were falling constantly they had to give up. Yet the courageous attempt considerably stimulated mountaineers throughout the world.

Also in 1970, a British party attempted the south wall of Annapurna. They had tried a variation route on Annapurna in 1969. First they climbed up to Glacier Dome, then turning to the west reached Roc Noir. After conquering the front peak they tried to follow the 7½-kilometer ridge to the main peak but had to quit halfway. In their 1970 expedition they wanted to scramble up the steep south wall directly to the summit of the main peak. It was terribly difficult rock-climbing, but they did it—at the cost of one member's life.

One more noteworthy achievement during 1970 was a Japanese party's climb of Makalu. The Japanese climbed Makalu previously, but this time they went via a variation route. They chose the long southeastern ridge, and after a painstaking struggle they succeeded. Perhaps from now on the only notable achievements in climbing in Nepal will be made over variation routes.

XII

After the Nepal Himalayas come the Sikkim Himalayas. As in the Garhwal, exploration in this area began quite early. Today, however, mountain climbing is strictly forbidden in Sikkim. On the Nepal-Sikkim border is Kangchenjunga, the world's third highest mountain. Darjeeling, in the northeastern corner of India, was a kind of holy place before World War II for people who loved the Himalayas. From the hills surrounding Darjeeling one can look directly up at the soaring peak of Kangchenjunga. The mountain probably achieved fame much earlier than other mountains in the Himalayas because of its fortunate location.

Kangchenjunga was also the earliest Himalayan mountain to be explored. From the mid-nineteenth century many natural scientists and explorers visited the region. None, however, ever dreamed of climbing to its rugged summit. The first man who considered climbing it was Freshfield, who travelled around its base to estimate the dangers and the chances for success.

In 1905, Freshfield attempted to climb up the Yalung Glacier on the southwest slope. He failed to get very far. The really determined expeditions began with a German party. The Germans tried twice, in 1929 and 1931. Both times they attempted the northeast ridge above the Zemu Glacier on the east slope. But the ridge was long and the monsoon season brought deep snow and terrible storms. They retreated both times. In 1930, G.O. Dyhrenfurth organized an international expedition which tried the Kangchenjunga Glacier on the north slope. Once onto the glacier they realized it was impossible to advance without risking a dangerous avalanche. They too had to retreat.

Kangchenjunga appeared impregnable, for none of the routes seemed feasible. Nevertheless, the mountain finally fell to the British. After two scouting expeditions in 1952 and 1954 they decided to go up the Yalung Glacier. On May 25th and 26th in 1955, two parties of two men each reached the summit. They stopped a few steps short of the highest point in keeping a promise made to local authorities not to tread on the spot considered the most sacred part of the sacred mountain.

The mountain group around Kangchenjunga is vast. Toward Sikkim in the east is Siniolchu, called by some people the most beautiful mountain in the world. Toward Nepal in the west is Jannu, called "the monster mountain" because of its grotesque appearance. The latter had long been thought impregnable mainly because of its formidable appearance, but in 1959 a French party, after three fierce assaults, conquered the monster.

East of the Sikkim lie the Bhutan Himalayas, and east of them the Assam Himalayas. The Bhutan and Assam mountains are the least known of the Himalayan chain. Both Bhutan and Assam now refuse to admit mountaineers, and the only peak in the Bhutan Himalayas on which men have stood is Chomolhari, at the far western end of the range. The British climbed it from Tibet.

Chomolhari is more appropriately considered a Tibetan rather than a Bhutanese mountain. As one enters the village of Phari Dzong by the old road leading to Tibet from India through Sikkim, one suddenly faces Mt. Chomolhari. It stands there in its complete splendor, and no traveller spares words of praise on viewing it.

In Tibetan *cho* means God, *mo* is a feminine suffix and *lhari* is a holy mountain. Chomolhari, therefore, means "the holy mountain of the Goddess," and it has been worshipped as such by the Tibetans. Chomolhari was scaled in 1937 by Spencer Chapman's British party. He and a close friend climbed with the help of three sherpas. He borrowed all of his equipment and had almost no money. But he succeeded, and nobody else has done so since.

Very few mountaineers have entered the Assam Himalayas. In 1939, Tilman attempted to climb Mt. Kangto but only reached a lesser mountain on the approach. There are several reasons why you cannot approach the mountains in Assam. There are dense jungle areas, for example, between the villages and the mountains. (Rumor said the jungles were inhabited by brutal savages, but the inhabitants turned out to be peaceful tribesmen.) Also, it rains a great deal in the region. Moreover, a deadly plague is rampant. The main reason today, however, is political difficulties with the Chinese concerning the border.

At the far eastern end of the Assam Himalayas stands Namcha Barwa, the last peak in the 2,700-kilometer stretch of Himalayas. It was discovered in 1912. Gyara Peri, 7,150 meters high, was discovered in 1913, just across the Brahmaputra River. Namcha Barwa and Gyara Peri will continue to occupy the thoughts of all Himalaya mountaineers for some time to come.

Afterword

Yoshikazu Shirakawa   *March 10, 1971*

I explored the South Pacific area, and the memory of great ocean expanses made the massive, icy mountains of the Himalayas tremendously impressive to me. Perhaps more impressive than a person might think who had never seen such water expanses. Likewise, earlier trips to Europe's Alps also motivated me to produce this book on the Himalayas. Actually, I had visited part of the Himalayas prior to going to the Alps, and while in the Alps kept hearing whispers urging me to return to the Himalayas. Although I thought my book on the Alps should be completed before I began a new project, I finally had to respond to my inner urgings. I left the work of editing ''The Alps'' to my publisher and flew to Kathmandu.

It is difficult to imagine that this remote and forbidding mountain chain is in the middle of an area experiencing a rapid growth in population. The mountains' frozen surface is plated with a thick layer of ice year round. And although all of the Himalayan mountains over 8,000 meters have been scaled, many parts of the region are as yet uncharted.

The Himalayas, bounded by Bhutan in the east and Afghanistan in the west, cover parts of seven different countries. In the vast 3,000-kilometer expanse there are fourteen mountains over 8,000 meters and hundreds more whose summits are above 7,000 meters. The mountains from 6,000 to 7,000 meters high are so numerous they have never been counted.

Everybody knows something about the Himalayas. They are extremely rugged mountains that were once under an ancient sea or lake and were formed at approximately the same time as the Alps and Andes. Everyone has heard of the Gurkha soldiers from this area, too. But most knowledge about the Himalayas is only superficial. How many people can really visualize the density of these mountains? What understanding do we have of the everyday life of the Gurungs or the sherpas?

I decided to cover as much of the Himalayas as possible on foot and to report my findings as thoroughly as I could. Although I knew that it would be a superhuman task for one man to do an exhaustive study in this manner, I hoped that I could compile a book which would fill in some of the gaps in our knowledge of the region.

Central Asia has been of great interest to the world since Marco Polo's reports of his travels awakened thirteenth-century European minds to the wonders of the East. Six hundred years before Marco Polo, the Chinese priest Hsüan-tsang made a great journey across Middle Asia, and translations by British and French scholars have made his ''Record of Western Lands of the Great T'ang Period'' available to us.

In 1848, Sir Joseph Hooker's ''Diary of the Himalayas'' described an expedition into the Sikkim Himalayas. The Schlagintweit brothers introduced the features of the Garhwal Himalayas. The British alpinist Gleam was the first to explore a number of ranges in the chain, including the Sikkim and Garhwal Himalayas. During the 1920's, the British General Bruce walked the northern side of the Himalayas all the way from Bhutan to Afghanistan and was highly praised for his accomplishment. He is said to have lifted the veil of mystery that surrounded the Himalayas, yet he could not enter Nepal, a region which includes a broad stretch of the Himalayas, because of the country's closed door policy at that time.

Probably no one ever made a more ambitious journey than the British mountain explorer Douglas W. Freshfield and the world famous Italian photographer Vittorio Sella. They circled an extremely wide area including the Baltoro Glacier and Kangchenjunga. Freshfield's book

"Round in Kangchenjunga" was written in 1903, and his book of photographs, "The Baltoro Glacier," introduced the Himalayas to the world.

One cannot neglect the contributions of Toni Hagen of Switzerland. The results of his continuous explorations and investigations into the nature and people of the region has been compiled in "Nepal." He recorded a wealth of information about the Himalayas and can be considered a leading authority on the subject. Studies by Hagen are so important that anyone who wants to know about the Himalayas must read his writings. Yet he knew only Nepal.

Not too many years ago a Japanese alpine photographer published an album under the title "The Himalayas." It is a very handy volume and has certainly helped to project an image of the Himalayas to the Japanese people. But this book features only a small area of Nepal, just one of the seven countries over which the Himalayan Range lies. We also have "Peaks in the Himalayas" by Kyuya Fukada, which is supplemented by a collection of photographs of the mountains taken by many different photographers. This was the first book of photographs to describe the entire scope of the Himalayas to Japan in the vernacular, but unfortunately the pictures were not taken by a single person and it is hard to grasp from the varying images a true picture of the mountains. I firmly believe that to document clearly the many features of the Himalayas a single photographer must be employed.

The Himalayas cover a tremendously vast expanse. The weather in the easternmost range greatly differs from that of the one farthest west. The eastern end is subjected to both dry and rainy seasons while in the west the weather is dry throughout the year. One is impressed by the stark contrast of high mountains and desert. In addition to geographic differences, one can see sharp contrasts in plant and animal life along the range. The lush green of the Nepal region bears little resemblance to the barren Pakistani desert mountains.

Even within Nepal the mountains differ greatly. If one sees only Everest and environs he cannot picture what the mountains in the Annapurna area look like. This is one of the reasons why I wanted to compile this book. I tried to see and record as much as I could about the entire region—its similarities and differences.

The Himalayas are both beautiful and perilous, and I wanted this essence to be captured and reported. There is an old saying that "seeing is believing." Since this area is so remote that few persons will ever visit it I hoped that I could bring the Himalayas to you. If I have imparted in any way a deeper understanding of the area then I have fulfilled my purpose in compiling this album. I hope that I have reported well enough that people of the world might better realize the nature of the planet on which they live and consider what is required for the survival of their species.

The motivations for writing this book are not new to me. I have explored 130 countries and have reported to the greatest extent possible the various aspects of each in the series "World Civilizations and World Geography," "World Civilizations" and others. The basic purpose for my explorations and writings is to impress upon others the necessity of re-examining the condition of the world in which we live.

Unfortunately, the very vastness of the globe limits any single individual's perspective. But I pay special interest to the comments of astronauts who have observed the earth from afar. One said it was a shame that the earth, covered with green and having abundant air and water, is being polluted. An Apollo 8 astronaut made the observation that the earth is like an oasis in the treacherous space of the universe. One of Apollo 11's crew said that when he thinks of the universe God created he wonders what man is. Commander Shepard, aboard Apollo 14, said he felt sad looking at the earth while returning from the moon and thinking that men were still fighting wars there.

Human intelligence enabled man to reach the moon. But the same intelligence invented nuclear weapons. The technology which brought about a high level of industrial development has also created a vast complex that is polluting and disrupting nature; it is frightening to hear that the snow in remote, non-industrial Greenland contains 500 times more lead than snow in its natural state; the people of Japan were shocked when an employee of a smeltery committed suicide because cadmium had virtually eroded her body; air pollution has become a common hazard in almost every major city in the world.

Professor Arnold Toynbee, a contributor to this book, wrote to me: "In photographing the beautiful places of the World, you are doing a great service. Your photographs will have preserved a record of what unspoiled Nature was like, if Man carries his present defacement of Nature to its miserable conclusion. But I hope your photographs will help to deter mankind from continuing on this disastrous course. This would be a great reward for your work." His words greatly encouraged me to continue working on this photographic series which I began some ten years ago.

Our scientists have made great strides: space travel is no longer a mere dream; the medical sciences have made great contributions to mankind; technological advances are being made at a tremendous pace. Yet we are experiencing domestic unrest, wars between nations are constantly being waged, and we are ruining our environment. I can only feel that every day, bit by bit, the world is being destroyed. My fear is that in doing my work I might inadvertently add a single stroke to the blueprint of a plan to desert the earth.

Photographing the Himalayas

Yoshikazu Shirakawa

The two main difficulties met in mountain photography are strong natural light and severe climatic conditions. Cameras used must have mechanisms simple but reliable enough to be operated under the worst conditions. Equipment must be lightweight, particularly in mountains like the Himalayas where transportation facilities are poor and heights of six and seven thousand meters are common. With these considerations in mind I chose the following equipment.

Cameras:	Asahi Pentax (6x7)	3
	Asahi Pentax (SP)	3
Lenses:	(1) for Asahi Pentax (6x7)	
	Super Takumar 55mm f/3.5	
	Super Takumar 75mm f/4.5	
	Super Takumar 105mm f/2.4	
	Super Takumar 200mm f/4	
	Super Takumar 300mm f/4	
	(2) for Asahi Pentax (SP)	
	Super Takumar 55mm f/1.8	
	Super Takumar 28mm f/3.5	
	Super Takumar 135mm f/3.5	

Since there would be no way to obtain replacements in the mountains, I carried three cameras and two of each size lens. I made the camera lens combinations as simple as possible. Oxygen is extremely thin at 7,000 meters and man's normal functions slow down considerably. I wanted to be able to change lenses and operate my cameras almost without thinking, even at high altitudes. A camera's operation must be simple and the photographer must be completely familiar with his equipment so that he can work under any conditions. These precautions let me complete my photographic expedition successfully despite the high altitudes in the Everest region—and despite attacks of mountain sickness.

To protect my cameras and accessory equipment during transport I wrapped everything in numerous vinyl coverings. My main concern was sand. It almost never rains in Nepal in the east and constant winds there blow a fine sand that could ruin all photographs if it got inside the cameras. West Pakistan and Afghanistan have desert regions and the same problem with sand is encountered there.

Protection against cold was another of my concerns with my photographic equipment. A camera mechanism must be kept operative even at temperatures 20-40 degrees below zero centigrade. I had the cameras and lenses winterized before leaving Japan but took special care to insert new batteries every five days. Although batteries are good for 10,000 shutter closings at normal temperatures, their efficacy drops 50 per cent at zero degrees centigrade. I did not discard used batteries, for they regain their effectiveness when returned to normal temperatures.

Throughout my expedition I did not attempt any tricky exposure techniques. My lens apertures ranged between f/16 and f/45, depending on conditions. The Asahi Pentax's "Spot-

meter'' accurately selected the exposure time, usually 1/30 second to one second. I exposed for 1-3 minutes when photographing the mountains in moonlight.

Although I think a fish-eye lens provides interesting photographs I decided not to use one on this expedition. I believed my task was to photograph the Himalayas in as natural a state as possible and therefore avoided techniques that might bend, elongate or otherwise change the mountains artificially.

I prepared 1,000 rolls of Kodak's Ektachrome Professional film but used only about 500 rolls, probably because there are fewer photographically interesting subjects in the Himalayas than in the European Alps and similar mountain ranges. I kept all exposed film at temperatures below zero degrees centigrade.

More difficult than taking pictures was getting exposed film back to Tokyo safely. Japanese friends in Nepal carried some film to Tokyo for me, and I decided to send the balance by air freight. However, forty rolls I sent on a plane from Kathmandu to Calcutta for further shipment to Japan were opened for inspection and ruined, and thereafter I carried film to New Delhi for direct airmailing to Tokyo. Mailing was not easy, for exposed but undeveloped film could legally be sent only by reporters registered with the Indian authorities, or by people who applied for and received special permission.

Moreover, an Indian friend told me that whether I registered a package or not it would probably not make it to Tokyo safely. He said that if I sent ten items to Japan, three might arrive. Much material I mailed from New Delhi never arrived in Japan.

For the record, I followed all prohibitions regarding photography in every country I visited, and faithfully kept all verbal promises I made about not photographing off-limit subjects. These included photographs of Tibet to the north while in Sikkim, and photographs of Nanga Parbat while in West Pakistan that would include the Tibetan skyline. I did take pictures of

Nanga Parbat from the north during numerous airplane flights but took no restricted photographs—although I could have by simply turning my camera slightly. Pakistani law forbids taking photographs to the north, and that information is announced to airplane passengers. I have seen pictures of the forbidden area in a collection of Himalayan photographs published in Japan, but believe it is wrong to publicize photographs that are, in effect, law infractions. The issue should not be shelved as being merely an individual's idiosyncracies, but should be recognized for its international implications.

I understand and sympathize with a photographer who sees a great mountain nearby but is told he must not photograph it. He probably could not help closing his shutter when he thought he might never have the chance again to take a similar picture. But that man should not expect to be patted on the back. He not only failed to appreciate the hospitality shown him but could possibly cause misunderstandings, even friction, between the two countries involved. I consider it regrettable that a Japanese would dare disregard the hospitality of a foreign country by doing something its law prohibits.

In compiling this album I took special care not to repeat the rude behavior of other Japanese. It will be a long time before the Himalayan countries are at peace with one another, but I look forward anxiously to the day when anyone who wants to can explore the Himalayas without having to obtain complicated permits. The day will come when one will be able to climb and photograph the Himalayas merely by possessing a passport.

Acknowledgments

My photographic expedition to the Himalayas was accompanied by unusual difficulties which my previous trips to Europe's Alps did not prepare me for. Obtaining permission to enter the mountain regions was the first obstacle to overcome before being able to challenge the problems of high altitude. This photographic album is the result of warmhearted and continuous assistance afforded me by the governments and peoples of many countries. I certainly need more space than is available to express my gratitude to them for making my expedition possible. Here I can mention only a few of the people to whom I am especially grateful.

I sincerely express my gratitude to His Majesty the King of Nepal and his brother Brigadier General Prince Sushil Shumsher J.B. Rana. Travel in the Himalayas is always filled with dangers and difficulties, yet my problems were greatly reduced in Nepal thanks to the special help of the King and his brother. I am afraid that I can express my gratitude only inadequately for the generous treatment afforded me by His Majesty. Of his special kindnesses, I particularly must mention his permitting me to use his personal plane. Flying gave me increasingly interesting views of the area's mountains. Brigadier General Prince Sushil Shumsher J.B. Rana, as the official in charge of civil aviation, personally planned my schedule of flights for aerial photography. Permission to photograph the Sikkim Himalayas was expedited through his kind offices.

Secretary G.B. Shah, Mrs. Bhinda S. Shah, Mr. G.B. Khnal and Mr. Arjun Bahadur Singn are Nepalese government officials who gave me great assistance. Mr. Rom Bahadur Thapa, National Police Administrator, introduced me to the chief of each rural police headquarters. His kindness let me complete my exploratory tour without undue trouble.

I also extend my thanks to Nepalese Extraordinary and Plenipotential Ambassador Prakash Chand Thakur and his Second-Secretary Amar Raj Bhandary for aiding and counselling me concerning governmental arrangements.

I entered the Himalayas six times, and each time I was greatly helped by Gartzen, my Chief Porter. He responded to my trust by continually demonstrating a strong sense of responsibility in his duties. His attention saw to it that my equipment was transported without damage. My young sherpa friend Annu is also owed special mention. My demands were usually unreasonable but he never complained. Without the devoted attention of Gartzen and Annu, marching in the high Himalayas would have been difficult and taking photographs would have been impossible. Words cannot express the gratitude I owe them for their patience and bravery.

To Japan's Ambassador to Nepal, Mr. Hidemichi Kira, First-Secretary Kunihiko Murono and Third-Secretary Toshisada Komori, I also must express my thanks. They first opened the door to Nepal for me.

Concerning the unsuccessful Indian part of my explorations, I must mention the efforts of the staff of the New Delhi office of Mitsui & Co., Ltd., especially the efforts of Messrs. Hidetoshi Onuki and Dhanesh Raizada. In India, applications for permission to make a photographic expedition must be accompanied by numerous request forms and certifications, all of which were promptly submitted by these people. I had expected to do their services justice with a successful trip, but to my great regret the strife on the subcontinent prevented me from completing my expedition through the Indian region.

In Bhutan I was helped by Japanese Ambassador Atsushi Uyama and Second-Secretary Ryuji Saito.

In Pakistan, I am greatly indebted to Mr. Shahsada Burhranudin Khan in Chitoral. I was welcomed by him as a close friend, and the plans for my travel in the Hindu Kush were laid with his help. The Japanese Embassy Chargé d'Affaires Shoichi Ban spared no efforts on my behalf in requesting permission to photograph the mountains. Although many of the requests were turned down, I cannot forget the kindnesses he rendered me.

Concerning permission to enter the Karakorum Range, I was greatly helped by Ambassador Akira Sono.

The exploratory tour to Afghanistan was accomplished with the constant help of Sultan Mohmood Ghazi. I owe much to the Afghanistan Vice-Minister of Foreign Affairs, Mr. Rawan Farhadi, for making arrangements for my aerial photography. I am also grateful to Ambassador Sashichiro Matsui and Second-Secretary Toshikazu Kato of the Japanese Embassy.

Thanks also go to many members of Japan's Foreign Affairs Ministry, especially to Foreign Affairs Minister Kiichi Aichi for arranging for the King of Nepal to write the introduction to this book, and to Mr. Nobuhiko Ushiba for writing official introductions to the Japanese ambassadors in the Himalayan countries. There were various frictions among the Himalayan countries during the time I was in the area, and had it not been for the assistance of Mr. Ushiba and the Japanese embassies I could not have completed my work. I am greatly indebted to them for their help. To these men and to many other members of the Foreign Affairs Ministry, including Mr. Kunio Muraoka, I humbly give thanks.

My thanks also must go to Mr. Hisatsune Sakomizu of the House of Counselors and to Mr. Eiji Yamazaki.

The staff of the photographic magazine *Asahi Camera* urged me to continue my work whenever I became discouraged. I wish to express my gratitude to each member of the editorial department of that magazine.

Financial aid, of course, was a primary factor in making my expedition possible. For financial help I am greatly indebted to Asahi Optical Co., Ltd. and Konishiroku Photo Industry Co., Ltd. The Japan Alpine Association's expedition to Mt. Everest cost 115 million yen, a sum spent to scale one mountain in the great expanse of the Himalayas. One can imagine, therefore, the great expenses involved in exploring a much wider expanse of those mountains. Porter costs alone were quite substantial.

The Managing Director of Asahi Optical Co., Mr. Hiroshi Hara, readily consented to my request for financial help. Other officials in the company gave me considerable support later. Letters from Director Shigenobu Hieda encouraged me whenever I became depressed in the mountains. I cannot forget these various kindnesses.

No words could fully express my gratitude to my assistants: Hiroshi Kihara, the cook, for example, at whom I often shouted impatiently about the food. When I think of his patience I feel particularly embarrassed. At the time, I never thought there were any difficulties in obtaining foodstuffs. But I realized later that he used some sauces he carried from Japan as if they were treasures. I cannot understand now why I should have ever complained about the taste of the food. Besides thanks, I offer him my apologies.

I also want to acknowledge Mr. Akira Tanioka's patience and cooperation. He commanded the sherpas, porters and other members of the party with efficiency and even bravery. His past experience and forcefulness got our entire party safely out of unusually heavy snow in the Sikkim Himalayas.

My Japanese friends in Kathmandu, Messrs. Minoru Kanezuka and Teruji Fujita, helped me substantially. I wish to record my thanks to them, too.

Travelling to other countries is not new to me, nor is exploring out-of-the-way places, for I have travelled around the world writing for newspapers and magazines, and taking photographs for commercial and other uses. But I had never experienced anything that equals my trip to the Himalayas in terms of the difficulties and dangers I encountered. The great trust of so many people, however, was always more than enough to encourage me and urge me on to complete my work.

Whenever I ran into difficulties I remembered the people who had worked so hard to help me. My work in the Himalayas is over for now. This volume attests to the cooperation of everyone who aided me, whether I had space to list them here or not.

Y. S.

MAPS OF THE HIMALAYAS

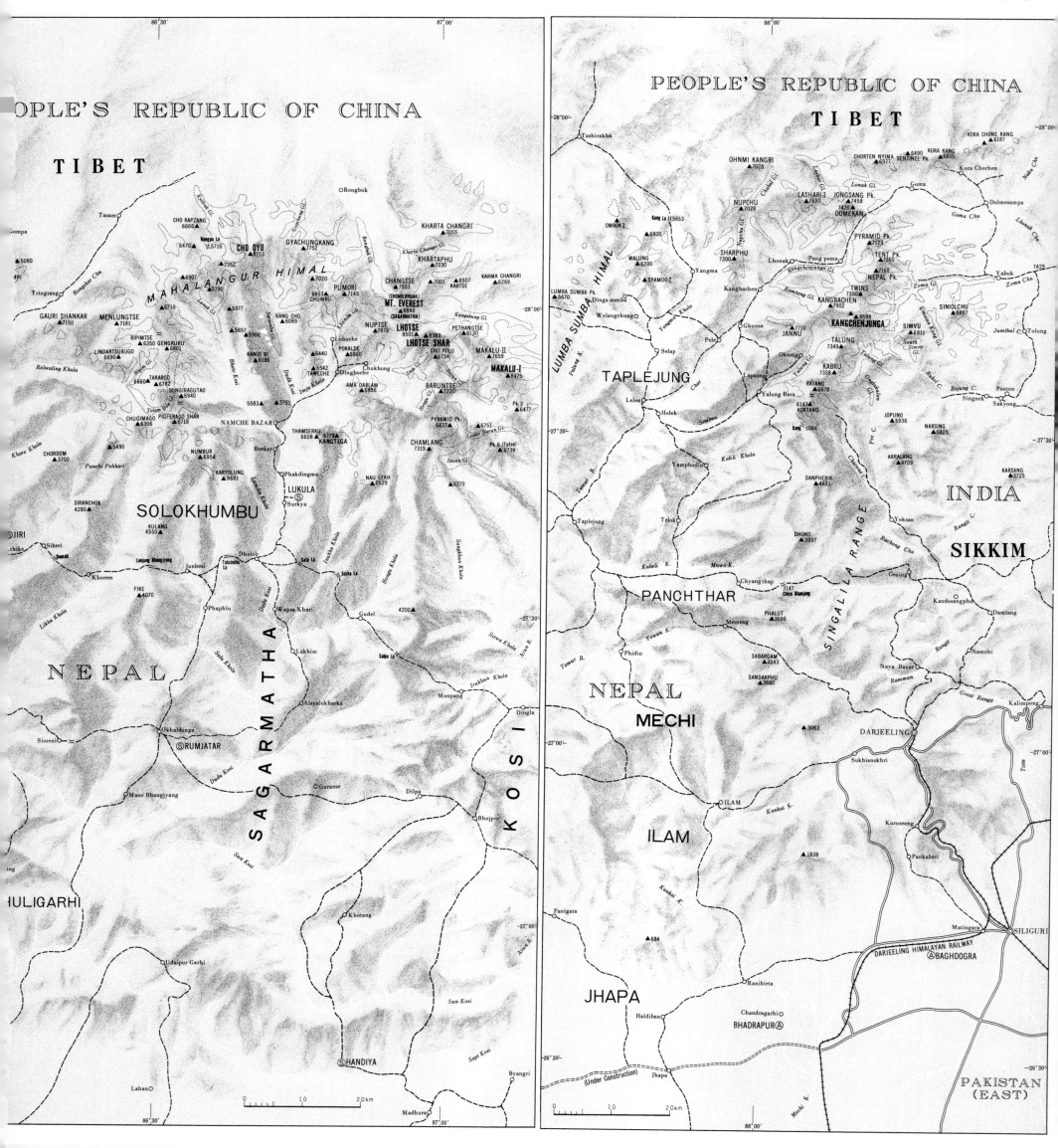

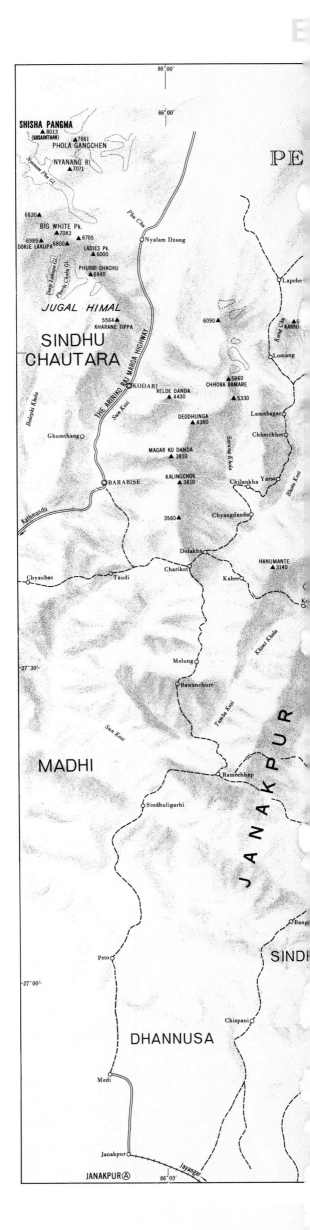

LIFT FOR MAPS

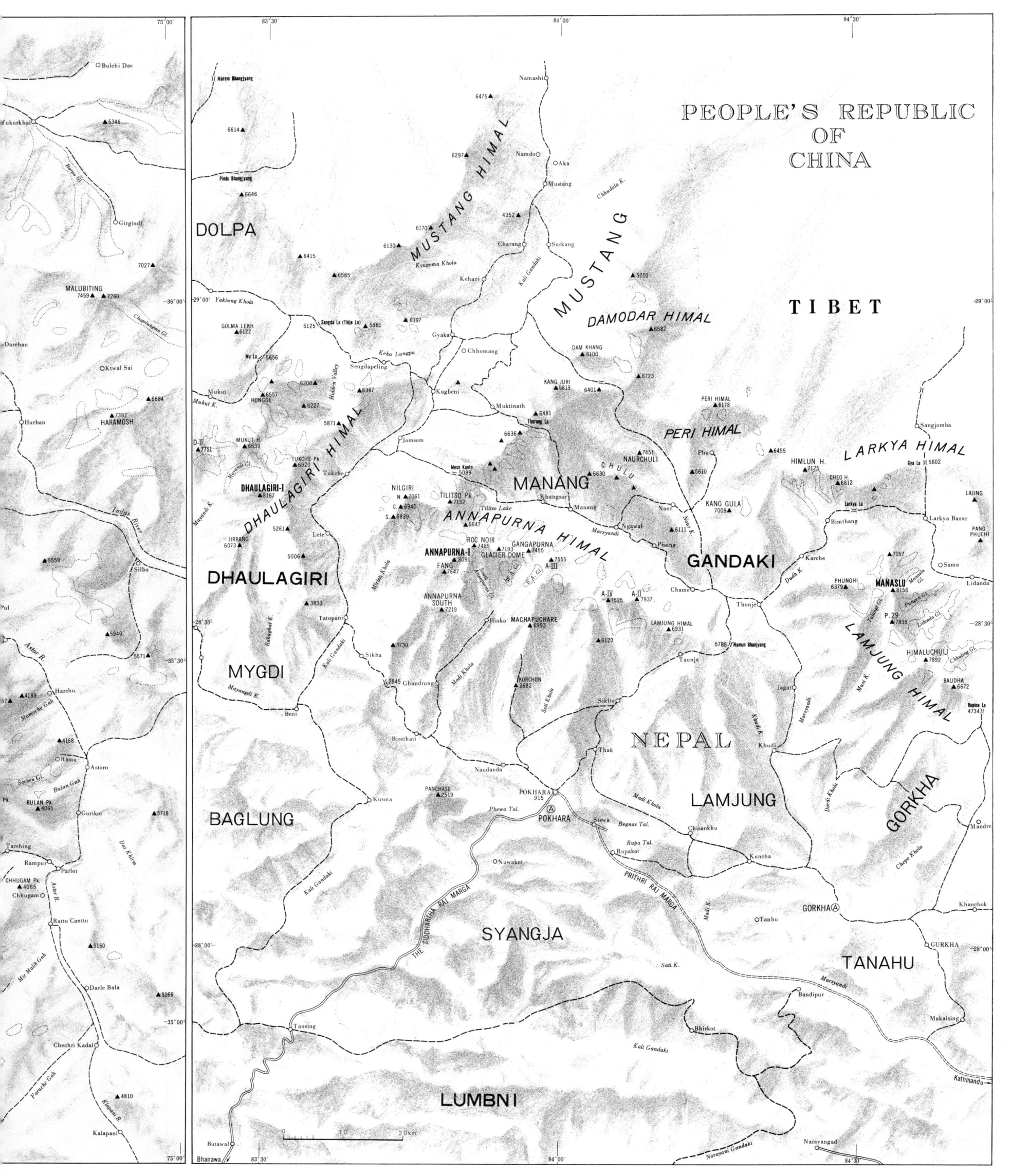

PEOPLE'S REPUBLIC
OF
CHINA

TIBET

NEPAL